Hiro,

A Bilko-sized blast
from the past. Enjoy
the ride - and the
memories of baseball
in L.A. before the
Dodgers.

Gaylon White
8-15-14

The Bilko Athletic Club

The Story of the 1956 Los Angeles Angels

Gaylon H. White

ROWMAN & LITTLEFIELD
Lanham • Boulder • New York • Toronto • Plymouth, UK
2014

Published by Rowman & Littlefield
4501 Forbes Boulevard, Suite 200, Lanham, Maryland 20706
http://www.rowman.com

Estover Road, Plymouth PL6 7PY, United Kingdom

British Library Cataloguing in Publication Information Available

Library of Congress Cataloging-in-Publication Data

White, Gaylon H., 1946-
The Bilko athletic club : the story of the 1956 Los Angeles Angels / Gaylon H. White.
pages cm
Includes bibliographical references and index.
ISBN 978-0-8108-9289-7 (cloth : alk. paper) -- ISBN 978-0-8108-9290-3 (ebook) 1. Los Angeles Angels (Baseball team : 1901-1957)--History. 2. Baseball players--California--Los Angeles--Interviews. 3. Bilko, Steve, 1928-1978. I. Title.
GV875.A62W54 2014
796.357'640979494--dc23
2013034818

™
The paper used in this publication meets the minimum requirements of American National Standard for Information Sciences Permanence of Paper for Printed Library Materials, ANSI/NISO Z39.48-1992.

Printed in the United States of America

To Don, my older brother, who became my first sports hero when he scored forty-eight points in an eighth-grade basketball game.

"What would life be if it weren't for the remembrances? We have the future of which we know nothing, we have the present, which is so close and moving so swiftly by that we can't make much of it, but the past is as clear as our memories will allow. It's the memories of the past that convince me how important what I am doing is in the present." —Jack Hannah, brother of Joe Hannah, a catcher for the 1956 Los Angeles Angels

Contents

Acknowledgments

I owe a huge thanks to more than one hundred players, sportswriters, umpires, and fans who shared their memories of Steve Bilko and the 1956 Los Angeles Angels.

One of the fans was John Schulian, an eleven-year-old in 1956 who went on to become an award-winning sports columnist and write in 1993 a masterpiece, *Of Stars and Angels,* for *Sports Illustrated* about Bilko, the Angels, and their cross-town rivals, the Hollywood Stars. The story appeared later in Schulian's book, *Twilight of the Long-ball Gods.*

"That was a labor of love," John said. "I can't tell you what I had for breakfast but I can tell you the lineups of the old Pacific Coast League teams." Schulian gives us another labor of love with the foreword of this book.

Dick Beverage, president of the Pacific Coast League (PCL) Historical Society and author of *The Los Angeles Angels of the Pacific Coast League,* the definitive history book on the Angels, connected me with players I couldn't find on my own.

Bill Swank, author of *Echoes of Lane Field,* a book on the San Diego Padres of the old PCL, convinced me to adapt the material I'd gathered on Bilko into a book on the 1956 Angels. He also provided pithy comments like "The very best era of baseball is when you were a kid."

Matt Dudas, a diehard Cleveland Indians fan, knew nothing about Bilko and the 1956 Angels before he volunteered to read the chapters as I churned them out. His insights made the stories more interesting and relevant to a younger generation of baseball fans.

Hank Inman is a former sportswriter and long-time friend dating back to the University of Oklahoma when we announced baseball games for KUVY, the student radio station. Hank is as avid a St. Louis Cardinals fan as I am a Chicago Cubs fan. We were together in 1984 at Three Rivers Stadium in Pittsburgh when the Cubs clinched a division title, their first of any type in thirty-nine years. We were listening to the radio two weeks later in a Cleveland Hopkins airport parking lot when the San Diego Padres' Steve Garvey hit a two-run walk-off homer to beat the Cubs in the fourth game of the National League Championship Series, the key blow in the Padres' winning the best-of-five series. Our shared history made Hank the ideal editor for critiquing the manuscript and making it better.

Leann DeBord, a former business colleague, was a jack of all trades, proofreading chapters, helping with the indexing, and coming to my rescue when Excel spreadsheets, PDF files, and the other mysteries of word processing threatened my sanity.

The UCLA Library' Special Collections Department is a gold mine of *Los Angeles Times* photographs from the 1950s. Helping me find the nuggets featured in this book was Simon Elliott, an all-star visual materials specialist if there ever was one.

It's customary for an author to thank his or her spouse profusely for their support and understanding during the long and arduous process of writing a book. My wife of nearly forty-nine years, Mary, had grounds for divorce many times as I spent countless hours away from home doing player interviews and poring through microfilm for newspaper stories that help bring the past to life again. Mary never complained, and she never questioned why I was spending so much time with people almost everybody else has forgotten. She understands the importance of telling their stories.

Preface

Davy Crockett was bigger than ever in 1955, and the number of raccoons was getting smaller and smaller.

From the mountain tops of Tennessee to the beaches of California, kids were wearing coonskin caps while singing "The Ballad of Davy Crocket" along with Fess Parker, the actor who played the legendary frontiersman in a television miniseries that was just as popular as the song. The Crockett craze connected with millions of kids across the United States.

Contrast this with baseball, the so-called national pastime. Baseball had a national following, but there were only sixteen major league teams and none west of Missouri. And there was no ESPN, cable TV super channels, or Internet to narrow the gap between East and West. East was east, west was west, and newspaper columns titled "Eastern Sports" reminded us of the difference.

In Los Angeles, where I was born and grew up, we had the Pacific Coast League (PCL), our own major league. The "big leagues" didn't arrive in southern California until 1958, when the Brooklyn Dodgers vacated Ebbets Field for the Coliseum in L.A.

Officially, the PCL was a minor league and considered open classification. All of the other thirty-two minor leagues in 1955 were class AAA or lower down to class D. With television providing more and varied forms of entertainment, attendance at major and minor league games was steadily declining. As high as fifty-nine in 1949, the number of minor leagues would shrink even more to twenty-eight in 1956.

My favorite team was the Los Angeles Angels—a name later adopted by the city's first major league team in the American League. They had a working agreement with the Chicago Cubs, and like the Cubs, the Angels' home ballpark was named Wrigley Field. They were both located in residential neighborhoods and their friendly confines almost identical in size and appearance down to the ivy-covered brick walls in left field.

We didn't need a front-row seat to see the faces of the players or hear their bantering. The crack of the bat, the popping of a mitt from a blazing fastball, and the yells of the vendors and fans could be heard almost anywhere in the ballpark. We didn't need binoculars to see a home run wreak havoc on one of the houses protruding above the left-field wall. We followed the house as closely as a pitched ball because the two could meet at any moment in a game. "No one would dream of sitting down for dinner without wearing a fielder's glove," wrote Ned Cronin of the house in the *Los Angeles Times*.[1]

I started going to Wrigley Field in L.A. in 1953 with my father, Reverend Hooper W. White, and my older brother, Don. That was the year we moved to Ontario, California, so Dad could pastor a church there. In late 1955 he changed churches again, this one in El Monte and closer to Wrigley Field—about thirty minutes via a new freeway. Baseball was a way for Dad to relax and escape the stress and pressure of the ministry. That was fine with me. I was ready to go to beautiful Wrigley Field any time he wanted.

It didn't matter whether the Angels were winning and that's good because usually they lost more than they won. In 1954, they finished nineteen games below .500 and sixth in an eight-team league. Our hope and excitement for the Angels in 1955 were greater than ever because of two hulking players—James Buster "Buzz" Clarkson and Steve Bilko. I didn't know anything about Buzz and Bilko until they arrived in L.A., Buzz at the beginning of spring training and Bilko near the end.

Everything is larger than life to a nine-year-old kid, which is how old I was at the time. No imagination was needed to pump up Buzz and Bilko. Not only were they big, they were shaped differently than the mostly slender players around them. The barrel-chested Buzz was about as round as a beer keg and moved like one. He appeared to play third base in slow motion, standing flat-footed as he flipped the ball to first base. "Just get it there in time to retire the batter," he said. "Saves wear and tear on the arm, too."[2]

At the plate, he lived up to his press clippings as a masher. To my eyes, Buzz was the second coming of Josh Gibson, the legendary Negro League slugger. Bilko was another Babe Ruth.

Many years later, Joe Garagiola, a teammate of Bilko's with the St. Louis Cardinals and Cubs and a long-time TV–radio announcer, told me, "I can see why Bilko would give you the hope of being the next Babe Ruth. When he hit a ball, he hit it. It sounded, it looked, and it acted like a home run."

I always wondered why Bilko went from being King Kong in the minors to a cream puff in the majors, as menacing as a Ding Dong cupcake.

In three monstrous seasons for the PCL Angels, he hit 148 homers. Fifty-five of them came in 1956 when he was Minor League Player of the Year and inspired the team's nickname, "The Bilko Athletic Club," and comparisons to all-time great minor league teams. Bilko's name was used for the main character in a hit 1950s television show that later became a movie starring Steve Martin as *Sgt. Bilko*. Hallmark even featured Bilko in a *Peanuts* greeting card booklet published several years after his retirement from baseball.

In 1,553 games in the minors, Bilko slugged 313 homers. In 600 major-league games, he managed only seventy-six. Six times he failed to stick with the Cardinals. The lowly Cubs let him go, followed by the Cincinnati Redlegs, Los Angeles Dodgers, and Detroit Tigers. Not until the American League expanded from eight to ten teams in 1961, adding the Angels, did Bilko find success in the majors.

In 1976, twenty years after Bilko's magical season in L.A., I spent a day with him at his home in Nanticoke, Pennsylvania. I was primarily interested in understanding why he wasn't as dominating in the major leagues as he was in the minors. I was researching a book on players who were great in the minors and flops in the majors.

My book on Bilko and other minor league stars was put on hold while I raised a family and worked in the corporate world, moving from Kansas to Ohio to Minnesota and, finally, to Kingsport, Tennessee, home of Dave Hillman, the ace of the 1956 Angels pitching staff. I did a telephone interview with Dave in 1976, but we didn't meet face-to-face until 2000.

Over lunch, Dave was thumbing through the 1956 Angels yearbook I brought with me. When Dave came to a photo of Hy Cohen, another Angel pitcher, he asked, "Whatever happened to Hy Cohen?"

A month into the 1956 season, Dave was nursing a sore right throwing arm. He had pitched to only one batter prior to facing the Seattle Rainiers in Seattle.

"They gave me the ball to pitch," Dave recalled. "They wanted to find out if I could make it, and if I couldn't, I would've been gone. Hy was 5–0 at that point. Of course, I made it. I beat Seattle. I was on my way.

"And then Hy was shipped out. That always bothered me. I've thought about it many times. Why was Hy shipped out? I don't know what happened to him. All I know is that he was gone."

The passing of forty-four years failed to ease Hillman's burden.

"I always felt in my heart that I was the reason he was sent out. He was a fine, good-looking boy. Whatever happened to him?"

Baseball is a game of revolving doors. Players come and go quickly, sometimes never to be seen nor heard of again. Dave's question made me curious to find out more about Hy Cohen and why a pitcher with a perfect record of five wins and no losses—the best in the league at the time—was sent to the lower minors.

I wound up interviewing twenty-six members of the 1956 Angels, including Cohen.

With few exceptions, the telephone numbers and addresses of the 1956 Angels and other players interviewed were listed in the phone book or available online, and they gladly talked with me.

When I called Frank DiPrima, a second baseman for the Angels in 1953, he was feeling the effects of medication he was taking for cancer. "You made me feel a lot better," DiPrima said as our conversation was coming to a close. "You made me feel good."

DiPrima died three and one-half years later at the age of eighty.

DiPrima and Gene Mauch traded places in '54, Mauch moving to L.A. and DiPrima to Atlanta, where Mauch was player-manager the year before.

I interviewed Mauch by telephone in August 2000, twelve years after he quit as manager of the California Angels. He had become a recluse, rarely talking with the media. We had a friendly, free-wheeling discussion about the 1956 Angels until I mentioned comments by Chuck Stevens, a member of the Hollywood Stars from 1948 to 1954 and an outspoken critic of the team. "I enjoyed the first twenty minutes of our talk and, then, I got in kind of a bad frame of mind," Mauch admitted.

"Sorry about that," I said.

"No, that's all right," Mauch replied. "I don't know what the hell gives him that much credibility. Oh, well, I like Chuck."

As the years passed and the book remained unfinished, Jack Hannah, brother of 1956 Angels catcher Joe Hannah, gave me a pep talk in the form of a letter. Jack was a major league pitching prospect until he hurt his throwing arm. He became an outstanding high school baseball coach and a songwriter-singer for the Sons of the San Joaquin. "How important is what you are doing?" Jack asked. "This is not the question. The question is: Just how important is what you are doing to *you*? I have never written a song because I wanted to impress anyone with my writing skill. I wrote it because God gave it to me. I'll let Him decide how He will touch others with it. God has a way of using, for His glory, what we do as a response to His 'nudgings' and 'whispers.'

"Don't discredit or minimize what you are doing with *your* story," Jack concluded. "You were impelled to do it. So finish it."

The Bilko Athletic Club is finished. My hope is that the stories of the 1956 Angels touch you as much as they did me.

NOTES

1. *Los Angeles Times,* September 15, 1956, A3.
2. *Ibid.,* July 20, 1955, C2.

Foreword

John Schulian

My first hard dose of reality was discovering that life is full of baseball cards you don't want. In my case, the cards featured Coot Veal and Bobby Del Greco and Harry Chiti, modestly talented journeymen doomed to play out their careers on dead-end teams, as obscure when they said goodbye as they were at hello. Who knew there could be so many Harry Chiti cards, or why? It seemed I got one in every package I bought. I traded cards with a neighborhood sharp named Richie Dillon and became the owner of more. He was twelve to my eleven and owned a Bob Dillinger mitt, and for that moment in time I looked up to him. Richie Dillon responded by fleecing me. I like to imagine that he later made a fortune from stock fraud or real estate scams. I also like to imagine that he got caught because even when he played me for a sucker, he made one big mistake: He gave me a Steve Bilko.

I forget whether it was from Bilko's mostly fruitless days with the St. Louis Cardinals or the Chicago Cubs, but that's beside the point. The important thing is that almost anywhere else a Bilko would have been one more card you didn't want unless you had a weird fascination with first basemen who were sluggers flummoxed by big league pitching, a subspecies that included Gail Harris, Lou Limmer, and Tookie Gilbert. But this was Los Angeles in 1956, and Bilko was pushing movie stars out of the headlines with all the home runs he was hitting for the hometown Angels of the old Pacific Coast League. In the world as I saw it, a Bilko baseball card symbolized things I had yet to put a name to. Good things.

I'd grasped the importance of homers at the age of three when a voice on our living room radio said Babe Ruth had died. A year or two later, a Hollywood Stars pitcher named Red Munger spotted my towhead in the stands and said, "Hiya, Whitey." The Stars were the Angels' crosstown rivals—oh, what bloody wars they waged—and I instantly became a Stars fan. My loyalty lasted but six years. Then Bilko hit town and turned me around.

You can attribute my change in allegiance to a failure of character if you like, but the truth is, he cast a spell on all of L.A. Even in the mid-1950s, with multitudes of transplants arriving daily, the burgeoning metropolis clung to its small-town heart. There were white picket fences in

Westwood, disc jockeys doing remote broadcasts from this or that Scrivener's Drive-In, and just enough innocence in the air to move people to embrace a big galoot who hadn't been able to cut it with the Cubs. Nobody seemed to care that Bilko was thriving in a minor league. To tell the truth, they didn't believe there was anything minor about the Pacific Coast League. It was billed as "the third major league" and Bilko served as a free-swinging exclamation point on that self-anointment.

So people wanted his autograph, wanted to shake his hand, wanted to buy him a beer, and there was something about him—the shy smile, the soft-spoken manner—that let it be known he was amenable to all three. Unfortunately, even before the arrival of the civic mantra that you can never be too rich or too thin, his admirers also wanted to know how much he weighed. That was Bilko's fate everywhere he played. He was always the fat guy. The standard guess was that he went 230 during the season and 260 after a winter's hibernation back home in Pennsylvania coal country. Today that kind of poundage is an everyday sight, though it's usually more sculpted than Bilko's Frigidaire shape and distributed on frames up to a half-foot taller than his 6'1". Just the same, I prefer to think he was ahead of his time.

If I seem a trifle protective of him, I am. I flinch when I read something uncharitable about his size, even though I've written about it uncharitably myself, most recently in the preceding paragraph. Likewise, I'm prone to boil over when someone who never saw him play describes him as a clumsy fielder. No less than Gene Mauch, his teammate on the Angels and one of baseball's grand strategists as a big league manager, praised his grace around first base, and Mauch wasn't one to sugarcoat his opinions.

What I'm saying, I suppose, is that Bilko is one of those rare athletes who will never stop being a hero of mine. My memories of him have nothing to do with how many helpings of mashed potatoes he could put away at a sitting and everything to do with his being tangible in a way Mickey Mantle and Willie Mays weren't. The West Coast Wrigley Field where he played was less than a half-hour drive from the house where I lived until I was thirteen, and if I couldn't be at Wrigley in person, at least all of the Angels' home games were on TV. That meant three seasons in which to watch him build his legend with a hundred and forty-eight homers for the Angels, three seasons in which he became so much more than just another vagabond slugger wandering baseball's hinterlands.

Even today, more than half a century after he last swung a bat in anger, if you mention Steve Bilko to people who care—I mean really care—about baseball, odds are they'll recognize the name. It's possible they'll also know something about his career, and I'm not talking about his twenty-one-homer season in St. Louis or his grand finale with the American League's expansion Angels. I'm talking about what he did in the Pacific Coast League when it was on the other side of the world from the majors and the aura around him bordered on mythological. It was as though he'd taken a leave of absence from being flesh and blood, or so it seemed to the kid I was then, the innocent who thought home runs began and ended with Bilko and held tight to a Bilko baseball card as proof that even a young swindler wasn't infallible. That time is gone, of course, but not forgotten, not ever.

Introduction

The Bilko Athletic Club is a journey back in time. Nearly sixty years have passed since mighty Steve Bilko and the '56 Los Angeles Angels flexed their muscles in stylish waffle-weave striped uniforms. A senior citizen center and recreational area have replaced the Angels' postcard-picture ballpark, Wrigley Field. The Pacific Coast League (PCL) still exists but its teams are scattered across the country, from Sacramento to Salt Lake City to Iowa to Nashville.

The 1950s oozed with a certain innocence that we'll never see again. *The Adventures of Ozzie and Harriet* on television made us feel good. Elvis Presley and Fats Domino had us rockin' and rollin' to the good times. "I like Ike" wasn't just a slogan that helped Dwight D. Eisenhower become president of the United States. He was genuinely liked by people in both political parties and won a second term in 1956 by a landslide.

There will never be another minor-league baseball team like the '56 Angels. Expansion five years later produced a major-league version of the Angels but it also triggered a talent drain in the minors that made it difficult to build strong, experienced teams. In fact, 1956 was a seminal year in the history of sports.

Fifteen-year-old Edson Arantes do Nascimento, also known as Pelé, made his debut for the Santos Football Club in Brazil. Pelé became the most celebrated soccer player in the world, leading Brazil to three World Cup championships.

Bill Russell powered the University of San Francisco Dons to their second straight undefeated season and National Collegiate Athletic Association basketball title. He went on to pace the Boston Celtics to eight-straight National Basketball Association titles from 1959 through 1966.

Johnny Unitas, an unheralded quarterback from the University of Louisville, broke in with the Baltimore Colts and, then, became one of the greatest National Football League (NFL) quarterbacks, elevating pro football to the lofty status it enjoys today.

Paul Hornung of Notre Dame won the Heisman Trophy and, then, starred for the great Green Bay Packer teams that won the first two Super Bowls.

The University of Oklahoma dominated college football, posting a 10–0 record to extend its winning streak to forty. This was the apex of the Sooners' forty-seven-game winning streak, a record as elusive as Joe DiMaggio's fifty-six-game consecutive hitting streak.

Rocky Marciano retired as world heavyweight champion with a perfect 49–0 record, forty-three of the victories by knockout.

Don Larsen of the Yankees pitched a perfect game in the World Series, the first and only time it has been done, and Mickey Mantle had his greatest year in a Hall-of-Fame career, leading American League hitters in batting average, home runs, and runs batted in (RBIs) to win a rare triple crown.

In Los Angeles, only Mantle's pursuit of Babe Ruth's single-season home run record matched the day-to-day drama of Steve Bilko's exploits with the '56 Angels. Stout Steve blasted tape-measure home runs as easily as he downed a six-pack of beer. He led Pacific Coast League hitters in eight categories, plus beer drinking in the clubhouse whirlpool. The Angels romped to the pennant.

"We had a helluva club and still finished 400 games out of first," said Jerry Casale, a pitcher for the San Francisco Seals, who placed sixth, twenty-eight-and-a-half games behind the Angels. Runner-up Seattle was sixteen games back. "That's how good Los Angeles was that year."

Novelist Harry Turtledove was seven years old in 1956. "Steve Bilko was my first baseball hero when he won the PCL Triple Crown in 1956. It's funny: I remember that he did that. I know Mickey Mantle won the American League Triple Crown the same year, but I don't remember it."

Bilko became John Schulian's own Mickey Mantle. "The 1956 Angels were more glamorous and charismatic because I was watching them with the eyes of an eleven year old," said the sportswriter-turned-screenwriter. "They meant something to me."

Bilko meant something to a lot of people.

"Big Steve was a big star in L.A.," said Irv Kaze, public relations director for the Angels in 1961. "When the major-league Angels came into being, the Coast League was already four years gone. But Steve's star transcended those four years."

George Goodale handled publicity for the Angels in both the minors and majors. "I have two pets in my baseball career," he said. "Bilko is one; Nolan Ryan is the other. They were just nice guys."

Steve Bilko is a baseball legend for many reasons. He was as big as King Kong. He could belt a baseball over the Empire State Building. He could consume massive quantities of beer. He also epitomized players who went from mashers in the minors to marshmallows in the majors.

"If he stayed healthy, he would've hit forty home runs in the big leagues," said Albie Pearson, a teammate with the Angels in 1961 and 1962 when Bilko was hobbled by injuries. "But it was late in his career."

Tommy Lasorda was a rival and teammate during the prime of Bilko's career in the 1950s. "If he were playing today, without question, you'd see a guy hitting fifty, sixty home runs," the former Los Angeles Dodgers manager said, adding for emphasis, "Easy."[1]

The difference between success and failure in the majors can be a few bad games, a more experienced teammate or a manager who doesn't like you. The careers of the '56 Angels were strikingly similar. All of them excelled in the minors only to struggle in the majors. Four didn't make it that far.

The Bilko Athletic Club is a story of success and failure—what the '56 Angels accomplished together as well as what happened to them later in their careers. And the best people to tell this story were the players themselves.

Despite winning 100 games in the minors, Hy Cohen felt his career, and entire life, was a failure until he saw the movie *Field of Dreams* about Moonlight Graham, a man who played one inning in the majors.

Casey Wise, the Angels' sure-handed shortstop, shared the frustrations and disappointments he experienced in the major leagues after showing so much potential in the minors.

Gale "Windy" Wade, the team's fearless centerfielder, would see his career ended by a fastball to the head from a former teammate.

Arm injuries cut short the promising pitching careers of Bob Thorpe and Dick Drott. Thorpe was working as an electrician when he was electrocuted at age twenty-four. Drott died of cancer at forty-nine, the same age as Bilko, who died of a heart attack in 1978.

A line in the poem, "Larson's Holstein Bull," by Jim Harrison reads: "Death steals everything except our stories."

It's important that the '56 Angels get the respect they deserve and their stories live on for future generations of baseball fans to enjoy.

The '56 Angels were not on the list of the top-100 minor league teams of all time compiled for baseball's 100th anniversary in 2001. The 1934 Angels were rated tops, followed by the 1921 Baltimore Orioles and the 1937 Newark Bears. No argument there. The travesty is that the '56 Angels were ignored in favor of lower-level teams, such as the 1924 Okmulgee Drillers (49th), the 1979 Saltillo Saraperos (75th), the 1978 Appleton Foxes (93rd), and the 1947 Lubbock Hubbers (97th).

"I managed three clubs in the big leagues that weren't as good as the '56 Angels," said Gene Mauch, the team's second baseman and biggest cheerleader. He cited the 1960 and 1961 Philadelphia Phillies and the 1969 Montreal Expos.

The amazing season of the '56 Angels unfolds through the stories of the players. Comments by other players and quotes from newspapers provide context and insight, creating a tapestry of the times.

Bilko was so popular in L.A. that his return in a Dodgers uniform in 1958 helped overcome stiff voter opposition to build Dodger Stadium at the desired location in Chavez Ravine where it became a model for future ballparks.

The Angels were torn apart after the 1956 season, players scattered and shattered by the ineptness of the Chicago Cubs, the parent club that signed and developed many of them. Ironically, the incompetence of Cub management contributed to the success of the Angels as Bilko was surrounded with other Cub castoffs determined to prove they belonged in the majors.

There are Bilko stories galore because, as Jim Brosnan said in a 2012 interview, "He was one of the special ones that did things that few of the others would even try to do." Brosnan and Bilko were teammates with the Angels in 1955. Brosnan went on to pitch in the majors for the Cubs, St. Louis Cardinals, and Cincinnati Redlegs and write two books, _The Long Season_ and _Pennant Race_, which gave fans their first real glimpse behind clubhouse doors.

Brosnan recalled the time in the Dominican Republic when Bilko turned down a sure bet for $1,000 with a young Dominican named Ramon Ibarre. Ramon was general manager of the team Brosnan and Bilko played for there and nephew of that country's iron-fisted dictator, Rafael Trujillo. The bet was that Steve couldn't consume two quarts of beer in an hour, drinking the beer out of a shot glass at minute intervals. He had to keep both hands on the table between drinks so he couldn't massage his stomach for relief.

"Theoretically, you can do it, but the beer plus the gas goes right to the brain and you become disoriented," Brosnan said. "Bilko had heard of this bet many years before when a great beer drinker named John Grodzicki, a pitcher for the Cardinals in the 1940s, tried it and fell on his face. Grodzicki was humiliated, but Bilko trained himself so he could drink beer without getting up to take a pee. He knew he could do it and he'd do it for nothing right in front of Ibarre. Bilko did it without any problem."

Kids idolized Bilko. "He was our Babe Ruth, Mickey Mantle, Ted Williams all rolled into one," said Bobby Grich, former all-star second baseman for the Baltimore Orioles and California Angels who grew up in nearby Long Beach, California.

Grich was seven years old when his father took him to Wrigley Field for his first professional baseball game. Bilko belted a home run. After the game, Grich rushed to the box seats behind the Angels dugout to get Bilko's autograph. "I looked around and found a stubbly pencil on the ground and tore up a popcorn box to use," Grich recalled. "There was a crowd of kids screaming, with outstretched arms pleading with Bilko to sign. I must have been the most determined because I stretched out as far as I could to make sure my popcorn shred was the farthest out. He saw my excitement and graciously took the stubbly pencil and signed on the grey inside piece of my popcorn box. You could hardly see the grey pencil on the grey sided box, but to me it stood out like a neon sign!

"I squeezed out from the crowd and looked up and screamed to my dad at the top of the stairs, 'I got Steve Bilko's autograph!' I ran for all my life all the way up to him and held out my prize for him to see. When we got home, I got out my scrapbook, taped it in and waited for the box score the next day to tape in next to the autograph. The lasting effect of that day was the result of me *never* turning away an autograph throughout my 20-year professional career if at all possible. I always remembered the thrill it was to me and tried to pass on that respect and remembrance of Steve Bilko to the kids that ever asked me for the same thing."

The story that best captures the Bilko mystique is the Palm Springs dentist who quizzed his patients about Bilko to certify they were true longtime Angelenos. Ninety-five percent passed the certification test. "Big Steve Bilko was a demigod to us early boomers growing up in the '50s," Edward Kuhn wrote the *Los Angeles Times* in 1990. "He was our Sultan of Swat . . . anything was possible when Bilko was up, and even when the Angels were far behind, no one would get his beer until Bilko had his turn at bat. Can you help my patients and myself by letting us know what happened to this man who deserves to be batting cleanup in Los Angeles' 'Field of Dreams'?"[2]

NOTES

1. *Oakland Tribune*, July 27, 2003.
2. *Los Angeles Times*, October 13, 1990, C3.

ONE

Of Buzz and Bilko

"While Bilko is regarded as baseball's answer to the guided missile, it was Buzz Clarkson who established the record for destruction of property." —Ned Cronin, *Los Angeles Times*, September 15, 1956

Most teams started the 1955 Pacific Coast League (PCL) season by getting rid of older players. The exception was the Los Angeles Angels. They welcomed thirty-seven-year-old Buzz Clarkson from the Class AA Texas League, where he hit forty-two homers the previous year. "Buzz apparently is the Jack Benny of baseball when it comes to counting backward," the *Los Angeles Times* reported on his arrival.[1]

"He was on Social Security even then," quipped Ed Mickelson, who played against Buzz in the Texas League and PCL.

Buzz did his apprenticeship in the old Negro Leagues, and like most black players hoping to get a shot at the majors, Buzz shaved three years off his real age.

Baseball players refer to a brief stay in the majors as a "cup of coffee." Buzz took his sip of the "cup" in 1952 with the Boston Braves where he appeared in fourteen games, getting five hits in twenty-five at bats for a .200 average. "The only thing against him is his age, which is indeterminable," one reporter wrote.[2]

Buzz returned to the Milwaukee Brewers in the Class AAA American Association, leading them to their second straight title. He was a big contributor to both, batting .343 in 1951 and .318 in 1952.

Bill Sweeney was the Angels' manager in 1955 until health problems forced him out. He was replaced in late May by Bob Scheffing, who would lead the team through the 1956 season.

One day in spring training, Sweeney was watching Buzz when he paused to ask a Seattle sportswriter, "Have you seen that man swish a bat?"

The writer agreed that it was a sight to see. "Everything Buzz hit was a line drive," he wrote. "Rival third basemen checked their premiums when he stepped in."[3]

In an exhibition game against the Cubs, Buzz slashed five hits, including two doubles, and batted in three runs.

Bobby Bragan, manager of the Hollywood Stars, also of the PCL, had seen Buzz play in the Texas League and winter ball and predicted he would hit twenty-five to thirty home runs for the Angels.

After watching Buzz in spring training, Max West, one of the PCL's greatest sluggers with 230 career homers, shook his head in amazement: "He hit some by the shortstop a foot each side and the shortstop didn't have time to stoop over, they were by him."[4]

"From what I've seen so far," Sweeney said, "I think the pitchers better pitch behind him."[5]

Steve Bilko was twenty-six when he joined the Angels in 1955 and was one of seven players the Chicago Cubs sent to L.A. ten days prior to the start of the PCL season. Bilko was with the Cubs when they played the Angels in an exhibition game in Mesa, Arizona.

"Sweeney kept looking at me and looking at me," Bilko recalled.

"Don't look at me!" Bilko told Sweeney. "I'm not going to California!"

"It turned out going to Los Angeles was the greatest thing to happen to me," Bilko said. "From that point on everybody knew, and I knew, that I could hit. I just hadn't got the chance. In Los Angeles, I was just left alone."

In addition to the 200-pound Buzz and 230-pound Bilko, the Angels had John Pramesa, a 210-pound catcher who hit .294 and eleven homers for L.A. in 1954.

This inspired L. H. Gregory, a sports columnist for *The Oregonian*, to write: "The Los Angeles infield is one of the most awesome sights in baseball, with three of the heaviest, heftiest, strongest and hardest-hitting men in baseball manning the defensive corners like bastions in a fortress."

"I've never seen anyone, Babe Ruth included, hit one much harder in thirty-one years of baseball," Sweeney told Gregory.

"Steve Bilko is the widest man across the chest and shoulders we ever laid eyes on," Gregory reported. "He's enormous."[6]

The six-foot-one Bilko hit twenty-one homers for the St. Louis Cardinals in 1953, but he also struck out a league-leading 125 times. The Cards sold Bilko to the Cubs in 1954 where he languished on the bench, hitting a mere four homers. "I felt I should've had a better chance to make the Cubs," Bilko said.

Sweeney's handling of Bilko was pivotal.

"Sweeney was kind enough to say, 'I don't care if you get a hit the rest of the year. You're still going to be my first baseman.' That really helped me. I figured, gee, this guy has faith in me that I'm going to hit. The season started and the first two games, I had two hits or something. Then I started to hit. Everything was coming along. I didn't have to worry about weight or anything."

Bilko blasted ten home runs the first month of the 1955 season, one of them a grand-slam and another shot was still climbing after clearing the left-field wall by thirty feet.

"Bilko is built like a tank, he's as solid as a tank and he packs the firepower of a tank," one L.A. sportswriter observed.[7]

But Paul "Tank" Younger, a muscular fullback for the Los Angeles Rams, protested the description of Bilko as a tank. "Tubby would be better for him," Younger suggested.[8]

Bilko reminded Joe Garagiola, a former teammate, of Humphrey Pennyworth, a big, strong blacksmith–athlete in the *Joe Palooka* comic strip popular during the 1950s. "He had this young face and yet he was a hulk of a man. Even though he was big enough to move buildings, he wouldn't crack an eggshell. He was a nice, gentle man. A big, lovable guy."

In the 1970s when Garagiola was announcing game-of-the-week telecasts, he recalled a Bilko home run on a barnstorming tour in New England. "There was a mountain beyond left field. I thought the ball was going through the mountain. That's how hard he hit it."

The Angels were rolling along with a 16–10 record, one game out of first place, as Buzz and Bilko pounded opposing pitchers. Bilko had eight home runs, Buzz had five. And then, Buzz slipped on Wrigley Field's wet infield grass while fielding a bunt. He broke a bone in his left foot.

When Buzz returned to action seven weeks later, the Angels were 35–40 and in fifth place. Without Buzz batting behind him, Bilko's batting average dropped seventeen points and his homers were fewer and far between. The local media and fans let him have it.

"Despite his occasional homers, he can't be depended on in the clutch," one sports columnist griped. "It aggravates them [Bilko's critics] to see poor Steve miss an outside curve by six inches."[9]

"The boo-birds poured it on Steve Bilko, the league's most controversial player, for his lackadaisical efforts," another writer reported. "They got so bad that Boom Boom, who has failed to hit in his last fourteen tries, threw his hands up in the air when they got on him hard."[10]

Bilko mused, "The fans have been on me since the first time I picked up a bat at Wrigley. It baffles me because it never happens any other place in the league or any other place I have played in the past. I don't know what they want. Maybe they expect me to hit a home run every time I come to bat."[11]

Bilko never criticized the fans. Instead, he joked, "All I can figure is that Los Angeles people like to holler at somebody, and even the nearsighted ones can't miss me for a booing target."[12]

Bilko celebrated Buzz's return to the lineup with four hits, including his eighteenth home run. He homered again the next game. Two days later Bilko went five-for-five in a game, belting two more round-trippers.

The Angels were the hottest team in the league the rest of the way, posting a 55–36 record and finishing in a tie with Hollywood for third place, four games behind pennant-winning Seattle.

Buzz hit .294 with thirteen homers and forty-six RBIs, despite playing in just 100 of the Angels' 172 games. Bilko's thirty-seven homers topped the league and he was runner-up in batting average (.328) and RBIs (124).

"The season will be remembered mostly because of that tremendous man, Big Steve Bilko," gushed the same columnist who questioned Steve's abilities earlier in the season.[13] Steve was named the league's most valuable player and he signed a contract for the 1956 season that waived his major league draft rights so no team could pick him in the winter draft.

In September 1955, *The Phil Silvers Show* made its debut on television with Silvers adopting the name Bilko for the scheming U.S. Army master sergeant he played—Ernest Bilko. The series, originally titled *You'll Never Get Rich*, was a big hit, making Bilko a household name nationally. The show was the basis of a 1996 movie, *Sgt. Bilko*.

Bilko was on his way to becoming a genuine celebrity. His name appeared in print so many times that, according to Angels' publicist George Goodale, "There wasn't a movie star that could touch him.

"Steve handled the attention very well," Goodale added. "He couldn't believe it. But all the adulation he got only served to make him want to do better. It goaded him into a more intense effort."

If you want to know how good a ball player is, ask another ball player who played with or against him.

Dave Hillman, the ace of the 1956 Angels pitching staff, and Jim Fanning, a catcher for the Angels in '55 and part of '56, played with Buzz at Beaumont, Texas, in 1954 before the slugger was traded to Dallas. Hillman had to stand on the pitcher's mound, sixty feet, six inches away from Buzz at home plate. "You could see sawdust coming out of that bat when he hit the ball. He'd hit 'em and the third baseman would just quiver."

Fanning recalled the sound of the ball hitting Buzz's bat: "In batting practice or even a game, you'd hear all of these cracks and you knew right away who was hitting. It had something to do with the way he held the bad when he made contact. It had a different kind of crack to it."

Ed Mickelson was a first baseman for Shreveport, Louisiana, in the Texas League in 1954, and Portland in the PCL in 1955, so he saw plenty of Buzz. In his memoirs, *Out of the Park*, Mickelson wrote, "One night he hit a ball at Joe Koppe, our shortstop, during a game against Dallas at Shreveport. Koppe leaped for the ball, just missing it with the tip of his

Figure 1.1. Steve Bilko, second from right, was as big as any movie star in Hollywood in 1956. Here, singer-actor Pat Boone, far right, shows ball autographed by Bilko to actress Shirley Jones and Gale Wade, Angels centerfielder. *Courtesy Gale Wade.*

glove. The ball kept rising, and it sailed on to clear the ten-foot-high wall in left-center for a home run."[14]

"He could hit a ball about as far as anybody I've ever seen," Mickelson said. "You have remembrances. And you remember Buzz Clarkson. When I wrote the book, I thought to myself: 'Did that really happen? Did Koppe jump for the ball and did it really start rising and go out of the ballpark?' And it did. It's amazing. But you start thinking, 'That couldn't be. Nobody can hit a ball that hard.'"

Mickelson wasn't alone in his thinking.

When Buzz entered the dugout shortly after belting a 420-foot single off the centerfield wall at Wrigley Field, Gene Mauch, the Angels' second baseman, said, "Buzz, I know how you hit the ball. But how do you hit it that hard? I can't believe it."

One of Buzz's blasts damaged his favorite apartment house. "The blow struck the green shuttered house opposite the left-field wall, bombing a hole right through the front door," the *Los Angeles Examiner* reported. "The residents poured out all the exits looking for enemy aircraft."[15]

Mickelson marvelled at "what a hitter he was—and must have been in the Negro Leagues in his youth."

From 1937–1950, Buzz played for various teams in the Negro Leagues, Mexican League, and the independent Provincial League in Canada.

In a barnstorming game in Puerto Rico in 1940, the story goes that Buzz came to bat against the great Satchel Paige with the bases loaded in the first inning. Satchel wanted to walk Buzz.

"Don't you know you're going to walk a run home?" the catcher asked.

"Well, I'd rather walk one home," Satchel replied, "than have him hit three or four home."[16]

Satchel walked Buzz to score a run, and, then, made good on his pledge of not allowing another run in the game. Fact or fiction, the story attests to the respect pitchers had for Buzz' power.

Buzz played winter ball in Puerto Rico throughout his career. In early 1955, he was player-manager for the Santurce Crabbers, guiding them to Puerto Rico's national title and the Caribbean Series championship. Willie Mays and Roberto Clemente, future Hall of Famers, played on the same team but Buzz batted in the clean-up spot.

"He was smart," Wade said of Buzz. "And he played a smart third base. He probably played better than a lot of younger, quicker guys because he shifted according to the hitters, and that's the key."

Buzz also was a good judge of baseball talent.

The 1955 season was Henry "Hank" Aaron's second in the majors. He batted .280 with thirteen homers as a rookie but was far from being a superstar. Mays hit .345 with forty-one home runs the year before and would slam fifty-one more in 1955.

"Keep an eye on that Aaron," Buzz told L.A. sportswriters in July 1955. "Over the long haul, I wouldn't be surprised if Aaron . . . proves a more valuable player than Mays."[17]

Buzz called everybody "Road" because he had trouble remembering names. That's fitting because he spent 1956, his last as a player, on the road, starting in L.A., stopping briefly at Tulsa in the Texas League, and winding up at Des Moines in the Western League.

Don Swanson pitched for all three teams, and saw most of Buzz's eighteen home runs that year. "Buzz could hit the ball as hard as ever," Swanson said. "He was just born too soon."

The Buzz and Bilko show wasn't over yet.

The Angels and Stars were scheduled to tangle in a best-of-five game playoff to decide the 1955 city championship.

The crosstown foes split their regular-season series, winning fourteen games apiece, as well as tying for third place in the PCL.

Figure 1.2.   James "Buzz" Clarkson, center, could hit the ball as hard and far as his Santurce Crabbers teammates shown here, left to right: Willie Mays, Roberto Clemente, Clarkson, Bob Thurman, and George Crowe. At age forty, Buzz starred for the 1955 Angels. He played briefly for the 1956 Angels. *National Baseball Hall of Fame Library, Cooperstown, N.Y.*

The Angels–Stars rivalry was one of the most intense in baseball.

"I would stack it up to the Dodgers–Giants, Yankees–Red Sox, and Cubs–Cardinals," said Irv Kaze, the Stars' publicist. "The rivalry was just as heated and emotional as any of those at their best."

Angel fans disliked everything about the Stars, especially Mark Scott, their radio play-by-play announcer. Scott closed every broadcast by saying, "And remember, sports fans, whether you win or lose, always be a good sport."

The Stars didn't always live up to that phrase on the field. One of their top players, Carlos Bernier, was suspended the year before for slapping an umpire. Bobby Bragan, the Stars' manager from 1953 to 1955, was one of the all-time umpire baiters.

In a game against the Angels earlier in the season, Bragan was so upset with the umpiring that he used eight pinch-hitters in one batting spot. "I told them when they got to the plate not to take a pitch, just call time and I'd send another hitter up," Bragan explained. "In other words, it wouldn't be possible for them to get a walk or strike out. I used all the players I had in the dugout.

"If you're going to make a joke of this game," Bragan said to the umpires, "I'm going to show you how to really make a joke of it."

After being ejected from a game for excessive arguing, Bragan sent the Stars' batboy out the next inning to coach third base in his place.

As the batboy trotted toward the coach's box, the home plate umpire said, "Don't let Bobby make a fool of you, son."

"He's not," the batboy replied. "I'm enjoying it."

Bragan's theatrics were captured in a *Life* magazine photograph show- ing him lying at the feet of an umpire, still arguing after being tossed out of the game.

The Angels were favored to win their first city championship in five years as all of the games in the playoff series were scheduled for Wrigley Field, where the Angels had an 11–3 advantage over the Stars during the regular season.

The Stars won the first two games prompting Bragan to predict a series sweep. That riled up the Angels, who won the next two games to even the series and force a decisive fifth game.

In that game, the Angels trailed 7–6 with two outs in the ninth inning, the tying run on third, and Bilko coming to bat. He already had three hits in the game and was batting .450 (nine-for-twenty) in the series. He had yet to park one. Buzz—five-for-twenty with two home runs—was on- deck, waiting to bat next.

Bragan brought in right-hander Joe Trimble to pitch to Bilko. "Trimble had a wonderful curveball—like Bob Feller's."

The Stars manager instructed his catcher, Bill Hall to "get a couple of strikes with the curveball, waste one and throw him another curve. Make him hit the curve."

The first pitch was called strike one. The second pitch was a ball. The third pitch was called strike two. Hall checked with Bragan on the next pitch. "Bobby, do we need to waste a fastball to him or just throw him another curve?"

"Go ahead and throw him another curve," Bragan said.

Trimble threw a fourth straight curve. Bilko took a lethal swing and missed. The mighty Bilko struck out. The Stars had beaten the Angels again.

NOTES

1. *Los Angeles Times*, March 8, 1955, C2.
2. *The Sporting News*, May 7, 1952, 12.
3. *Seattle Times*, July 7, 1955, 25.
4. *Los Angeles Mirror-News*, April 5, 1955, Part III, 1.
5. Ibid., April 5, 1955, Part III, 1.

6. *The Oregonian*, April 12, 1955, 6M.
7. *Los Angeles Times*, April 24, 1955, B6.
8 *Los Angeles Times*, April 30, 1955, B2.
9. *Los Angeles Mirror-News*, June 2, 1955, Part III, 1.
10. *Los Angeles Mirror-News*, August 11, 1955, Part III, 3.
11. *Los Angeles Herald-Express*, June 1, 1955, B2.
12. Ibid.
13. *Los Angeles Mirror-News*, September 12, 1955, Part III, 1.
14. Ed Mickelson, *Out of the Park: Memoir of a Minor League Baseball All-Star*, (Jefferson, NC: McFarland & Company, Inc., 2007), 131.
15. *Los Angeles Examiner*, August 15, 1955, Section IV, 1.
16. Larry Moffi and Jonathan Kronstadt, *Crossing the Line: Black Major Leaguers, 1947–1959*, (Jefferson, NC: McFarland & Company, Inc., 1994), 75.
17. *Los Angeles Times*, July 20, 1955, C2.

TWO
The Best Minor League Team I Ever Saw, Bar None!

"They captured my imagination as no other team ever has—Bob Speake and Jim Bolger flanking Windy Wade in the outfield, Casey Wise turning double plays with [Gene] Mauch, Elvin Tappe behind the plate, George Freese at the hot corner, and over at first . . . Bilko . . . Bilko . . . Bilko. . ." —*Of Stars and Angels* by John Schulian, *Twilight of the Long-ball Gods*

The rivalry between the Los Angeles Angels and Hollywood Stars was one of the fiercest in baseball history.

From 1926 through 1957, the old Pacific Coast League foes played, argued, and brawled with each other and sometimes in reverse order. To start another battle, all you have to do is mention the 1956 Angels as one of baseball's greatest minor league teams.

"The best minor league team that I ever saw, bar none!" said Gene Mauch, the 1956 Angels scrappy second baseman who went on to be a major league manager for twenty-six years.

"It was a good team in a lousy league," countered Chuck Stevens, a first baseman for the Stars from 1948 to 1954. "The league was very weak that year."

The PCL had its own "open" classification—a notch above Class AAA and as high as a player could go in the minors.

As for the quality of the league in 1956, San Francisco manager Joe Gordon said it was much stronger than when he was in it five years earlier, explaining, "There are twice as many good players, and the pitching has improved tremendously."[1] He went so far as to suggest that the Angels could finish second to the New York Yankees in the American League if they added two top-flight pitchers.

11

The debate has been going on since the middle of the 1956 season when Angels' manager Bob Scheffing rated his club as the best he ever saw in the minor leagues.

Frank Kelleher, an ex–Hollywood Star and Newark Bear, disagreed, claiming that the 1937 Newark team was superior.

Mauch started his campaign for the '56 Angels as "best minor league team ever" near the end of the season as they rolled to a 107–61 won-loss record, finishing sixteen games ahead of their closest competitor.

They belted 202 home runs, two shy of the league record; posted a team batting average of .297; and scored 1,000 runs in 168 games or nearly six runs a game. Six players belted twenty or more home runs and had batting averages of .300 or higher. Four players batted in 100 or more runs. Six players, including the entire infield, were named to *Look* magazine's PCL all-star team for 1956. And Steve Bilko hit one mighty home run after another to earn Minor League Player of the Year honors and inspire the team's nickname: The Bilko Athletic Club.

Mauch was standing nearby when a sportswriter asked Dwight "Red" Adams to compare the three L.A. championship teams (1944, 1947, and 1956) for which he pitched.

"Tell him that this is the best club," Mauch urged Adams.

"Gene was so high on the '56 ball club and for good reason," Adams said. "I couldn't give the guy a definite answer. The circumstances were a lot different. The league was a lot different. It's pretty hard to just go by records."

Other Angels needed no prompting from Mauch.

"There was no other team in the minor leagues that could compare with us in 1956," said Gene Fodge, a pitcher. "It was the team of teams."

"We were the best minor league team in the whole damn minor leagues," claimed Johnny Briggs, another pitcher.

"We never thought we could be beat, even if we were behind by six, seven or eight runs," recalled George Freese, a power-hitting third baseman. "It was a fabulous team. Best minor league team that was ever put together in baseball."

"The '56 Angels team was better than the Cubs of '56," Bilko said, echoing the view of many people who saw both teams play.

"I played on a lot of teams," said Casey Wise, a switch-hitting shortstop, "and this one exemplified a team better than any other. I guess that's what made it a great team. We scored so many runs that the pitchers, I'm sure, were fighting each other for the chance to get out on the mound. It was just a good solid team all-around. It didn't really have any serious flaws."

Wise was a member of the Milwaukee Braves in 1958 when they won the National League pennant and fell just short of winning their second-straight World Series, losing to the Yankees in seven games. Many years later, Wise received a questionnaire from the Braves' publicity department, asking about his biggest thrill in baseball.

"I was reluctant to put something about the minor leagues in there but I said, 'Being part of and playing for the Los Angeles Angels in 1956.' That is about as good an answer that I could come up with. It was the epitome really of what you think of with success. You're an important part of the team. The team was cohesive and pulling for each other. And Bilko was hitting home runs. It doesn't sound like a lot now but fifty-five home runs in those days was pretty impressive."

In 1956, the single-season record for home runs in both the major leagues and PCL was sixty. After hitting twenty-three home runs in the first fifty games, Bilko was being called the "greatest thing to happen to the Angels since wings" and "to Los Angeles since Shirley Temple and Rin Tin Tin."[2]

The *San Francisco News* wrote, "Since all of the Angel games, except Friday night, are on TV, Mr. Bilko's long-ball hitting has grown to proportions in Los Angeles almost equal to Phil Silvers' maneuvering sergeant of the same surname."[3]

"The name, 'Bilko,' was made to remember," said John Schulian, a sports columnist turned television screenwriter. "Two syllables, punchy with a K. It was made for headlines because it's short. It goes all over the place."

Bilko's name was all over the country because of the hit television show starring Phil Silvers as Sgt. Ernest G. Bilko.

The real Bilko had to deal with more important matters such as his weight. It was an issue that former U.S. President Dwight Eisenhower even commented on when they met in 1961: "They tell me you're off about thirty pounds in weight."[4]

When the media asked what he weighed, Bilko politely answered, "Somewhere between 200 and 300 pounds." He weighed himself on the first day of spring training and the last day of the season and let his thirty-two-ounce bat do his talking in between.

After Bilko socked his forty-first homer in a game at San Francisco's Seals Stadium, the *San Francisco Chronicle* reported, "If Mickey Mantle had hit the homer, his full length tape measure would not have been long enough. But it was hit by Steve Bilko and passed off as just another homer. The ball cleared the left-field wall (365 feet) and also a parking lot in back of left field. It was a 600-foot homer—if it was a foot."[5]

On August 26, Bilko had fifty home runs with twenty-four games to play. Meanwhile, Mantle had forty-four home runs and was in hot pursuit of Babe Ruth's major-league record.

The two sluggers were so popular in 1956, a presidential election year in the United States, that Ned Cronin, a *L.A. Times* columnist, proposed that Mantle run for president with Bilko as his vice president: "A vote against Mantle and Bilko is a vote against home, mother and bottled beer."[6]

Mantle finished with fifty-two home runs. Bilko went twelve days in September without a home run to wind up with fifty-five. The bulky Bilko even outdid the speedy Mantle in the triples department—six to five. Altogether, Bilko paced the PCL in eight categories: home runs, batting average (.360), runs batted in (164), hits (215), runs scored (163), walks (104), total bases (410), and slugging percentage (.683).

Up and down the West Coast, sportswriters were dreaming up nicknames for Bilko such as Stout Steve the Slugging Seraph or simply Stout Steve, Sergeant Bilko, Sergeant of Swat, Big Boy, Boom Boom, Mr. Biceps, Angel Atlas, and the Ambulant Atomic Energy Plant from Southern California. A new cult hero was born, and "The Bilko Athletic Club" was being hailed as one of the greatest minor league teams in baseball history.

Figure 2.1.   Sluggers Steve Bilko, left, and Mickey Mantle were so popular in 1956 that one L.A. sports columnist suggested Mantle run for president and Bilko vice president of the United States. In this photo taken before an exhibition game in 1958, Mantle shows Bilko his favorite bat. *Associated Press Wirephoto/National Baseball Hall of Fame Library, Cooperstown, N.Y.*

For all of the attention focused on Bilko, the '56 Angels were far from being a one-man team.

"That team had just about everything as far as the minor leagues go," said Eddie Haas, a twenty-year-old outfielder who started the season with the Angels before being sent to the lower minors. "It had power, speed, older players that could play."

Except for the twenty-three-year-old Wise, all of the regulars had played in the majors, several displaying flashes of brilliance.

At thirty, Mauch was the oldest and most experienced, bouncing around the National League with five different teams and managing the Atlanta Crackers in the Southern Association prior to landing with the Angels in 1954.

Freese, twenty-nine, played in fifty-one games for the Pittsburgh Pirates in 1955, hitting for a .257 average.

Bilko, twenty-seven, broke in with the St. Louis Cardinals in 1949, and in his first full season in the majors in 1953, rapped twenty-one home runs and batted in eighty-four runs. "He was good enough then," said Ralph Kiner, a seven-time home run champion in the majors. "I thought he should've stayed."[7]

Catcher Elvin Tappe, twenty-seven, appeared in forty-six games for the Cubs in 1954.

Left-fielder Bob Speake, twenty-five, was an early-season sensation with the Cubs in 1955, socking ten homers in his first ninety big league at bats.

Gale "Windy" Wade, twenty-seven, was the Cubs' centerfielder to begin both the 1955 and 1956 seasons.

Right-fielder Jim Bolger, twenty-four, already had three brief trials with the Cincinnati Reds and a full season in 1955 with the Cubs.

At one time or another, the pitching staff included Adams, Marino "Chick" Pieretti, and Harry Perkowski, all thirty-something minor-league veterans with experience in the majors. Pitchers Dave Hillman, Hy Cohen, and Bob Thorpe pitched for the Cubs in 1955. Thorpe and Johnny Briggs began the 1956 season in Chicago before arriving in L.A.

As dominating as Bilko was in 1956, Mauch was the team's sparkplug. He was also one of the PCL's most fiery and cunning competitors.

"Gene Mauch is a notorious cheater," wrote a *Sacramento Union* columnist. "He's been known to wheel on the double play and make his throw to first when no closer than a yard to the bag."[8]

"He knew how to cheat on batters, how to cheat on the double play," said Richie Myers, a shortstop for Sacramento and later L.A. "I always respected him as a player playing against him. And, then, I got to know him more playing with him. He played hard. And he played to win."

"He'll beat you any way he can, and I can name ninety-nine ways he can do it," Scheffing said.[9]

While his .348 batting average, twenty home runs, and eighty-four RBIs in 1956 were all career highs, Mauch's greatest value was as a leader. He was a master at devising trick plays, stealing opponents' signs and, if necessary, getting in the face of a teammate.

"He expected the very best from everybody," said Adams. "He was totally into the game. If he saw you losing a little bit of that focus, he would remind you in whatever way it took."

Bob Anderson, the Angels' twenty-year-old relief ace, credited Mauch for making Bilko the great hitter that he was in 1956.

"Steve was a guess hitter, and Gene was as good at picking up signals from an opposing pitcher as you could possibly imagine. So Steve was an even better hitter."

Soon after winning the championship, the Angels sold Mauch to the Boston Red Sox. The next month the Cubs tabbed Scheffing to be their manager for the 1957 season.

"He helped me plenty," Scheffing said of Mauch. "If I had known I was going to manage the Cubs, we would have never sold him to the Red Sox. I'd have held onto him as a player, coach or something." [10]

Of his baseball acumen and that of his teammates, Mauch said, "My brother-in-law [Roy Smalley, shortstop for the Cubs in the early 1950s] said about me one time that 'he never heard Mauch say he was a genius, but he never heard him deny it either.' No, I wasn't. But I knew how to play and so did the rest of them."

Five players, including Mauch, managed in the majors. Tappe guided the Cubs' misguided College of Coaches experiment; John Goryl, an infielder who was farmed out a month into the season, managed the Minnesota Twins; Haas, the Atlanta Braves; and Jim Fanning, a catcher, the Montreal Expos.

Fanning was responsible for establishing the scouting bureau that major league teams still use today. Adams became a highly respected pitching coach for the Los Angeles Dodgers.

Lorenzo "Piper" Davis, the only black player on the team, was player-manager of the Birmingham Black Barons. For the Angels, Piper was an outstanding pinch hitter and supersub.

"He goes in at any position and for three or four games does just as well as the man he replaces," Mauch said. [11]

The thirty-nine-year-old Piper was a catalyst, spending much of his time in the bullpen warming up the team's young pitchers and giving them the benefit of the wisdom he gained from playing in the Negro Leagues.

"Piper knew his role and he played it well," Speake said. "That was the beauty of Scheffing managing people. He let both Piper and Gene do their thing."

Scheffing was affectionately called Grump because he was known to tell his players, "When the game is close, don't be over near me because I'll be grumpin' and groanin' about everything."

Joe Garagiola and Scheffing were teammates on the St. Louis Cardinals and became best friends. "You have to understand that Scheffing is a very happy man inside," Joe said. "He just hasn't told his face about it."[12]

Actually, Scheffing was mild mannered and easy going, imposing few rules on his players. "It was like a big family and he was our dad or big brother," Adams said. "He was the guy for that ball club."

Scheffing admired Casey Stengel, manager of the Yankees from 1949 to 1960, when they won ten American League pennants and seven World Series titles, calling him "the master psychologist of all baseball managers."[13] Scheffing was not a bad psychologist himself, leaving Bilko alone to be himself and letting Mauch operate like a manager on the field.

"Bob was a handler of men, not ball players," said Speake. "Bob appreciated Gene's baseball wisdom and leadership ability on the field, and he just let it go, let it develop so that Gene could help younger ball players and also be part of that winning tradition. Bob had the knack of sitting back and letting you do your thing."

"He let us be as creative as we wanted to be and he had great trust in us," Mauch said. "After all the years I managed, I learned it's far more important that the players know that the manager respects them than it is for them to respect the manager. Scheffing was a helluva manager—the best manager I ever played for."

When Scheffing became manager of the Angels early in the 1955 season, they had a 25–25 record and Bilko was struggling. Scheffing went to Bilko and said, "Don't worry about anything. You'll start hitting."[14]

Perhaps the best decision Scheffing made was switching Wise from second base to shortstop.

Two months into the season, the Cubs sent Myers to L.A. He was considered the best shortstop in the league the previous year at Sacramento. "I can't break in," Myers told a Sacramento sportswriter soon after reporting to L.A. "Casey Wise and the club are just going too darned good."[15]

Wise batted .287 and had Scheffing praising his defense: "He's not a spectacular player but you'll notice he makes the plays and makes most of them look easy."[16]

That pretty much described the infield defensively.

"None of us were real flashy but when the ball was hit to us, the routine outs were outs," Mauch said. "We didn't screw up."

Freese batted fifth in the lineup behind Bilko and when teams pitched around Stout Steve, he made them pay with 113 RBIs. "With ducks on the pond he's their most dangerous hitter," said Royce Lint, a pitcher for the Portland Beavers. "I should know. He's got at least twelve or fifteen RBIs off me this year."[17]

The outfield of Speake in left, Wade in center, and Bolger in right was fast and fearless.

"They would run through a brick wall to catch a ball," Hillman said.

"That's what walls are for," quipped Jim Brosnan, who played with Wade, the chief fencebuster, in L.A. and Chicago.

"Speake makes catches every game that are just out of this world," Mauch told a reporter in 1956. "He can go and get just about anything that's still in the park."[18]

"Both Bob and Jim were capable centerfielders," Wade said. "The reason I played centerfield was because I couldn't play either one of the other fields. We had the advantage of that great speed, and I've said many times that you couldn't shoot a 30.06 rifle between us in the outfield. Because when one guy was catching the ball, the other guy was behind him backing it up. We could play hitters and bunch 'em. It was very difficult for anybody to get base hits on us in that outfield."

"It was a real good outfield not only defensively but those guys put up big numbers hitting, too," Haas said. "They played hard every inning of every day. I mean, they were hard-playing players. I was young but after awhile it just dawned on me how hard those guys played every day and every inning. We could be down eight-nine runs in the eighth or ninth inning and you'd see one of them make a diving catch. That's what made them an outstanding outfield."

Wade played with a death wish, sliding head first, barreling into infielders to break up double plays, and literally crashing through outfield fences.

"He didn't give a damn how many outs there were," Mauch said. "If he wanted to run and dive for the ball, he ran and dove for it. It didn't matter. He was just daring. There were no reins on Gale Wade."

"Winning one ballgame to me was a whole season," Wade explained. "If it meant taking a catcher out at home plate or knocking out the second baseman with a rolling block, I did it. I sacrificed my body to win ballgames."

This daring style of play and a gregarious personality earned Wade the nickname "Windy." He hit for a .292 average, batted in sixty-seven runs, and, despite playing only 101 games, poked twenty home runs and a team-high seven triples.

The offensive numbers for Speake and Bolger were even more impressive. Speake posted a .300 average with twenty-five home runs and twenty-nine doubles, scoring 107 runs, and driving in 111 runs. Bolger batted .326, belted thirty-seven doubles, and twenty-eight home runs.

"Nobody on the club had more timely at bats than Bolger," said Mauch, citing his RBI total of 147, second in the league only to Bilko.[19]

"Jim could do about anything you'd want," said Coats. "He could run. He could throw. He had good power."

"When he had that cotton-pickin' uniform on and he had a bat in his hands, you just had to get out of the way," said Fanning. "He'd swing a bat in the dugout. He'd swing it in the tunnels, in the clubhouse. I mean he was a menace. He was intense."

Fanning and Joe Hannah shared catching duties until the Angels acquired Tappe from the Cubs in late May. Tappe was the proverbial strong-fielding, weak-hitting catcher.

"He could almost throw out of a telephone booth," Adams said. "I can remember him taking just a little tiny short step as he was catching the ball. It was almost like bouncing it off of him. He had wonderful footwork. Good hands. Just a good defensive catcher."

Scheffing had a young, capable defensive catcher in Hannah but he wanted the more experienced Tappe to mentor the team's young pitchers.

"He won't hit too much," Scheffing said, "but with El behind the plate our pitchers won't miss his hits. If he could hit even .240 he'd be in the majors."[20]

Tappe exceeded all expectations by hitting .267—a whopping 156 points higher than his average the previous year.

The Angels really had two different pitching staffs—Grump's old men and his kids.

As an "old" catcher, Grump liked having a few "old" pitchers around to balance the inexperience of the team's kid pitchers. Pieretti, Adams, and Perkowski provided that balance as well as a combined seventeen victories.

Adams was one of the PCL's craftier veteran pitchers. "He made a living off of dummies and kids," said Mauch. "He could make a kid look foolish, and dummies, he could get them out the same way four and five times. Brilliant."

Signed by the Angels in June after he was released by Portland, Adams won six games and mentored the youngsters.

"It says a lot for Scheffing," Adams said. "I guess that he felt that he needed us old, broken-down guys around."

"We had older guys in the right places," added Briggs, one of the kid pitchers. "We had Adams and Tappe helping the pitchers, and we had Mauch in the infield."

Mauch was also helping the pitchers. "You could hear Mauch all over the place," Briggs said. "He was always telling somebody something."

The kid pitchers were Drott; Anderson, Thorpe, Briggs, and Fodge. Drott was the youngest at nineteen years old, and Fodge the oldest at twenty-four.

The quintet posted a 56–33 won-loss record, Fodge leading the way with nineteen victories, followed by Drott's thirteen and Anderson's twelve.

Anderson was used exclusively as a relief pitcher, making seventy appearances to set a league record. His ERA of 2.65 was the best on the team.

Drott made the jump from Class B to the PCL look easy, leading the league in strikeouts with 184. "Dick Drott had the best curveball I ever saw in a nineteen-year-old kid," Mauch said.

Anderson had a wicked fastball to go with his imposing size of six-foot-four, 210 pounds. Mauch compared Anderson with Troy Percival, one of the game's top closers when he pitched for the California/Anaheim Angels from 1995 to 2004.

"We knew one thing. If we had a lead going into the eighth inning, the game was over. Everybody in the league was scared to death of Anderson. Scared to death of him. He was just wild enough."

Thorpe won seven games and Briggs five after starting the season with the Cubs.

"You can't name too many ball clubs that had that many good young arms on it in the minor leagues," said Adams. "There was tremendous talent . . . a lot of potential."

Bridging this mix of old and young pitchers were Hillman, twenty-eight, and Raymond "Moe" Bauer, twenty-seven. In baseball terminology, they were journeymen—well-traveled players who are reliable but not star performers.

That changed with the Angels as Hillman led the Angels pitching staff in wins (twenty-one), shutouts (three), complete games (fifteen), and innings pitched (210). His 3.38 ERA was tops among the starters. "But for a sore arm that kept him inactive for the first five weeks, Hillman would have, at the very least, twenty-five enemy scalps dangling from his belt right now," one writer offered.[21]

Bauer, a left-hander with an outstanding curveball and pinpoint control, was a finesse pitcher who nicely complemented the power pitching of Anderson out of the bullpen. He appeared in forty-nine games, posting a 6–1 record and 3.16 ERA.

"Hillman would give you innings," said Coats. "He might not have the world's best stuff but he'd hang around long enough for you to have that hot inning or two and score some runs. He won a lot of games when other pitchers would've been out of the ballgame."

The pitching staff was considered the weak link of the '56 Angels.

Kelleher, the ex-Newark player, said Hillman was the only pitcher good enough to play for the 1937 Bears.[22]

"The pitching staff was subpar and, as a result, the 1956 Angels were probably a level below the greatest teams of PCL history," Richard Beverage wrote in a book chronicling the history of the team from its beginnings in 1903.[23]

Nobody denies that the Bilko Athletic Club was the most destructive in the last twenty years of the league's existence. "We had the big bomber at first base," said Coats. "And we had Speake, Freese and Bolger who could hit the ball out of the ballpark at any time. And we had Casey and Mauch—they were going to get on. We could put two or three innings together pretty quick. We never thought we were out of a ballgame. And the other team sensed that."

Opposing pitchers attest to the team's greatness.

"It was the best team that I had ever faced," said Sacramento pitcher Roger Osenbaugh.

"They had a powerhouse," said Charlie Beamon, a pitcher for the Vancouver Mounties who had success against the Angels. "I beat 'em a couple of times but it was a struggle. You had to really be on top of your game."

Anderson went on to pitch parts of six seasons in the majors with the Cubs and another with the Detroit Tigers.

"I remember some things with the Cubs," he said. "I remember a lot about the '56 Angels. I was in awe of Steve Bilko. I was in awe of Gene Mauch. George Freese was a tremendous guy. Jim Bolger received very, very little recognition but was an outstanding ball player. And Gale Wade had some of the best acting talent I've ever seen in my life. He could make a pitcher think that he was in agony and then come by and lash the next one right by his ear. I was in awe of the way they all played together."

In 1937, the New York Yankees were again the best team in baseball, easily winning the American League pennant and breezing past the New York Giants in the World Series.

A strong case can be made that the second-best team in baseball that year was the Newark Bears, a Yankees farm team in the International League. In those days, the league was Class AA, then the highest level in the minors.

The 1937 Bears are the team that Kelleher cited as the greatest minor league team of all. And he's not alone. The Bears won 109 regular-season games, plus 12 more to win their league playoffs and the Little World Series. They won their league by twenty-five games, batted .299 as a team, and averaged almost six runs per game—all numbers strikingly similar to the '56 Angels.

The biggest difference between the two teams is the success their players had in the majors. Only one Newark player failed to make it to the majors compared with four Angels—Bauer, Coats, Davis, and Hannah. Newark's Joe Gordon and Charlie Keller went on to star in the big leagues, with several others enjoying some success. None of the Angels found stardom in the majors. Drott came the closest, winning fifteen games as a rookie with the Cubs in '57. He won only twelve more games the rest of his career.

"I thought Anderson and Drott would have big, big careers," Mauch said. "For various reasons, they didn't quite make it as big as I thought they would in the big leagues."

Bilko was labeled the "Paul Bunyan of the Bushes" and became the poster boy for minor-league greats who flopped in the majors.

The criteria used by many to measure the greatness of a minor league team are how many of its players become big league stars. This doesn't make any more sense than measuring great college football and basketball teams based on what their players did in the pros.

Consider, for example, the 1974 Pawtucket Red Sox of the International League. Two of their players, Fred Lynn and Jim Rice, became big league stars. But Pawtucket finished last in its division with a 57–87 record, hardly qualifying it as an outstanding minor league team.

The Angels' Wade played centerfield for the 1954 Indianapolis Indians, champions of the American Association with a 95–57 record. The Indians were led by three future major league stars—pitchers Herb Score and Sam Jones, and Rocky Colavito, a slugging outfielder.

"We had some hard throwers and power hitters but it was not as good a club as the '56 Angels," Wade said. "We had more experienced players in L.A. Every single guy at every single position played smart baseball. That was the difference. That's what made it a great ball club."

Few have the knowledge to compare teams from different leagues and eras because they didn't see them play. That leaves us with records and statistics to evaluate them. And they can be misleading.

"Everything is relative," said Schulian, the former sportswriter. "The '56 Angels weren't trying to win ballgames in the National League; they were trying to win games in the Coast League against Coast League teams."

For all their dominance, the 1956 Angels couldn't beat their backyard nemesis, the Stars.

Rube Samuelson, a sports columnist for the *Pasadena Star-News*, mused,

> "Why can't the Angels chop
> Down the Hollywood's mammy?
> Hush, child, a hex is on –
> The ye olde double whammy."[24]

The Stars earned local bragging rights for the sixth straight year, winning fourteen of twenty-four games, sweeping four doubleheaders and blanking the Angels four times. "How do you explain it?" Scheffing asked.[25]

One claim that can be made with a certain degree of confidence is that the '56 Angels were the last great minor league team. The majors began expanding in 1961, diluting the talent in the minors and changing them forever.

Figure 2.2. **A strong case can be made for the 1956 Los Angeles Angels as the last great minor league team.** Front row, left to right: John Briggs, pitcher; Arnold Tesh, batboy; Bob Scheffing Jr., batboy; Billy Meyers, batboy; Joe Hannah, catcher; Elvin Tappe, catcher; Dave Hillman, pitcher. Second row, left to right: Bill Heymans, assistant secretary-treasurer; Marino Pieretti, pitcher; Bob Scheffing, manager; John Holland, president; Jackie Warner, coach; Don Lauters, utility; George Goodale, publicity director; Billy Holman, clubhouse boy. Third row, left to right: Joe Liscio, trainer; Steve Bilko, first base; Casey Wise, shortstop; George Freese, third base; Gene Mauch, second base; Bob Speake, left field; Gale "Windy" Wade, centerfield; Jim Bolger, right field. Back row, left to right: Gene Fodge, pitcher; Bob Thorpe, pitcher; Dick Drott, pitcher; Dwight "Red" Adams, pitcher; Raymond "Moe" Bauer, pitcher; Lorenzo "Piper" Davis, utility; Bob Anderson, pitcher; Bob Coats, outfielder. *Courtesy Dave Hillman.*

The debate over the '56 Angels was kicked up several notches in 1999 with the publication of *The Grand Minor League,* an oral history of the old PCL.

Stevens, the ex-Star, threw a spitball at the Angels: "I thought they were overrated in a bad league, and I can name five ball clubs in my history that could have beaten them hands down any day of the week."[26]

That raised the ire of the Angels, especially Mauch.

It was the Angels–Stars rivalry all over again. You could almost see Mauch's neck turn red, the veins ready to pop: "I know Chuck Stevens very well. He was a good player. And a self-styled analyst that doesn't know his ass from fourth base."

Stevens argued that "the league weakened terribly" around 1954–1955. "Up until that time, it was just a step below the major leagues."

"I'm not going to say anything that would lessen the great year that our guys had," Mauch said. "The only difference that I can think of is that Hollywood wasn't quite as good in '56 as they were in '54."

"A couple of the Hollywood clubs that I was on would have loved to have played those guys," Stevens said.

"The Stars teams wouldn't make a pimple on our elbow. He doesn't want us to be as good as his '52 and '53 Hollywood teams. He wants to be part of the best team. And he just missed it by a few years," Mauch quipped.

"If you look at the rosters of some of the great minor league teams," Stevens said, "you'll see the names of guys who went on to distinguish themselves in the majors. That's not the case with the '56 Angels.

"Well, I really don't know how to answer that," Mauch said. "I do know this. We all had career years at the same time.

"The only guy who thinks it was a helluva ball club is Gene Mauch. And Mauch has been wrong before."

"I'm not going to get in an argument with Chuck. He might be right but you would never get me to say it."

"Get the '56 Angels out of Wrigley Field and put the Stars and the Angels in Seals Stadium and we would beat their brains out."

"I can't get over Chuck saying that. It irritates the hell out of me."

Enter Freese: "I know what we did and the statistics we had so I don't care what anybody says. Bilko could hit a ball over the fence with his forearm."

"You can criticize the Pope if you want to," Haas lamented. "You can't please everybody."

What critics fail to appreciate is the '56 Angels were mostly a bunch of major league rejects who bonded with each other to achieve goals and dreams they could never realize on their own. For one glorious season, Bilko was a chip off Babe Ruth's block and the Sultan of Swat everyone expected him to be. He inspired many of his teammates to career years that made "The Bilko Athletic Club" baseball's last great minor league team.

NOTES

1. *Los Angeles Examiner*, August 1, 1956, Section 3, 4.
2. *San Francisco Chronicle*, July 21, 1956, 2H; June 20, 1956, 2H.
3. *San Francisco News*, June 1, 1956, 16.
4. *Baseball Digest*, May 1961, 41–42.
5. *The Sporting News*, August 1, 1956, 25.
6. *Los Angeles Times*, August 26, 1956, A3.
7. *Los Angeles Examiner*, August 18, 1956, Section II, 1.
8. *Sacramento Union*, July 26, 1956, 5.
9. *The Sporting News*, August 15, 1956, 27.
10. *The Sporting News*, April 27, 1960, 6.

11. *Los Angeles Times,* September 8, 1956, A1.
12. *St. Louis Globe-Democrat,* October 31, 1985, 2B.
13. *Los Angeles Times,* May 9, 1956, B6.
14. *San Francisco Examiner,* June 2, 1956, Section II, 2.
15. *Sacramento Union,* June 5, 1956, 7.
16. *The Sporting News,* April 3, 1957, 17.
17. *Los Angeles Times,* July 31, 1956, Part II, 2.
18. *Los Angeles Times,* September 8, 1956, A1.
19. Ibid., September 8, 1956, A1
20. Ibid., July 17, 1955, B6.
21. *Los Angeles Times,* September 5, 1956, Part II, 2.
22. *Los Angeles Herald-Express,* August 17, 1956, D1.
23. Richard Beverage, *The Los Angeles Angels of the Pacific Coast League,* (Jefferson, NC: McFarland & Company, Inc., 2011), 182.
24. *Pasadena Star-News,* June 19, 1956, A4.
25. *Los Angeles Herald-Express,* September 12, 1956, D5.
26. Dobbins, *The Grand Minor League,* Emeryville, CA: Duane Press, 88.

THREE

Little Wrigley

"Wrigley Field is a picture. Architecturally it is in a class by itself. Money was not spared in making it the finest." — *Sporting News*, October 29, 1925

The name of the ballpark lives on in Chicago. Wrigley Field is worshiped as much as a shrine as it is for a place where baseball is played. Only a fortunate few remember the original Wrigley Field in Los Angeles— "Wrigley's Million Dollar Palace" opened in 1925 by William K. Wrigley, the chewing gum magnate and owner of both the Cubs and Angels.

Until the end of its days in 1957 as home for the Angels in the Pacific Coast League, Wrigley Field was the "Toast of the Coast." There was no finer minor league ballpark anywhere.

A concrete-and-steel double-deck grandstand fanned out from a nine-story office tower that also served as a memorial to veterans of World War I. On each side were clocks measuring fifteen feet in diameter and, instead of numerals, capital letters spelling out "Wrigley Field." At the top of the tower was an observation deck where "one can see the beautiful mountains of Southern California, all the adjoining suburbs and the ocean." [1]

The grandstand seated 18,500 fans, the right-field bleachers 2,000, providing a capacity of 20,500.

"The playing field is one of the largest in the country measuring 345 feet from the home plate down each foul line to the fence and 427 feet to a point in centerfield," the *Sporting News* reported. [2]

The brick wall in left field was nearly fifteen feet high and in later years was covered with ivy to emulate Chicago's Wrigley Field. A wire screen, nine feet in height, ran parallel to the right-field bleachers.

Four home runs were hit in the first game and three in the second, prompting the *Los Angeles Examiner* to comment, "Wrigley Field, the

Figure 3.1.   Wrigley Field was a clone of its namesake in Chicago with ivy-covered brick walls and dimensions friendly to power hitters like Steve Bilko. *Courtesy Dave Hillman*

home of the Angels and home runs. That's the way the official stationery will have to read if the pace set in the last two days at the immense new enclosure is maintained."[3]

The ballpark was designed by Zachary Taylor Davis, the same architect who created Cubs Park and the Chicago White Sox' Comiskey Park. Davis made the park in L.A. like the one in Chicago both as it existed in 1925 and how Wrigley wanted it to be.

Cubs Park was renamed Wrigley Field the next year and eventually expanded to its current seating capacity of 41,159. In 1930, lights were added in L.A., and night baseball was played there fifty-eight years before Chicago's Wrigley.

Boxing took center stage at L.A.'s Wrigley in 1939 when Joe Louis, the world heavyweight champion, knocked out Jack Roper in the first round. A crowd of 30,000 witnessed "a furious fight with cold murder on every punch."[4]

Knowing a bargain and good location when they see one, movie directors started using L.A.'s Wrigley regularly.

In the 1930s, actor-comedian Joe E. Brown starred in *Elmer the Great* and *Alibi Ike*, both movies about players trying to help the Cubs win the pennant.

The 1940s brought us *The Pride of the Yankees* with actor Gary Cooper playing Lou Gehrig, the courageous New York Yankee, and *It Happens Every Spring* with actor Ray Milland playing a college professor who concocts a potion that, when applied to a baseball, is repelled by wood. For the latter, the exterior of L.A. Wrigley was altered to resemble Chicago's Wrigley.

One of the more noteworthy 1950s movies filmed at the ballpark was *The Winning Team* with Ronald Reagan portraying Grover Cleveland Alexander, the alcoholic pitcher who won 373 games.

Meanwhile, some of the greatest players in baseball history passed through L.A.'s Wrigley on their way to the big time—brothers Joe and Dom DiMaggio played for the San Francisco Seals, as did Lloyd "Little Poison" and Paul "Big Poison" Waner; Ted Williams and Bobby Doerr for the San Diego Padres; and Bill Mazeroski for the Hollywood Stars.

Some of the Cubs' best players in the 1940s and 1950s honed their skills with the Angels—outfielders Andy Pafko and Frank Baumholtz; infielders Randy "Handsome Ransom" Jackson and Gene Baker; and pitchers Warren Hacker, Omar "Turk" Lown, Don Elston, and Jim Brosnan.

Another pitcher, Cal McLish, went on to star for the Cleveland Indians. Tommy Lasorda, a pitcher, and George "Sparky" Anderson, a second baseman, were teammates on the 1957 Angels. Both were inducted into the Hall of Fame after outstanding careers as managers.

Despite its movie celebrity status, the ballpark operated in the shadow of Wrigley Field in Chicago.

Players familiar with both often referred to it as Little Wrigley and every time there was talk about the PCL becoming a third major league or one of the sixteen teams in the majors moving to the West Coast, the shortcomings of the ballpark were magnified. Its location at 42nd Place and Avalon Boulevard in the deteriorating Watts area of L.A. was strike one. Parking for only 800 cars was strike two. The short power alleys that made it a home run haven was strike three.

In 1954 Bill Veeck, a former owner and baseball maverick, was hired by P. K. Wrigley, son of William, and then owner of the Cubs and Angels, to come up with a plan that would make the ballpark acceptable to the majors.

Veeck proposed enlarging the playing field and extending the double deck grandstand along the base lines to create a completely enclosed park with seating for up to 55,000 people. There would be parking for 10,000 cars.

Veeck presented an artist's conception of this future Wrigley Field. The cost of the project was $7.5 million, including $2 million for the purchase of Little Wrigley by the Los Angeles Coliseum Commission, which would operate it along with the nearby Coliseum, home of the Los Angeles Rams professional football team.

"The new Wrigley Field should be baseball's most modern park," Veeck said, "with every convenience for the fans—escalators, nurseries, snack bars, powder room facilities and restaurants. It should have all these features plus many others."[5]

"Bill talked to all the important people, collected the facts, evolved a working plan and lined up capital," P. K. said. "Now it's up to somebody to do something."[6]

Nobody did.

"Don't be confused by all this foofaraw about converting Wrigley Field into a major-league ball park," wrote *L.A. Times* columnist Ned Cronin. "The thought of enlarging its seating capacity to 50,000 and making it immediately available to the first major-league outfit that feels the urge to head west smells like something that came right out of an opium pipe."[7]

Instead, Cronin urged using public funds to build a new stadium in Chavez Ravine, a poor Mexican American community near downtown L.A. "It has the area necessary for ample parking, is centrally located from the standpoint of the freeway pattern."[8]

Perhaps Little Wrigley wasn't up to big league standards, but L.A. fans were clearly ready for the majors.

In March 1955 the New York Giants and Cleveland Indians played a two-game exhibition series at Little Wrigley in what was billed as a flashback of the 1954 World Series, won by the Giants in four straight games.

A crowd of 17,893 watched Willie Mays hit three consecutive home runs in the first game, a 4–2 Giant victory. Mays' first homer sailed over the 345-foot sign in left-center field, the second into the bleachers in right-center, and the third over the right-field screen.

Attendance for the second game was 24,434. Fans squeezed onto the field along the left-field line and stood at the back of the grandstands. An estimated 2,000 failed to get inside at all. The Giants won 7–3 behind a pinch-hit homer by Dusty Rhodes and a spectacular catch by Mays in deep center field—virtual replays of their World Series feats that doomed Cleveland.

Cronin used the near-record turnout to castigate baseball commissioner Ford Frick for issuing a gag order to major league team owners on moving a franchise to L.A. In an open letter to Frick, Cronin wrote, "If a major league owner doesn't know enough to give a gold mine a wide berth, he still has you, Mr. Frick, to keep him out of nervous disorders."[9]

Over the next two years, there was constant media speculation as to what franchises would move to the West Coast and when. Finally, in February 1957, the Dodgers and Giants announced plans to relocate to Los Angeles and San Francisco for the 1958 season.

That settled the issue of major league baseball in L.A. The rendering of Veeck's vision of the "Wrigley Field of the Future" was featured in the

1956 Angels yearbook, but elsewhere the ballpark's future remained in limbo.

The Dodgers paid lip service to playing at Little Wrigley while exploring the possibilities of using the Coliseum or the Rose Bowl in Pasadena.

In January 1958, Little Wrigley was at the center of a controversy involving a remark by Frick on national television that he didn't "want to see Babe Ruth's home-run record broken by playing in a cow pasture." He added, "The foul lines aren't bad and left field is about the same distance as right field, but how about some of those hitters like Mays pulling one? They will hit it into the next county." [10]

The Dodgers defended Little Wrigley briefly, suggesting that the centerfield bleachers could be moved further away from home plate and a twelve-foot arching screen added atop the brick wall in left center—"a favorite target for Steve Bilko and other power hitters." [11]

Within the span of four days, the Dodgers said they were playing in Little Wrigley and, then, the Coliseum.

"I'm not going to burn my bridges, but as of now my feeling is that the Dodgers will use Wrigley Field in 1958," Dodgers president Walter O'Malley said initially. [12] The Dodgers quickly changed course, agreeing to play in the Coliseum until a new stadium was ready.

Over the next four years the Dodgers played in the Coliseum, site of the 1932 and 1984 Summer Olympics and primarily a football and track facility. Distances down the foul lines were ridiculously short—251 feet in left and 300 feet in right. To make it semisuitable for baseball, a forty-foot net was erected in left, with both fields angling sharply to center field, 440 feet from home plate. "We don't want to acquire a reputation for Chinese home runs," O'Malley quipped. [13]

Little Wrigley was a "cow pasture," but the Coliseum's left-field fence that became known as the "Chinese Wall" was no problem. "I don't think Babe Ruth's record is in particular danger," Frick said. "Foul lines are not especially important where home runs are concerned. The rest of the wall in right center, left center and dead center determine whether you'll get a lot of homers." [14]

After thirty-three years and some 4,000 minor-league games, Little Wrigley was snubbed by the majors in favor of a football stadium—the ultimate insult.

While the Dodgers were setting one attendance record after another at the 101,000-seat Coliseum, Little Wrigley waited to see if the American League followed the money to L.A.

In 1958, Floyd Patterson defended his heavyweight championship fight at Little Wrigley by knocking out Roy Harris in the twelfth round. The ballpark was also used as the location for *Damn Yankees*, the cinema version of the musical about a Washington Senators fan who leads his team to the American League pennant. The *Los Angeles Times* used the occasion to poke fun at the Dodgers: "There was the thought that the

Dodgers, lounging in last place, might profitably emulate . . . the dancing on toes, split leaps and graceful whirls. But then things are bad enough."[15]

Soccer invaded Little Wrigley in 1959 with England's national team embarrassing a United States all-star team 8–1. Later in the year, the television series *Home Run Derby* was filmed at Little Wrigley and aired the next year. It would emerge again in the 1990s on ESPN Classic, inspiring the home-run hitting contests now part of baseball's annual all-star game.

In 1961, the American League expanded from eight to ten teams, adding the Los Angeles Angels and Washington Senators.

For one glorious year, the Angels played at Little Wrigley. At long last, the finest minor-league ballpark of its time was in the majors.

If ever a player and ballpark were made for each other, it was Steve Bilko and L.A.'s Wrigley Field.

"His years with the Angels were an ideal marriage of ballplayer to ballpark," observed Chuck Stevens, a first baseman for the Hollywood Stars from 1948 to 1954 and the Seals when Bilko entered the PCL in 1955. "Bilko played in a lot of other ballparks and a lot of other leagues, but in L.A. it was inevitable. When I heard Steve was coming to the Angels, I said he's going to put some numbers up."

Stout Steve did just that—thirty-seven homers in 1955; fifty-five in 1956; and fifty-six in 1957.

Of the 148 home runs Bilko slugged with the Angels, ninety-eight were at Little Wrigley. He became known as Wrigley Field's "home pro."

"It was more-or-less on the same order as Wrigley Field in Chicago," explained Bilko. "Most of the minor league parks then were built the same as the major league parks. Rochester was the same as Sportsman's Park. Montreal, at that time, was the same dimensions as Ebbets Field in Brooklyn. They figured if a guy can play in this park he could come up to play in the major league park. After I got out to California and I hit a lot of home runs, I always wondered how I would do if I played a full year in Chicago."

Stout Steve's power was greatest to left-center and right-center so Little Wrigley was just what the doctor ordered for a return trip to the majors.

Ralph Mauriello grew up in the Los Angeles area, pitching for the 1957 Angels and compiling an 11–5 won-loss record and team-high eight complete games. "Part of the problem with Wrigley Field was with the way it was shaped."

Mauriello used his engineering background to figure out why so many pop fly balls went for home runs.

"When I was in high school, I remember reading in the papers about the strange air currents at Wrigley Field," Mauriello recalled.

Spring training for the Angels was at Wrigley Field.

"The very first day I went to run my wind sprints in the outfield, I understood why there were so many home runs hit in the ballpark. The reason is that it's 339 down the right-field line, 340 down the left-field line, and 412 to center. Those sound like very comfortable numbers. But the outfield walls were straight. And the angle between the foul line and the left-field wall was something like seventy-five degrees. I never measured it but I went home—and since I was a math major—laid out the ballpark on grid paper.

"I had four points—home plate, left-field corner, right-field corner and centerfield. I drew straight lines between the left-field corner and centerfield and between the right-field corner and centerfield. And then I took out an engineering scale and measured it and it was 325 feet over the third-baseman's left shoulder. The shortest distance from a point to a line is perpendicular. And if it's seventy-five degrees down the left-field line, somewhere in left field it's perpendicular and it's closer—325 feet. And it was 345 over the right shoulder of the shortstop. So that's why the ball was going out of the ballpark."

What did all this have to do with Bilko's success at Little Wrigley?

"It may have given him a few home runs that would have been outs," Mauriello said. "But for the most part, he hit the ball so hard and so far that it was scary."

In his seventeen years pitching in the United States and Japan, Joe Stanka said there were only two hitters he worried about ripping his head off with a line drive. Bilko was one of them.

"That was always on my mind because I was scared," said the six-foot-six, 200-pound Stanka. "You make just a very little mistake inside and it was out of the park. So I tried to keep the ball away from him and that meant they came back through the box a lot."

Stanka pitched for the Sacramento Solons in 1956 and 1957.

"One time I'll never forget it because it scared me to death. Bilko hit a ball back through the box above my head so hard that it dug up a little of the outfield grass. That was how hard it was hit."

"Bilko had ungodly power," agreed Roger Osenbaugh, another Sacramento pitcher. "The thing with Bilko was to drive him off the plate and then go outside with him. However, the problem with pitching Bilko away was he had so much power to all fields that a fastball or pitch away, he could bring right through the box. And pitchers were certainly aware of the fact that Bilko could come through the box with a line drive that could do you some serious harm."

With the power-packed 1956 Angels lineup, teams couldn't pitch around Bilko. "If you tried, other guys would sting you," Stevens said.

The Angels slammed 202 home runs—two shy of the league record. Bilko accounted for thirty-six of the 136 that the team belted at Little Wrigley.

"Bilko's home runs were home runs," said Gale Wade. "He didn't hit these cheap fly balls."

"Home runs that Steve Bilko hit weren't *just* over the fence," said Jim "Mudcat" Grant, a pitcher who faced Bilko in both the minors and majors. "They were *way* out there."

Six Angels hit twenty or more homers, including Wade and Gene Mauch.

"There was a nice little breeze to right-centerfield all the time," Mauch explained. "I hit two home runs one day and both of them were with a man on and nobody out. I was just trying to hit a fly ball to right field or a ground ball to second. And I hit two balls in the bleachers."

The large number of day games at Little Wrigley in 1956 slightly inflated the team's home run numbers. "But Wrigley Field didn't have that much to do with our success," Wade maintained. "The type of ball club that we had was going to do well in any ballpark."

The longest home run Angels' publicist George Goodale ever saw Bilko hit was at San Francisco's spacious Seals Stadium. "It was over the left-field fence and across a small parking lot. It landed on the fly in front of a liquor store—well over 500 feet. Jim McGee of the *Call-Bulletin* measured it."

"I'll always remember the one he hit in Oakland," Wade said. "I was on second base. He hit a line drive. The pitcher actually ducked. I figured it's a line drive to the centerfielder. So I turned around to face the outfield and watch the centerfielder going back. That damn ball kept climbing. It went over the centerfield wall."

A policeman saw the ball ricochet off a factory building. "Impressed both by the keening whine of the projectile as it passed overhead and the distance of the factory from the baseball orchard, the gendarme marked the point of impact, fetched a measuring tape and reported his findings at the Oaks' front office," Lenny Anderson wrote in the *Seattle Times*. "The overall flight of the ball from Bilko to bulkhead was 552 feet." [16]

As an umpire in the PCL, Cecil "Cece" Carlucci had the best view of all.

"Bilko was a big teddy bear—as relaxed as he could be. He never looked back at the umpire. You didn't even think he was going to swing and, then, boom!"

"Steve Bilko was in the wrong place at the wrong time," Osenbaugh concluded. "If he had been in the major leagues the years he was hitting in the Coast League, he would've torn them apart."

The hysteria around Little Wrigley in the majors can be traced directly to Bilko.

"Steve was a good guy but if he could hit all those home runs, why the hell he didn't stay in the big leagues hitting home runs?" asked Chuck Stevens.

The media was particularly skeptical of Bilko after he failed to stick in the majors with the Cards and Cubs early in his career and, then, later with the Dodgers and Cincinnati Redlegs.

In 1960, the Detroit Tigers picked Bilko in the winter draft after he hit .305 and twenty-six homers for Spokane in the revamped PCL. Steve appeared to be a good fit for Detroit as Tigers Stadium was a home-run hitter's park and Tigers manager Jimmy Dykes planned to play Steve every day.

Red Smith, a nationally syndicated sports columnist, approached Dykes at spring training and asked, "How's your first baseman?"

"Bilko? Fine, he can move around there all right. Be kind. Write something nice about him."

So Smith wrote,

> That's easy to do. Stephen Thomas Bilko has been coming up to play first base for one club or another since the dawn of history. He has hit as high as .360 in the top minors and as low as .220 in the majors. There are 235 sweet-natured pounds of him. He needs to feel wanted.
>
> When he was with Cincinnati he shared an apartment with three other players. Steve did the cooking. He was a wonderful cook. His roommates appreciated him and sent him a Mother's Day card, but the Reds sent him to Los Angeles, who sent him to Spokane.[17]

The general feeling among the media and baseball establishment was that if Bilko could hit that many home runs at Little Wrigley, what would Mays, Mickey Mantle, Henry Aaron, and other power hitters do?

This was the basis of Frick's "cow pasture" comment and concern that baseball's most coveted record, Ruth's sixty home runs in a single season, was in jeopardy of being broken by a shower of cheap fly balls.

The irony is that the mark was broken in 1961 by the Yankees' Roger Maris but only two of his sixty-one homers came at Little Wrigley.

The Bronx Bombers were duds at Little Wrigley, managing a mere thirteen home runs while losing six of nine games. Mantle hit for a measly .206 average (seven-for-thirty-four) and just two of his fifty-four homers came at the bandbox that New York sportswriters had ridiculed for years.

Adding to the Yankees' embarrassment, the M & M Boys were outslugged by the Angels' diminutive Albie Pearson, who smacked three homers. "You don't need much muscle in this park," Little Albie said. "Anyone can hit one over the fence here, even me."[18]

The joke goes that the 140-pound Albie stood six-foot-five when he started the season in centerfield between hulking Bob Cerv in left and Bilko in right. By the end of the season, he had ran himself down to five-foot-six. "I was never five-six," Albie said. "I call everybody over five-five, 'Sir.'"

If it hadn't been for expansion, Bilko's major-league career would have likely ended in Detroit where he hit .207 with nine homers. But the American League's addition of two teams gave Steve another chance.

As part of the player draft, the Angels and Senators had a choice of one unprotected major leaguer from each of the other eight teams. The Angels plucked the thirty-two-year-old Bilko from the roster of Detroit's Denver farm club. "This could very well be my last chance," Bilko wrote the Angels when he returned a contract signed for an estimated $12,500. "I couldn't think of a better place to make a last stand than Wrigley Field." [19]

The major-league Angels were a microcosm of the old PCL—a rag-tag bunch of oldsters and youngsters. And it was only fitting that they play their first season in what was Little Wrigley's first and last season in the majors.

Figure 3.2.   Steve Bilko was back with the Angels in 1961, this time the big league version created by the American League's move to Los Angeles. During a visit to the Angels spring training camp in Palm Springs, President Dwight Eisenhower autographed Bilko's glove and told Angels manager Bill Rigney, far right, that Bilko and the 240-pound Ted Kluszewski, third from left, would "make a couple of good bodyguards." *Los Angeles Public Library Photo Collection.*

Besides Bilko, some of the veterans making their last stand were first baseman Ted Kluszewski, third baseman Eddie Yost, catcher Earl Averill, and pitchers Ryne Duren and Art Fowler. The hot-shot prospects included outfielder-first baseman Lee Thomas, outfielder Ken Hunt, shortstop Jim Fregosi, catcher Bob "Buck" Rodgers, and pitchers Ken McBride and Dean Chance. Another member of manager Bill Rigney's merry band of misfits was Leon "Daddy Wags" Wagner, a free-swinging slugger who had an unorthodox habit of gripping the bat with his hands apart.

Dick Young, the outspoken *New York Daily News* columnist, predicted that neither "L.A. nor Washington will win forty games; no pitcher will win more than eight."[20] The Senators won sixty-one games. Seven pitchers from the new teams won eight or more games.

The "Over the Hill Gang," as the Angels were called, finished eighth in the ten-team league but won seventy games, the most in the first year by any expansion team. "Everybody wanted to do so good that they did better than they thought they could," Bilko explained.

Bilko played right field and shared first base with Kluszewski and Thomas. He popped twenty home runs (twelve at Little Wrigley), Kluszewski fifteen, and Thomas twenty-four. Wagner had twenty-eight, Hunt twenty-five, and Averill twenty-one as the Angels parked 189—second in the league behind the world champion Yankees' 240.

A single-season record of 248 homers was hit at Little Wrigley, 122 by the Angels and 126 by opponents. The previous record was 219, set four years earlier at Cincinnati's Crosley Field. "I needed a three-dollar seat to catch some of the balls that Mantle hit," Pearson said. "I mean, they were rockets. It was amazing the way the league kind of dwarfed that park."

"I gave up a couple of home runs there that were cans of corn in another park," Duren said.

Milt Pappas, a pitcher for the Baltimore Orioles, summed up the feelings of most pitchers when he said, "I was never so happy to see a stadium vacant as that place."[21]

"One of the worst clubs ever assembled," Jimmy Cannon, the dean of media critics, declared after seeing the Angels play. "They are in these uniforms because they proved their inefficiency."[22]

On becoming a sports columnist for the *L.A. Times* earlier in 1961, Jim Murray wrote, "I hope Steve Bilko has lost weight. The last time I saw him in the Coliseum, the front of him got to the batter's box full seconds before the rest of him."[23]

Like Little Wrigley, the Angels got no respect.

The Angels began the season on the road, losing seven of eight games.

They came home to an old ballpark, all gussied up for what could've been mistaken for a World Series game instead of the home opener. Everybody knew that this would be Little Wrigley's only season in the majors before the Angels moved in with the Dodgers at their new stadium in Chavez Ravine the following year.

Richard Nixon, previously vice president of the United States, attended the inaugural, sitting next to Casey Stengel, the former Yankees manager, and his wife, Edna. Nixon had recently lost to John F. Kennedy in the 1960 presidential election. Casey confided to a reporter, "Edna offered Mr. Nixon a job as president of our next bank, but he hasn't given her an answer yet."[24]

For fans subjected to watching the Dodgers play in the colossal Coliseum where there was no roof and beer was prohibited, it was like the good, old days.

"This is the life," one long-time Angels fan said. "A beer in my hand, a roof over my head and a seat near the diamond. I almost forgot how good we used to have it."[25]

Bilko was in the starting lineup, playing the outfield for the first time in his pro career. The Angels had new caps featuring a halo on top. "When I came to the ballpark the day I was to play right field, I see this cap in my locker with this white thing around the top. I yelled to our clubhouse manager: 'What's this? A bull's eye so I'll get hit on the head?'"

One of the Angels' batboys was Scotty Keane. He was ten years old when he started following the Angels in 1956. Bilko became his hero.

"They say Yankee Stadium was a cathedral," Scotty said. "Wrigley was the cathedral of minor league ballparks. It looked super. The fans were right on top of the action. The dugouts were small. Going up and down the stairs to the clubhouse, people could see you. I remember the accessibility of the players. Whether they stopped or not, you could see them coming in and out of the dugout."

Scotty was kneeling in the on-deck circle when Bilko pinch-hit in the ninth inning of the final game of the season against the Cleveland Indians. A couple of hours earlier at Yankees Stadium in New York City, Maris hit his sixty-first home run to break Ruth's record.

"I'm down at the end of the bench with Eddie Yost," Bilko said. "It was sunny and we were half asleep."

Rigney hollered for Bilko to get a bat.

"I didn't pay any attention to him because I figured the season is over for me."

Eddie poked Bilko.

"Hey, he wants you to hit."

"You're kidding."

Eddie wasn't joking. Bilko got up off the bench, mumbling, "I might as well go and make the last out."

With a victory, the Angels could edge the Minnesota Twins for seventh place. The Indians had a lock on fifth.

Cleveland's Tito Francona entered the game needing two hits to bat over .300.

"It was my first year," said Tom Satriano, the Angels' third baseman who was twenty-one at the time. "I'm green."

Tito was a left-handed hitter so Satriano moved in to discourage him from bunting down the third-base line. Rocky Bridges, playing second base, signaled for him to back up.

"Confused, I look at Rigney. And he motions with his hands to back up. I back up a couple of steps. I look over at Rigney and he has me back up some more."

Duren was pitching for the Angels. "He is not a good defensive pitcher. And he's slow."

Tito bunted. "I've got no chance of throwing him out."

Tito was now on first. "Duren had one of the worst pick-off moves to first base of any pitcher. And, yet, the next pitch he picks Tito off first base."

Tito came up a second time. "I'm determined that he's not going to bunt on me again. I moved in to take the bunt away." Rigney signaled for Satriano to back up.

"I don't get it. But I back up."

Tito bunted again. "It's a lousy bunt—just to the left of the pitcher's mound. Ryne picks up the ball and looks at it like he's trying to read the signature, winds up and throws an average-speed fastball to first base. Tito is safe."

The Indians were leading 8–4 with two outs in the bottom of the ninth inning.

"I go up to hit," Satriano continued. "Rigney calls me back. Steve's going to pinch-hit for me."

Bilko needed one more homer to give him twenty for the season.

Jim "Mudcat" Grant was pitching for the Indians. Ironically, they faced each other in the next-to-last PCL game played at Wrigley Field four years earlier. "Pitching to Bilko in 1957 was like pitching to Mickey Mantle," Mudcat said. "Sooner or later he was going to get you."

Mudcat reared back and threw what Satriano described as "a batting practice fastball down the middle." The Angels' Dean Chance recalled Bilko swinging at a pitch over his head.

"I didn't think that I could lose the ballgame," Mudcat said. "And I thought the fans wanted me to challenge Bilko. It was a lot of fun to see this big guy—and a wonderful man—do this thing. You didn't try to give him a fat one. But you challenged him to see what he could *really* do."

"The toughest thing to do in the game is pinch-hit," Satriano said. "If anybody could do it, Bilko could. He was so grooved with that home run swing of his . . . it was an oiled swing."

Bilko swung.

"Bam!" Satriano exclaimed. "He crushes it for a home run. Finally, it dawned on me: quid pro quo."

"I thanked Mudcat Grant as I was going around second base," Bilko said.

"Don't feel bad," he told Mudcat. "You've got such a big lead and I needed this homer."

You could almost hear Bob Kelley, the Angels' play-by-play announcer in their PCL days, giving his signature home-run call based on a beer sponsor's slogan: "It's mild and mellow!"

"They were all in on it—except me," Satriano said. "Tito knew. Bilko knew. Rigney knew. Bridges knew. Duren knew. Mudcat knew."

"I didn't have the least idea of any stuff like that going on," Mudcat said. "But if it did, it wouldn't surprise me either. He was a real good guy. He was a crowd pleaser. And he was a home run hitter."

Scotty already was in tears knowing that his dream job in the dream ballpark was about to end. And, then, Bilko socked the ball 400 feet over the brick wall in left field, producing tears of joy. "I don't care how he did it. The fact that he hit the last home run is just unbelievable."

In 1992, when Mudcat saw the movie *Babe* starring actor John Goodman as Babe Ruth, he had a flashback to Bilko running around the bases. "I thought about Steve Bilko, man. He had this Babe Ruth-like figure. And his thing was hittin' home runs."

A Hollywood scriptwriter could not have written a better ending. On the last day of the season with two outs in the ninth inning of the last game ever played at Little Wrigley, Stout Steve Bilko hit the last home run.

NOTES

1. *The Sporting News*, October 29, 1925, 3.
2. Ibid.
3. *Los Angeles Examiner*, October 1, 1925, Section III, 2.
4. *Los Angeles Times*, April 18, 1939, Part II, 1.
5. *The Sporting News*, December 29, 1954, 9.
6. *Los Angeles Times*, February 6, 1955, B7.
7. *Los Angeles Times*, February 8, 1955, C3.
8. Ibid.
9. Ibid. March 23, 1955, C3.
10. *The Sporting News*, January 22, 1958, 5.
11. *Los Angeles Times*, October 4, 1957, 6.
12. *Los Angeles Times*, January 14, 1958, 1.
13. *The Sporting News*, January 29, 1958, 3.
14. *Los Angeles Times*, January 28, 1958, C1.
15. *Los Angeles Times*, May 27, 1958, Section IV, 3.
16. *Seattle Times*, May 12, 1955, 22.
17. Red Smith, *Red Smith on Baseball*, (Chicago: Ivan R. Dee, 200), 250–51.
18. *Los Angeles Times*, May 7, 1961, N2.
19. *Los Angeles Herald-Express*, February 11, 1961, A8.

20. *The Sporting News*, December 28, 1960, 2.
21. *Los Angeles Times*, August 7, 1991, C1.
22. *Los Angeles Times*, April 27, 1961, C1.
23. *Los Angeles Times*, February 12, 1961, N1.
24. *Los Angeles Times*, April 28, 1961, C3.
25. Ibid., C2.

FOUR

A Major League of Our Own

"To a lot of us out here, we looked at the PCL as a major league—a third major league."—Bob Hunter, Baseball Hall of Fame sportswriter, as quoted in the *Los Angeles Times*, October 19, 1990

The Pacific Coast League was both heaven and haven to its players.

"I felt like I died and went to heaven," said Ed Mickelson, who played for the Portland Beavers from 1955 to 1957. "We flew everywhere; they weren't flying in the major leagues. Nice cities. Wonderful restaurants. It was more first class in many ways than the major leagues."

"We were so far away from the baseball world in the Midwest and East Coast, it was our own haven," said Bob Speake, the 1956 Angels' left-fielder.

For Speake and most of his Angels teammates, home was Missouri, Illinois, Indiana, Ohio, Pennsylvania, North Carolina, West Virginia, Tennessee, and Florida. Only four players were born in California. The Coast League became the team's domain just as it had for countless players over the years.

"You had a lot of guys that had been there for a number of years," Speake said. "And they prided themselves for having played their career in the Pacific Coast League."

And why not?

"This was *the* major league," said Irv Noren, a former New York Yankees outfielder who grew up in Pasadena, California. "That's all there was out here."

The big leagues ignored the West Coast until 1958, when the Brooklyn Dodgers moved to L.A. and the New York Giants to San Francisco. This followed three other franchise shifts—the Braves from Boston to Milwaukee in 1953; the St. Louis Browns to Baltimore, where they became the

43

Orioles in 1954; and the Athletics from Philadelphia to Kansas City in 1955.

"Major league baseball today is not a national game, but a sectional game," Gordon Cobbledick wrote in the March 1954 issue of *Baseball Digest*. "The concentration of eight franchises on the Eastern seaboard, seven of them within a space of 225 miles, gives the business little appeal for the millions in other sections."[1]

Max West attended high school in the L.A. area in the 1930s, focusing more on tennis than baseball. "I didn't pay any attention to major league teams," he said. "They were on the other side of the country."

Max played three years in the PCL before breaking into the majors with the Braves in 1938. "I didn't know the names of any big league players except Joe DiMaggio, and I knew about him because he played in the Coast League."

In a spring exhibition game against the New York Yankees, the twenty-one-year-old West hit a "grass-cutter" that went through the legs of the Yankees' first baseman. "We've got several first basemen in the Coast League better than this guy," Max thought to himself.

He learned later the first baseman was Lou Gehrig, one of baseball's all-time greats. "I didn't know who Lou Gehrig was."

For kids on the West Coast in the 1950s, the PCL was our own major league. "The majors were a voice from another room," novelist Harry Turtledove said of the 1956 season when he was a seven-year-old in L.A. "The PCL was in my room, if you know what I mean."

We could relate to the teams in the league because they were in the same time zone. The ballparks were small enough to allow us to get close to the players. And, most important of all, the players were accessible, many of them living and working among us.

West operated a sporting goods store in nearby Alhambra. Lou Stringer, a second baseman for both the Angels and Hollywood Stars, was a car salesman. Roger Bowman, a twenty-two-game winner for the Stars in 1954, ran an upholstery shop in Santa Monica.

The PCL was "one step above AAA, and a half-step below the majors," according to Roger Osenbaugh, a pitcher for the Sacramento Solons. Osenbaugh signed with Sacramento in 1952 shortly after the PCL was awarded Open Classification status. "Open Classification was baseball's plan to make the Coast League the third major league, and I thought it would be great to join the majors with my hometown club."

PCL owners began campaigning for major league status following the 1946 season, when attendance reached an all-time high of 3.7 million. That fall the Cleveland Rams, defending champions of the National Football League, relocated to L.A., and the San Francisco 49ers began play as part of the fledging All-America Football Conference.

"What is the difference between a major and a minor league?" asked Bob Cobb, owner of the Stars, in 1948. "Size of parks, attendance, prices of admission and players' salaries. That's about all.

"Suspend the draft for six years and we can bring our rosters and parks up to big league standards. We are a cosmopolitan people out here, more so than in the majority of eastern cities. People from every outside state have moved to the West Coast."[2]

Major league owners stonewalled, eventually elevating the PCL to Open Classification in 1952 and offering a plan that, among other things, required upgrading and expanding the league's ballparks. Players also were given the option of waiving their right to be drafted by major league teams.

One of the first to sign the no-draft clause was Chuck Connors, a first baseman for the Angels in 1952. Connors had played in the majors with the Dodgers and Chicago Cubs. He aspired to be an actor, and in L.A., he had the stage needed to land the starring role in *The Rifleman*, a popular television series from 1958 to 1963.

In a story written for *Sport* magazine, Connors related a conversation he had with Fred Saigh, then owner of the St. Louis Cardinals.

"I was sorry to see you sign away your right," Saigh said to Connors.

"On the contrary, Mr. Saigh, I didn't sign away a right. I established one."

Connors went on to explain, "I now have the right—which I never had before—to decline being drafted by the major league.

"By signing the no-draft clause I can help determine my immediate future and my post-baseball career, which is of vital importance, too."[3]

The 1953 season opened with Connors pursuing an acting career full time and PCL president Clarence "Pants" Rowland predicting the league will be "on a par with the major leagues in three to five years. We may not be recognized as a third major league by then, since things like that take time and patience. But eventually they'll have to recognize us. Sooner or later we'll catch up with them, and our champion will meet their champion in the World Series."[4]

In retrospect, the PCL never had a chance. Major league owners wanted West Coast cities for themselves and had no intention of granting the PCL major league status.

"If they had taken the PCL and made it a third major league, the quality of ball players would've been maintained rather than diluted as it was by expansion teams later on," said Bobby Usher, an outfielder for the Angels and San Diego Padres from 1952 to 1956, who also spent six seasons in the majors.

"Geographically, Pants Rowland had the right idea," said Eddie Bockman, a player, manager and scout during his sixty-three-year baseball career. "You've got a major league team in Seattle. You've got two in the Bay Area and two in the Los Angeles area. You've got San Diego, and, then, you absorb Houston and Arizona. There are your eight teams. That's better than the way it is now."

The PCL's hopes for major league status were long gone by 1956. The quality of play was being criticized as inferior to previous years. The Oakland franchise had relocated to Vancouver, British Columbia, requiring more travel, and teams no longer played week-long series against each other. The players were unfazed.

"To me, it was the nearest thing to the big leagues," said Steve Bilko. "The only difference was in the big leagues you'd see four good starting pitchers. In the Coast League, you'd see three good starting pitchers. That's how close it was."

"Every team, especially in pitching, had at least three or four position players that had played in the major leagues," said Mickelson. "On the pitching staff, where they had eleven or twelve pitchers, there would always be four or five who had pitched in the major leagues."

"A lot of fellows were trying to get into the Coast League," said George Freese. "It was the best league going as far as money and playing conditions were concerned."

Bilko and several other players signed no-draft clauses so they could stay in the PCL.

"I signed the clause," Bilko said, "for the simple reason I didn't want to get drafted by some club and the first two weeks of the season if I wasn't hitting ten home runs already, it would be see you later. I'd rather play every day than go and sit on a bench somewhere and play maybe fifty games all year and then they'd say, 'Geez, you can't hit up here.'"

The Hollywood Stars were a farm team of the Pittsburgh Pirates in 1952. Whenever Stars manager Fred Haney wanted to fire up his players, he yelled, "Hustle you guys or I'll send you back to Pittsburgh."

The PCL's top teams arguably were better than the St. Louis Browns, the Chicago Cubs, the Pittsburgh Pirates, and other perennial losers in the American and National Leagues during the 1950s.

"The Angels would've finished well up in the first division if they had played in the major leagues that year," said Russ Kemmerer, a twelve-game winner for the Seals in 1956. "They were a real tough ballclub to beat."

The 1952 Pirates supplied Joe Garagiola with enough humorous material for a highly successful career in broadcasting and three books on baseball. When Garagiola arrived in Pittsburgh after being traded by the St. Louis Cardinals, a consistent pennant contender, he said it was like "getting out of a Cadillac and into a wheelbarrow."[5]

The Pirates lost 112 games in 1952, the most by a Pittsburgh team in sixty-two years. They finished a whopping fifty-four-and-a-half games behind the National League champion Brooklyn Dodgers.

The Pirates were not alone in their futility.

In 1951, Bill Veeck purchased the Browns for $2.5 million. "It was the worst collection of ball players I had ever seen. It hurt to look at them."[6] The Browns finished last with a 52–102 won-loss record.

Veeck's strategy for the 1952 season was simple: "We've sold half our players and hope to sell the rest. Our secret weapon is to get a couple of Browns on every other club and louse up the league."[7] He succeeded as the Detroit Tigers, losers of 104 games, replaced the Browns in the cellar.

The Browns lost 100 games the next year and then moved to Baltimore.

Even though they were in the majors, the Kansas City Athletics gained a reputation for being a Yankees farm team because they traded many of their best players to New York. True to form, the 1956 Athletics lost 102 games to finish last in the American League.

The Baltimore Orioles and Cubs weren't that much better in 1956. After seeing them play in spring training, one observer proclaimed them the worst teams he'd ever seen. "Never saw so many kids in all my life," he said, adding, "In big league baseball you can't get by without half a dozen real pros."[8]

Collier's magazine summed up the Cubs this way: "Great at second and short, sad almost everywhere else."[9]

When Angels' manager Bob Scheffing was asked in spring training which of the eligible Cubs he'd most like to have for his 1956 team, he named only two players—Gale Wade and Jim Brosnan, a pitcher.

Wade wound up in L.A., playing centerfield on a championship team. Brosnan remained with the Cubs who finished last with their worst record of the decade.

The presence of "real pros" made the PCL a valuable testing ground for young big league prospects.

Joe DiMaggio got his start in the PCL. So did Ted Williams, Bobby Doerr, Paul and Lloyd Waner, and Bill Mazeroski—all future Hall of Famers.

One of the pros in 1956 was Larry Jansen, a pitcher who had a 30–6 record for the Seals in 1946. He won 122 games in the majors, including twenty-three in 1951 for the pennant-winning Giants. Jansen was back in the PCL in 1956, posting an 11–2 won-loss record and earned run average of 2.58 for the Seattle Rainiers.

"When I went up, I didn't think there was that much difference," Jansen said. "Even when I came back I said, 'Well, it's still very close to the big leagues. Because they had so many players like me who came back from the big leagues. The kids had to learn real fast. They had to be able to play. And they could play."

The nineteen-year-old Mazeroski appeared in eighty games for Hollywood in 1956 before moving up to Pittsburgh, where he starred at second base for seventeen years.

Rocky Colavito, twenty-two, went up to the majors to stay after hitting twelve home runs in thirty-five games for San Diego. Colavito would go on to slug 374 homers in the big leagues.

Other young Coast League players on their way up to the majors in 1956 were outfielders Albie Pearson and Floyd Robinson; infielders Frank Malzone and Felix Mantilla; catcher John Romano; and pitchers Ryne Duren, Luis Arroyo, Bob Purkey, and Charlie Beamon. Some of the old pros were infielders Vern Stephens, Ferris Fain, Eddie Basinski, and Dick Sisler; and pitchers Allen "Two Gun" Gettel, Elmer Singleton, Max Surkont, Gene Bearden, and Bill Werle.

Beamon was nineteen in 1954 when he broke into the PCL with the Oaks. In 1956, he was 13–6 with the Vancouver Mounties before joining the Orioles and winning two games, one of them a four-hit shutout against the Yankees.

"I didn't see that big a difference in the majors," said Beamon. "You had the Yankees and two or three other good teams but the rest of them were the same as Coast League teams."

Gettel, nicknamed "Two Gun" because he was a pistol-packing cowboy when he wasn't pitching, won thirty-eight games for six teams in the majors and 103 for Oakland and San Diego in a PCL career that spanned from 1949 to 1956.

"When I first went to Oakland, we could've played any major league club and beat 'em," Gettel said. "Some of the guys in the Coast League could hit just as good as the boys in the majors."

Gettel pitched briefly for the Cardinals in 1955 before returning to the PCL with San Diego. "When I went up to the Cardinals and then came back, I didn't see a whole lot of difference but that they were playing better ball in the Coast League than they were in the majors."

"You had a lot of guys who were veterans," said Werle, a sixteen-game winner for Portland in 1956. "If they couldn't play in the major leagues, they wanted to play in the Coast League."

Werle also pitched in the American Association. "It was an easier league to pitch in because the hitters were so much younger."

"The difference between the two leagues was that the Coast League had established major-league caliber players," Kemmerer said. "There were a lot of players who wouldn't go to the majors because they made more money playing in the Coast League."

"You had more hard throwers in the American Association," said Wade. "The old saying was that if a fireballer came into the league, everybody got together and voted him out. They didn't like hard throwers."

Pitchers in the Coast League relied on their experience and a wide assortment of pitches that sometimes included the spitball, an illegal pitch.

"Whenever I hit against Max Surkont or Elmer Singleton and a couple of people were on base in a tight game, I knew damn well I was going to get a spitter coming up there," said Mickelson. "That was a heck of a pitch to try to hit because it came up like a moderately speed fastball that you were going to clobber and the next thing you know, it quickly dropped straight down."

"Gene Mauch and Piper Davis used to warn me about the guys who threw spitters," said Eddie Haas, the Angels' twenty-one-year-old outfielder.

"It was a bunch of veterans who knew how to play the game," Mickelson said. "On any given day some of the pitchers would be back in the form they were in the major leagues. They may have lost a little bit on their fastball. But they had a lot more savvy. They knew how to pitch."

"The old timers that were up in the majors and came back down like I did, well, that makes a big difference," said Gettel. "When you're in the majors, you figure out a hitter and you don't forget."

In 1947, the Giants offered Jansen less money than he made the year before in San Francisco.

"That's all we're going to pay you," Giants owner Horace Stoneham said. "Either come here or stay there."

"Sell me back to San Francisco," Jansen said.

Jansen got Stoneham to agree to a $7,000 raise if he proved he could win in the big leagues. He won ten of his first fourteen decisions to get the raise and went on to win twenty-one games. "They didn't pay us much, I tell you."

On retiring from baseball, Jansen coauthored a book titled, *The Craft of Pitching*. He was a master at throwing a slider, a pitch that looks like a fastball until it breaks laterally and down. "I was one of the first to go to the big leagues with a good slider," Jansen said.

"You didn't have the hard throwers that you had in the International League or American Association," said Charlie Silvera, a catcher for Portland prior to joining the Yankees in 1948. "Most of the pitchers had been in the major leagues. They knew how to pitch and could make it tough for a young hitter."

"The pitchers were smarter," Wade said. "It was the smartest league I ever played in."

The PCL was the jumping-off place to the majors for the most successful managers of the 1950s.

Casey Stengel led the Oakland Oaks to the 1948 title before leading the Yankees to ten American League pennants and seven World Series championships in twelve years.

Charlie Dressen succeeded Stengel in Oakland and went on to manage the Dodgers to a second-place finish in 1951 and National League pennants in 1952 and 1953.

Fred Haney guided Hollywood to PCL championships in 1949 and 1952 and then managed the Milwaukee Braves to two National League pennants and a World Series crown.

The list of managers who led teams in both the PCL and majors is impressive: Pepper Martin, Jimmy Dykes, Paul Richards, Rogers Hornsby, Mel Ott, Augie Galan, Bobby Bragan, Stan Hack, Fred Hutchinson, and Joe Gordon, to name a few.

"There was a real who's who," said Bragan. "It gave the league additional prestige."

The greatest and most respected Coast League manager of all shunned the majors.

Francis "Lefty" O'Doul was the highest paid manager in the game in the late 1940s, making as much as $50,000. He managed his hometown team, the San Francisco Seals, for seventeen years and four other PCL teams for six.

"My grandfather used to tell me that if the pilgrims had landed on the West Coast instead of in Massachusetts, they never would have left California and the East never would have become populated," O'Doul explained. "As for my going to New York, Chicago, or anywhere else you might mention, I feel I'm already in the big leagues." [10]

Lefty's teams won four championships, but he was best known as a tutor of young hitters. Joe DiMaggio played two years for the Seals before Lefty took over in 1935 and helped Joe hike his batting average fifty-seven points to .398. Under Lefty's watchful eye, Dom DiMaggio increased his average over a three-year period from .306 to .360. And in a single season, he transformed Gene Woodling into a dangerous pull-hitter, improving his average ninety-six points to .385.

"Lefty loved the Coast League," said Dino Restelli, a hard-hitting outfielder who played six years for him in San Francisco. "He'd say, 'I'm here at home. I could be mayor if I wanted to. I have my own bar and restaurant in downtown San Francisco. I play golf all year long. Why would I go to the big leagues for $20,000?'"

"Lefty was a colorful manager," Bragan said, recalling a game in San Diego when O'Doul managed the Padres. "I heard a couple of Navy guys hollering at Lefty, giving him hell about something. He said, 'Listen, if you don't shut up, I'm going to send a Marine up there and clean you out.'"

Lefty was just as effective with pitchers as he was hitters.

"I walked a lot of guys so I was always in trouble," said Beamon, a pitcher for Vancouver when Lefty managed there in 1956. "He was patient enough to give me a chance to work my way out of it."

The best example of Lefty's unorthodox management style was a game in San Francisco involving Duren, a flame-throwing pitcher for Vancouver. The Seals scored two runs in the eighth inning as the Mounties "started having error problems" to go with Duren's control problems.

"Lefty came to the mound and said, 'Well, you're all right. I just thought I'd come out here and break this thing up a little bit. Could be the fix is on, couldn't it?"

Lefty headed back to the dugout. Another error in the bottom of the ninth helped the Seals score three runs and cut the Mounties' lead to 7–6. Lefty paid Duren another visit.

"I'm going to take you out of here," Lefty said. "I think the fix is on. It's obvious that you didn't have anything to do with it."

"I'm not coming out, Lefty," Duren said.

"I've got to take you out. This is my second trip out here."

"No, you don't. You can take yourself out."

"You can?"

Lefty called the umpire over to confirm that he could remove himself from the game instead of Duren.

"You'll have to get out of the dugout," the umpire advised Lefty.

"By God, I'm thirsty anyway," Lefty said. "I'm going up to the clubhouse."

"I struck out the next two guys and we won the game," Duren said. "I was so angry that I didn't care if my arm flew off. My fastball was back. From that point on, I had a winning record. I went from a 1–6 record going into the game to finish 11–11 and come within a strikeout of leading the league. I was a major league pitcher at the end of the season."

Coast League teams didn't need mascots, loud rock 'n' roll music, and jumbo scoreboard television screens with animation to entertain fans. They had colorful characters like Chet "Chetsy" Johnson, a pitcher who left everybody laughing except his manager.

"The funniest thing Chet could do would be to win twenty games for me," said Tommy Heath, Chet's manager at Sacramento in 1956.[11]

The PCL had more than its share of quirky, sometimes wacky players that made it hilariously different from other leagues.

One of the wackiest was Billy Schuster, a shortstop who played in the league from 1940 to 1952. Facing Schuster for the first time, a pitcher fielded a ground ball hit to him. As he started to throw the ball to first, he saw Schuster running right at him and sliding. "He didn't know what to do," said Rinaldo "Rugger" Ardizoia, a pitcher for the Stars at the time. "Someone had to yell at him to throw the ball to first base. He finally did, and he came back to the bench and said, 'That man is crazy.' That's something we already knew."[12]

At six-foot-three and 200 pounds, power-hitting Joe Brovia made no secret of his contempt for pitchers who threw him curveballs and other off-speed pitches. "Throw the ball, you cunny-thumb sucker," Joe yelled, trying to provoke a fastball that he often jacked out of the park.

Brovia and Marino Pieretti, a pitcher for the '56 Angels, were room-mates when they played together in Portland and Sacramento.

"Joe hated pitchers with a vengeance," Pieretti said. "No matter who they were, they were terrible. All pitchers were bad except when I was his roommate. The sportswriters would say, 'Joe, you don't like pitchers. What about your roommate?' Joe would say: 'He's on my side; I like him.'"

Dwight "Red" Adams, another Angel pitcher, played with Brovia in Portland.

"We'd just wait for him to come back to the dugout when he'd make an out because we knew he was going to do something funny," Adams said. "One game he hit a couple of line shots right at somebody. That just killed him when he hit a ball hard and didn't get a base hit. He came back to the dugout and he was beside himself. He looked up at the sky and, like he was talking to the Lord, said, 'Are you living up there?'"

Chetsy Chet won 111 games in the PCL, including twenty-two for the Seals in 1950. But he is remembered more for his comical antics than his pitching.

"One day I overhead a fan say 'Look at that left-hander, what a screwball' and it gave me ideas," Chet said.[13]

If a ball was hit hard and close to Chet, he'd pull a fan out of his pocket and start fanning himself.

If someone got a long hit off him, he'd pull out a yo-yo and begin playing with it.

"It was really pantomime," said Osenbaugh, a Sacramento teammate.

"I have always felt the fans come out to watch more than a ballgame," Chet said. "They want a show, laughs, color."[14]

And Chetsy Chet gave it to them.

He carried a little black book in his back pocket that he pretended to use for help in pitching to hitters. "If Bilko hit one out, he'd tear a page out of the book," umpire Cece Carlucci recalled.

"He hit a home run against the Angels one day and it took him five minutes to go round the bases. He was hugging Chuck Connors at first, went to the second baseman, hugging him. Went to third jumping up and down, kissing the base. When he got to home plate, he hugged me."

"He was a great showman," said Mauch. "He moved the outfielders all around when I came to bat. And when Bilko came up, he lay down behind the mound and hid because he didn't want to pitch to him."

Off the field, Chet was almost normal.

He was walking with two other Solons pitchers, Osenbaugh and Milo Candini, in downtown Seattle, on their way to a movie theatre. They came to a crosswalk that was blocked by a large Packard sedan being driven by an elderly man. A woman was on the passenger side of the front seat.

"People were going around the car in both directions," Osenbaugh said. "Milo and I walked around the front of the car. At the same time, Chet opened the back door of the car, got in and slid across the seat to the far-side door, opened it, and got out.

"Milo and I were aghast at what Chet did. We saw three emotions in eight seconds from the people in the car. One was fear. As he was sliding across the seat, they both became angry. When he got out of the car and shut the door, they laughed. Chet didn't say a word. He had a real gift for that kind of stuff."

The inevitable happened in 1958.

Major league baseball finally arrived on the West Coast, the Dodgers taking up residence in L.A. and the Giants in San Francisco. The media was excited. The politicians were smiling. And Walter O'Malley and Horace Stoneham, the owners of the Dodgers and Giants, already were counting their millions.

"If there was a groundswell of opinion for the Dodgers move to Los Angeles, it was in Brooklyn in Walter O'Malley's office," said John Schulian, a former sportswriter. "He was the one who wanted it."

For those of us who grew up on PCL baseball, we didn't want to see it go away. But that's what happened.

The Angels moved to Spokane where they became the Indians. The Stars became the Salt Lake City Bees. And the Seals became the Phoenix Giants. The league expanded in the 1960s to include, at various times, teams in Dallas, Denver, Honolulu, Indianapolis, Little Rock, Oklahoma City, Tacoma, and Tulsa.

The old PCL was history and the new one, a geography teacher's nightmare.

"It was a great league," said Eddie Basinski, an infielder for the Portland Beavers from 1947 to 1957. "It could've been a third major league except for Horace Stoneham and Walter O'Malley. They ruined it. They were greedy and wanted the West Coast for themselves."

The PCL was revamped and returned to Class AAA status. The no-draft clause was eliminated. The reserve clause in player contracts that bound a player to a single team remained until it was challenged in the 1970s and players won the right to be free agents.

Looking back on his baseball career played under what he called "chattel mortgage," the Angels' Speake was philosophical.

"The pendulum was way out of sync in baseball prior to free agency. Teams were owned by families. Players were under reserve clause contracts. The ball club owned the ball players, and if you didn't like it, you went home.

"The Cardinals traded Curt Flood to the Phillies. Curt said he wouldn't report; baseball said he had to. So Curt sued, won his case and the reserve clause was changed to free agency. The single greatest change in baseball was the player representative, which meant big money and long-term contracts.

"In '55 the Cubs told Steve Bilko he was going to L.A. and Steve went, no questions asked. The pendulum has swung from one extreme to the other."

Few people are aware of the old PCL.

"You don't play the game," Osenbaugh said, "to have people think that you were a good ball player or that you played in a good league. But the Coast League was a great league."

"It was a minor major league," added Jim "Mudcat" Grant, an eighteen-game winner for San Diego in 1957 before going on to win 145 games in the majors. "You got a chance to pitch against some ballplayers that were good enough to play in the major leagues."

"A lot of things that went on in the Coast League didn't go on in the other leagues," said Basinski. "It was strictly baseball in the American Association and, of course, strictly baseball in the major leagues. But the Coast League was in a league of its own."

NOTES

1. *Baseball Digest*, March 1954, 75.
2. *Baseball Digest*, May 1948, 43.
3. *Sport*, July 1952, 22.
4. *Sporting News*, April 15, 1953, 40.
5. *Life*, August 13, 1956, 93.
6. *Reader's Digest*, May 1952, 93.
7. Ibid., 96.
8. *Los Angeles Times*, March 16, 1956, C1.
9. Ibid., C1.
10. *Dell Baseball Stars*, 1951, 72.
11. *Los Angeles Times*, April 6, 1956, 2.
12. Dick Dobbins, *The Grand Minor League: An Oral History of the Old Pacific Coast League*, (Emeryville, CA: Woodford Press, 1999), 234.
13. *Pasadena Star-News*, April 5, 1956, A5.
14. Ibid., A5.

FIVE

An Unforgettable Season

"When you talk about Los Angeles in 1956, it was a joy to go to the ballpark. That was the most enjoyable time in my life." —Dave Hillman, pitcher, 1956 Los Angeles Angels

The Angels pulled a shocker on February 4, 1956, signing Sam Brown, an all-America tailback for UCLA with electrifying speed.

"To the public, Brown is a great football star, but to the talent hunters of professional baseball, he is a better baseball player than a footballer," the Angels proclaimed in their '56 yearbook.[1] That was a bold statement.

The five-foot-ten, 170-pound Brown earned the nickname "First Down" by averaging 6.2 yards per run, piling up 829 yards on 144 carries and scoring nine touchdowns as UCLA rolled to a 1956 Rose Bowl match-up against Michigan State, which the Bruins lost in the last minute to finish with a 9–2 won-loss record. He was dazzling on kickoff and punt returns, averaging 22.2 yards on kickoffs and 13.8 yards on punts.

"Trying to tackle the nimble-footed tailback is something like trying to grab a handful of smog," one writer wisecracked.[2]

The Cleveland Browns of the National Football League drafted Sam in the twenty-second round even though he had made it clear baseball was his game. "I always wanted to be a professional baseball player," Sam said.

Brown played baseball at McClymonds High School in Oakland and two years each at West Contra Costa Community College and UCLA. One of his high school teammates was Frank Robinson, the Hall of Fame outfielder. "I could've signed to play baseball when I left high school but I was determined to play college football."

In high school, Brown attracted the attention of Clarence "Brick" Laws, owner of the Oakland Oaks, a member of the PCL until '56 when the franchise was moved to Vancouver. In 1949, Laws stunned the New

55

York Yankees by signing Jackie Jensen, an all-America halfback for the University of California at Berkeley.

"I can't figure a minor league club taking a player away from the Yankees or other big league clubs," said Del Webb, co-owner of the Yankees. "I don't think it has ever happened before in history."[3]

In 1950, Jensen was sold to the Yankees with Billy Martin, a second baseman for the Oaks. Jensen would go on to star for the Boston Red Sox, winning the American League's Most Valuable Player award in 1958.

To Laws, Brown was "another Jackie Jensen" and he was determined to sign him.[4] So were four major league teams, including the Brooklyn Dodgers and New York Giants.

"He has enough power to knock a ball a mile," said Jack Fournier, the Angel scout who signed Sam. "As for his speed, well, he can run with any of them. I've followed him for two years and I'm sold on the boy."[5]

Sam lived up to his press clippings in spring training.

One day at Wrigley Field, Angels' manager Bob Scheffing was standing behind the batting cage, watching and waiting to be impressed by one of several prospects trying to make the jump from the lower minors. Sam stepped to the plate. He let three bad pitches go by, and, then he dumped a perfect bunt down the third-base line.

The frown on Scheffing's face suddenly turned to a smile. Sam made the smile bigger with a wicked cut at the next ball, sending it whistling through the infield.

"Wrists," said Scheffing. "That's where he gets his power, from wrist action. You should have seen one he hit over the left-field fence yesterday. It went on a line, and so fast that it cleared the fence before he had taken two steps toward first."[6] And he raved about Sam's base-running and athleticism: "He runs the bases like a veteran. He is a smooth, natural athlete."[7]

Early in the exhibition season, Sam was hitting .500 and flexing the power that had everybody talking. After a game against Pepperdine College, Sam was being called "Home Run" Brown, slugging two homers to match a pair by Bilko. Buzz also homered, creating grand visions of things to come. The team's veterans recognized Sam's potential and worked with him to sharpen his skills.

Pitcher Harry Perkowski hit line drives to Sam in the outfield during practice. "I learned to be a better judge of line drives off the bat by him hitting them to me all the time," Sam said.

Gene Mauch talked baseball with Sam and "how I should be going back on the ball in the outfield rather than shuffling back. I should get back and, then, come forward on the ball."

At UCLA, Sam played against the Angels in spring training games. He also had followed the exploits of Bilko during the 1955 season. "I watched him with that real thin-handled bat and how he'd whip it around. The ball would just shoot off the thing."

Bilko used a 32-ounce bat, much lighter than most power hitters. This allowed him to buggy-whip the bat like a golf club.

Steve offered Sam batting tips mixed in with some good-natured ribbing. "He was always teasing me about something."

Buzz shared his vast baseball experience with Sam and was planning to take him to Puerto Rico to play ball the following winter.

Sam batted a solid .297 for the spring. "I found that I could hit the ball but I just didn't have the experience of being a good outfielder."

A week before the Angels' season opener, Sam was sent to the Chicago Cubs' minor-league training center at Lafayette, Louisiana. From there, he went to Magic Valley, Idaho, the Cubs' affiliate in the Class C Pioneer League.

Sam was a future star and the Angels wanted him to play every day while learning the intricacies of playing the outfield from George "Shotgun" Shuba, a Magic Valley coach and formerly an outfielder for the Dodgers. Scheffing planned to bring Sam back to L.A. Unfortunately, Uncle Sam called before Scheffing.

From 1948 until 1973, men were drafted to fill vacancies in the U.S. military that couldn't be filled voluntarily. Sam was notified on his twenty-third birthday (April 4, 1956) that he would be in the Army for the next two years.

Sam reported to Magic Valley but "wasn't allowed to get in any of the games because I was going into the Army and I wouldn't be of any use to the team."

He served eighteen months in Germany, playing baseball and football for Army teams. On being discharged, Sam concluded that at age twenty-five, he was too old to start over again in baseball, so he tried out with the Cleveland Browns. "That didn't work out because when I hit the Browns, geez, they had a powerhouse—Jim Brown, Bobby Mitchell, and Leroy Bolden. They had a good backfield."

Sam returned home to Oakland to work for the U.S. Postal Service and then went back to UCLA to get his degree and become an elementary school teacher in the L.A. area. "It just wasn't meant to happen," Sam said of his once-promising baseball career.

Few people are aware Sam ever played for the Angels. "Me and the guys knew when we talk baseball," he chuckled.

"Oh, it was a great experience," Sam said. "I enjoyed it very much. I just wish I had been a more experienced player and that I could've stayed with the team for the whole year."

Day games and Wrigley Field in Chicago were synonymous with each other until 1988, when the Cubs finally let there be lights at their ballpark. Games were played under the lights at Little Wrigley in 1930—five years before the first nighttime major-league game. So the Angels' decision to play all day games except on Fridays was big news.

It became even bigger when nobody showed up. Only 1,677 fans attended L.A.'s home opener. The crowds got even smaller—604, 428, and 326.

One columnist wrote, "One of these days when the public address announcer gives the lineups he won't have to say: 'Ladies and gentlemen.' Better he look over the house and say: 'Dear Sir.'"[8]

A survey conducted by the Angels during the offseason found that more of the 400,000 retired people living in the area would attend day games. "They didn't want to go out at night," said Angels' publicist George Goodale.

Another reason offered was increasing nighttime competition for baseball from television and drive-in theaters. By playing and televising day games, the Angels believed they could better promote themselves and chewing gum, the primary product of their owner, P. K. Wrigley.

Perhaps the most logical explanation is that Wrigley, a staunch opponent of nighttime baseball, wanted to start conditioning fans to attend day games in anticipation of a big-league team coming to L.A.

"Late in the season, we began playing night games on both Thursdays and Fridays," Goodale said. "In 1957 we went back to all night games except weekends."

The switch to day games didn't increase attendance, but it produced more home runs. Not only did the ball travel farther in the drier and thinner afternoon air, the hitters could see the ball better than under Little Wrigley's lights.

"Trouble with this league," said Max West, a star in the majors and Pacific Coast League before entering the sporting goods business, "the lights stink. In the big leagues, one cluster has got as many lights as all of these—Wrigley Field's—put together."[9]

West even suggested Buzz might hit sixty homers if the Angels played all day games at Little Wrigley.

West was behind another new wrinkle in 1956—the Angels' "waffle-weave" uniform described as a "winner's uniform" by Bob Speake: "You had to be a winner to wear it to keep people from laughing at you."

A wide blue-and-red waffle-weave stripe encircled the shoulders and ran down the sides of the pants. "The thought that went through my mind when I got to L.A. and saw the uniform in my locker was *softball*," Speake said. "This can't be true."

"Inserting the waffle-weave stripes was my idea," West said. "The players liked them because they gave them freedom. They were much cooler than the regular uniforms."

"It wore well," Speake said.

Gene Mauch modeled the new uniform at a press conference that was more like a fashion show.

"This," Angels' president John Holland proudly announced, "is our new waffle-weave uniform—a revolution in baseball. It's the first time a

Figure 5.1. Bob Speake wearing the '56 Angels "waffle-weave" striped uniform. *Author's collection.*

wide, football-type shoulder band of knitted-weave nylon has been intro-duced on the shoulder line."[10]

The uniforms were inspired by the football jerseys worn by Brown and his UCLA teammates the year before.

"They'll make a hit with the hemlines," Jeane Hoffman wrote in the *L.A. Times*, "even if they stumble all over the baselines!"[11]

"Bilko loved the uniforms," West said.

"Nobody can laugh at the ball club for what we accomplished," Speake said.

In fact, the '56 Angels laughed all the way to the PCL pennant.

Time has a way of tricking our memory.

Gil Stratton, an umpire before becoming an actor and sportscaster, liked to tell a story about Bilko hitting three home runs against Pepper-dine College in an exhibition game at Little Wrigley in 1956. Stratton was the home plate umpire.

"The college kids are really on Bilko," Stratton said. "The first time he comes up, he hits one over the right-field wall—a shot. The second time he comes up, he hits one over the left-field wall—a shot. The third time he comes up, I said, 'Well, you got one over right and one over left, might as well go for center.' Sure enough, he hit one into the center-field seats. So next time he's up, I said, 'Damn, Steve, that was really something. I don't think I've ever seen anybody do that—hit three home runs to all three fields.' He said, 'Damn hot dog kids pissed me off.'"

It's a wonderful tale and mostly accurate. The only problem is that Bilko hit only two home runs that game. But, hey, Stratton was a PCL umpire who, as a sportscaster, opened his show with the line, "Time to call 'em as I see 'em."

Besides, Bilko walloped so many home runs during spring training, a calculator was needed to keep count. Stout Steve's ten homers were about all the Angels had to brag about after finishing the spring with a 5–11 record against PCL rivals.

Scheffing was still trying to figure out how to replace the loss of six pitchers who had won seventy-five of the Angels' ninety-one wins the year before. "Oh, we've got other troubles, but they're minor by comparison." [12]

The outfield was worrisome.

The Cubs were high on Don Eaddy, a natural third baseman they wanted the Angels to test in centerfield. "Who's to say he can or can't," Scheffing grumbled. [13]

"He just can't miss," Cubs coach Ray Blades said of Eaddy. "We don't know where he'll play yet this year, but he's a big leaguer on defense now. It's just a question of his hitting." [14]

Eaddy's .133 batting average prompted Scheffing to complain he didn't "even make a loud noise when he connects." [15]

He was equally unhappy with Prentice "Pidge" Browne, the Texas League's home run king with thirty-three the year before. "He hasn't shown me that he can play in this league." [16]

Browne and Eaddy soon were out of the league. The Angels opened the season with Bob Coats in left field, Jim Bolger in center, and Eddie Haas in right.

"Eddie was one of those natural talents," said Angels' pitcher Bob Anderson. "We just loved to see the guy hit."

"He was a line-drive hitter," said Carroll Beringer, a pitcher who later played with Haas in the Texas League. "He could hit the best fastball you could throw."

"He was a big-league hitter," Coats said. "I thought he'd be a big-league star. And I think he would've if he hadn't had that terrible accident."

Playing for the Milwaukee Braves in a spring exhibition game three years later, Eddie broke his right leg when he stepped into a hole and crashed into a flagpole while making a running catch. He missed the entire 1959 season because of the injury.

Figure 5.2. Angel brass gave Steve Bilko a customized checkup at the start of spring training in 1956. Manager Bob Scheffing, lower left, checks his waistline; president John Holland checks his right arm; while Wid Matthews, director of personnel for the Chicago Cubs, feels his left arm. *UCLA Charles E. Young Research Library Department of Special Collections, Los Angeles Times Photographic Archives.*

In 1955 at Des Moines in the Class A Western League, Eddie was hitting .323 with twelve home runs before he crashed into a fence chasing a fly ball and broke a shoulder. In three seasons as a professional, he had a batting average of .327.

Eddie's debut with the Angels was memorable in more ways than one.

"I was the new kid on the block," Haas said. "I thought I was going to be tough. A lot of other people chewed tobacco. I was going to chew, too."

Eddie hit home runs in both games of a day–night doubleheader at San Diego to start the season.

In the first game he had trouble with a line drive hit to him in right field. "I was going to come in and make a spectacular catch and the ball sunk more than I thought and it hit the ground right in front of me, bounced up and hit the heel of my glove and, then, my elbow and Adam's apple."

"He fell down and we all rushed out there and he was turning blue and white," recalled shortstop Casey Wise.

Eddie had a big chaw of tobacco in his mouth at the time.

"I had to swallow," Haas said. "But I didn't tell anybody. I thought I'd be all right."

Eddie finished the first game and started the second even though "between games, I was turning green." Nobody knew he had a problem until he went to catch a pop fly in shallow right field.

"It was my ball all the way so I hollered, 'I got it.' But the longer I looked up, there was about three, four, five balls up there. And I didn't know which one to catch. I dove at one of them and it was the wrong ball."

"He was not a good fielder," Wise added. "But he could sure swing the bat."

Eddie was batting .275 with four home runs in late May when the Cubs returned Wade to the Angels. With Wade in center and Bolger in right, "it was ring around the roses in left field and right field," he said. "We had a logjam out there and I was a young guy so that's the reason they sent me out."

At Des Moines, Eddie could play every day and work on improving his defense. He made six errors in forty-one games at L.A.

"That bunch could hit," Haas said. "If you look back at those averages they had that year, I mean, man, I was low on the totem pole. I had to be sent out."

Eddie continued to follow the Angels even after returning to Des Moines where he hit .320 with eleven homers. "I kept track because, first, a lot of those guys were helpful to me. Second, I was kind of in awe of some of the seasons they were having. Bilko's year was just phenomenal. Bolger knocked in 147 runs. When you get into numbers like that, I was curious to see how things went after I left."

Eddie played briefly in the majors for the Cubs and Braves but spent most of his eleven-year career in the minors where he hit .293 with eighty-nine homers. He went on to become a coach, minor-, and major-league manager (Atlanta Braves, 1985), and scout.

Of the many valuable lessons Eddie learned from his Angels teammates, one in particular stuck out. "There were no speed guns back in those days," Eddie explained. "But I remember one phrase all those guys used if we played against a young kid that was probably throwing ninety-five to ninety-eight miles an hour: 'He's fast but he won't last.' Sure enough, about the second or third time around the batting order, he would lose a little bit, and they would sit on that fastball. And, boy, they would annihilate him."

The four most electrifying words in L.A. in 1956 were "And here comes Bilko!" The signature phrase of Bob Kelley, the voice of the Angels, was used to stir radio listeners when Steve Bilko came to bat with runners on base and a rally brewing. "And here comes Bilko!" Kelley proclaimed time and again.

In the Angels' ninety-second game on July 7, Bilko walloped his thirty-seventh homer, matching his total for 1955. There were seventy-six games to play and good reason to believe he would reach the magic number of sixty—the PCL record for home runs in a single season.

One L.A. newspaper published a "tale of the tape" comparing Bilko with Rocky Marciano, the reigning world heavyweight boxing champion: weight—Bilko 230, Marciano 187; chest—Bilko forty-eight, Marciano thirty-nine; thigh—Bilko twenty-six, Marciano twenty-two. The headline concluded: ROCK JUST SMALL BOY BESIDE BILKO.[17]

Stout Steve was both feared and respected by pitchers in the league.

"You respected what he could do," said Russ Kemmerer, a twelve-game winner for the San Francisco Seals in 1956 who would go on to pitch ten seasons in the majors. "You respected his power, his athletic ability and he, in turn, knew that you might not be winning a hundred games but at the same time you had the ability to get him out and when you got him out, he acknowledged it. Ted Williams was a lot like that. There was just respect."

"If you got the ball over the middle of the plate or on the outside, you could kiss it goodbye," said Eddie Erautt, a pitcher for the San Diego Padres. "You had to pitch him inside. He was so big that he just couldn't get around inside."

"He was just like Ralph Kiner," said Larry Jansen, referring to one of baseball's most feared home run hitters in the 1940s and 1950s. "Don't make a mistake."

"Steve looked like King Kong up there," said Jerry Casale, a hard-throwing twenty-two-year-old right hander for the Seals. "I looked at facing him as a challenge because I knew if you could get people out like him, you had a chance to go one step higher. This is what you'd have to face if you got to the big leagues."

Bilko was hitting .371 with forty-five homers going into a game July 31 against Casale and the Seals at Little Wrigley.

"Stop Bilko and you stop the Angels," Seals manager Joe Gordon told his pitchers.

He ordered them not to give Bilko anything good to hit even if it meant walking him every time. "We can't afford to let Bilko get those homers. Even when he isn't swinging at full power, or gets only part of the ball on his bat he can murder you."[18]

In the third inning, Wade tagged Casale for a two-run homer, putting the Angels on top 3–2. Up stepped Bilko.

"I threw a fastball that took off on me, and it went and knocked him right on his ass," Casale said, "and then Gene Mauch and the Angels' dugout started giving it to me: 'You guinea this! You dago that!' All kinds of everything: 'You're going to come up, Casale. We're going to get you, you son-of-a-bitch.' I'm listening to all this stuff until the end of the inning.

"I'm saying to myself, 'What the hell is the matter with them? I didn't try to knock Steve down.' He was an easy out for me. Of course, he was dangerous and a helluva good hitter. But I was able to handle him."

Bilko struck out.

Casale low-bridged the next batter, George Freese, before striking him out. And, then, he fanned Speake.

When the six-foot-two, 200-pound Casale batted the next inning, he was telling himself to stay loose. Dick Drott was pitching for the Angels and he threw so hard that hitters often referred to his fastballs as bullets.

Drott reared back and fired. "It wasn't a case of cream puffs at twenty paces, but one of bullets at sixty feet, six inches," one observer reported.[19]

"I swear to God that if I didn't put my arm in front of my heart, it would've broken my heart," Casale said. "It hit me on the left forearm. It blew up on me, and I went down and I saw stars. I couldn't believe that a pitcher would throw at another pitcher, especially as hard as I was throwing in those days. You wouldn't want to do that."

Gordon rushed from the Seals dugout to check on Casale.

"Jerry, I'm getting you out of here."

"Joe, go sit down. I'll take care of this matter myself."

Jerry could hardly wait to take the mound the next inning. "I knew Drott was the second batter. I almost walked the guy in front of him just to get to Drott."

Seals catcher Hayward Sullivan signaled for a curveball.

"No way, baby, no way," Jerry said to himself as he shook off the sign. "I'm going for the fastball and you know where it's going to be."

Drott squared around to bunt.

"He's looking straight at me. And I aimed the ball right for his mouth."

Drott quickly moved the bat to protect his face. The ball smashed Dick's right pitching hand, fracturing the index finger. He would be out of action for fifteen days.

"I thought it broke all his fingers. If he doesn't put that bat in front of him, the ball would've gone right in his face. That's how mad I was."

Casale dropped his glove and ran toward the Angels dugout trying to get Mauch. "I couldn't get close to him. Good thing I didn't get my hands on him."

"It was a rugged, body-denting struggle that at one time came precariously close to an all-out war of fists as Casale and his starting opponent, young Dick Drott, threw at each other, and pin-pointed their targets with blazing, exploding fastballs," Bob Stevens wrote in the *San Francisco Chronicle*. "Casale started it, and finished it."[20]

Jerry struck out Bilko three times to beat the Angels, 7–3.

"I'm not going to say that I wasn't trying to brush Steve back," Casale said. "I was just trying to pitch him in tight. Because with those big arms of his, if you pitched the ball out over the plate, he'd just hit it out of Los Angeles, and that ballpark was so small, you couldn't make any mistakes. Boy, he could pop them out of there in a heartbeat."

Bilko belted his forty-sixth homer the following day as the Angels went on a thirty-seven-run scoring binge to beat the Seals four straight. They were 16–8 against the Seals overall.

"Some players you can intimidate, others you can't," Kiner said. "Some players wake up and hurt you if you throw at them. They've found they can't scare Bilko, and if they do low-bridge him, he's going to be all the tougher."[21]

"The guy who tries to stick the ball in my ear had better do a pretty thorough job of it," Bilko warned. "I might get up."[22]

The craggy-faced Scheffing answered to the nickname of Grump bestowed on him by a fellow Cubs coach after a rough day on the golf course.

Even Grump was grinning as West claimed the air-cooled uniforms he designed for the Angels were responsible for their beginning June in first place with a 33–17 record, three games ahead of runner-up Seattle.

Through June 3, Bilko was batting .411 with twenty-three home runs and fifty-seven RBIs; Bolger was doing a thin-man's imitation of Bilko with eleven homers and fifty-one RBIs; Speake was close behind with nine homers and thirty-six RBIs; Mauch was hitting .366; and, since blowing into town in late May, Wade was batting .353 with six home runs in thirteen games. The Angels were hitting .294 and averaging more than six runs over fifty-four games.

After seeing L.A. in action, Cincinnati Redlegs general manager Gabe Paul called the Angels "the greatest bunch of major league prospects I've seen on one team in many a year."[23]

"You can't win if you haven't got the horses," said Scheffing, quickly pointing out he had quite a stable going for him.

"I have no radical theories about managing. The most important jobs for a manager are to keep his pitching staff organized and to maintain good morale on the ballclub. There are sixteen managers in the majors, and if you lined them all up and asked them what they would do in a given situation on the field, you'd get sixteen answers that were pretty much the same. You win games by hitting and throwing and running."[24]

Games are also won by a manager making the right decisions in terms of who stays and goes.

At third base, Scheffing released Clarkson in favor of Freese, who was hitting only .229 at the time. In the outfield, he replaced Haas and Coats as starters with Wade and Speake, even though both were playing well. At catcher, he played Elvin Tappe over Joe Hannah, hitting around .300 when he was benched.

He shook up the pitching staff by releasing two pitchers, Don Swanson and Hy Cohen, who were responsible for seven of the team's nineteen victories. In fact, Cohen's 5–0 record was the best in the league.

"It was a gutsy move," Speake said. "A lot of it had to do with the two kids, Dick Drott and Bob Anderson, needing more experience. He decided to go with the kids, and he was proven right."

On the same day Cohen was cut, Drott whiffed fourteen as he combined with Marino Pieretti and Anderson to tie the league record of nineteen strikeouts in a nine-inning game. The veteran Pieretti and two youngsters, Bob Thorpe and Johnny Briggs, were added in May, and Dwight "Red" Adams, another crafty vet, in June.

Briggs won three straight, Adams five, Dave Hillman seven, and Gene Fodge nine. Drott led the league in strikeouts. Anderson was voted the PCL Rookie of the Year for his outstanding work as a relief pitcher.

Injuries to Hillman, Briggs and Drott made pitching a constant concern for Grump. He expertly plugged the gaps.

The Angels lost nine of their last twelve games in June to slip to second place behind Seattle. They were back in first place in mid-July but by only a one game margin after being routed 15–3 by the Rainiers.

The following day Hillman and Fodge pitched the Angels to a doubleheader sweep of the Rainiers. Bilko, Wade, and Bolger slammed home runs.

The Angels turned up the heat in July and August, posting a 47–19 record to open a twelve-and-a-half game lead over Seattle with sixteen games to play in September.

"I can remember a burning desire we had to clinch it in Seattle," Speake said.

The Angels won the first game of their five-game series against the Rainiers as Hillman notched his twentieth victory. After dropping the second game, L.A. reeled off three more wins, the third an 8–1 romp behind Fodge to wrap up the championship.

"Proof of this team's greatness is the fact that it played its best ball against the strongest rivals," Scheffing said.[25]

The Angels were 16–8 against second-place Seattle and 18–6 against Portland and Sacramento, the third- and fifth-place teams. At one point, L.A. beat Portland fifteen straight times.

"They were pretty much unbeatable," said Portland's Ed Mickelson. "We had a good team. They had good pitching. They had good hitting. They had everything. That was just a dream team."

Scheffing cited two turning points, both in August.

The first was the Angels sweep of a five-game series against Sacramento after the Solons had taken five in a row from the Rainiers. The second was the Angels rebounding from three consecutive defeats to Vancouver to win nine of their next eleven games.

"That bunch just got after it every day," Haas said. "I don't know whether they were trying to get back to the major leagues or whether they thought that's the way baseball had to be played. But I look back on that team and I think: 'Man, they all thought they could play defense; they all thought they could hit. And they did. They won that thing by sixteen games."

Earlier in the season, Bilko promised Adams he was going to give his first baseman's mitt to Red's six-year-old son, Dwight, when the Angels clinched the pennant.

"Dwight thought Bilko was Superman," Adams said.

Moments after winning the title, Bilko walked over to Red and tossed him a new glove, the same one he used in games.

"It was pretty touching," Adams said, choking back emotion. "I thought he'd forget."

Moe Bauer and his son, Paul, were in Atlanta to see the Montreal Expos, managed by Mauch, play the Braves.

Moe called a batboy over to his seat near the dugout and handed him a ring. "Take this to Coach Mauch and ask him if he'll see the person who owns this ring."

Moments later Mauch looked up into the stands, quickly recognizing his old teammate, as skinny as ever. "Hey, Moe, come on down."

When people asked Moe about the '56 Angels, he showed them the championship ring given the players. "It's not a World Series ring, but it's a beautiful ring—the most beautiful minor league ring I've seen. There are only twenty-five or so of them around."

Moe died in 2005. Paul now wears his father's ring on his right hand.

Speake wore his Angels championship ring every day until 2011 when Bruce, his oldest son, celebrated his fifty-sixth birthday. "This way I know the ring will stay in the family."

The oval-shaped gold ring features a baseball diamond over two crossed bats, topped by a crown with diamonds. Four small diamonds representing infield bases flank a big round diamond in the middle. The initials L.A. are on one side of the baseball diamond, and the numerals fifty-six on the other. At the bottom are the letters "PCL."

Mauch was involved in the design of the ring just as he was in virtually every other aspect of the team.

"Scheffing was our manager but Mauch was the cat's meow on the field," said Haas. "He told everybody where to go, what to do.

"Mauch had a big impression on me as a kid. Some of the things I didn't understand until I got older. Once I played another four or five years and, especially when I started managing, I reflected back on some of the things that he just harped on. They were very helpful."

The Angels closed the 1956 season with Steve Bilko Day. That evening Angels' president John Holland treated the players and their wives to a performance by Nat "King" Cole at the swank Coconut Grove in L.A.'s Ambassador Hotel.

For Speake, the gathering symbolized the esprit de corps from Holland at the top of the organization down through Scheffing and the players. "It was just like a big family."

"You won't find that happening very often," Fodge said. "It was a fine thing and that's just what 1956 was all about."

Cole, a big Angels fan, mingled with the players and then entertained them with a medley of hit songs, including "Unforgettable":[26]

> Unforgettable, that's what you are
> Unforgettable through near and far

The players soon scattered near and far but they had their rings to remind them of an unforgettable season.

NOTES

1. *1956 Los Angeles Angels Yearbook*, 11 (1st ed.).
2. *Los Angeles Times*, October 28, 1955, C3.
3. *San Francisco Examiner*, May 27, 1949, 23.
4. *Los Angeles Examiner*, February 4, 1956, Section II, 1.
5. *Los Angeles Herald-Express*, February 4, 1956, A10.
6. *Los Angeles Times*, March 20, 1956, Part IV, 2.
7. *Los Angeles Herald-Express*, March 21, 1956, D5.
8. *Los Angeles Times*, May 6, 1956, B6.
9. *Los Angeles Mirror-News*, April 5, 1955, Part III, 1.
10. *Los Angeles Times*, March 27, 1956, 37.
11. Ibid.
12. *Long Beach Press-Telegram*, March 16, 1956, A13.
13. *Los Angeles Herald-Express*, April 3, 1956, C4.
14. *The Sporting News*, March 14, 1956, 15.
15. *Los Angeles Times*, April 9, 1956, C1.
16. Ibid.

17. *Los Angeles Mirror-News*, August 6, 1956, Part III, 2.
18. *San Francisco Examiner*, July 31, 1956, Section II, 4.
19. *Los Angeles Times*, August 1, 1956,Part II, 1.
20. *San Francisco Chronicle*, August 1, 1956, 1H.
21. *Los Angeles Examiner*, August 18, 1956, Section 2, 1.
22. *San Francisco Chronicle*, May 12, 1956, 2H.
23. *The Sporting News*, June 6, 1956, 15.
24. *Ibid.*, June 13, 1956, 33.
25. *Los Angeles Times*, September 5, 1956, A1.
26. Bourne Company, New York City.

SIX

Stout Steve, the Slugging Seraph

"The big man was Bilko, and I'm talking about more than the excess poundage that inspired a *Los Angeles Times* headline saying NOT EVEN MRS. BILKO KNOWS HIS WEIGHT. I'm talking about the feats that enabled Stout Steve, the Slugging Seraph, to block out the big league sun for my generation of L.A. kids." —*Of Stars and Angels* by John Schulian, *Twilight of the Long-ball Gods*

The Herculean strength and home run–hitting ability of Steve Bilko captivated kids and sportswriters alike. When Bilko appeared on the national scene in 1950, Red Smith, the renowned sports columnist, described Bilko as "a great, lummocking, broad-shouldered, wide-beamed broth of a boy."[1]

Bilko didn't look like a ball player. "He looks as if he had just climbed down off a beer truck—or rolled off the back of one, for that matter," wisecracked Jim Murray, sports columnist for the *Los Angeles Times*.[2]

"Stout Steve, the Slugging Seraph," said John Schulian, a former sports columnist, relishing the alliteration of the moniker as much as the memory.

Schulian was ten years old and a fan of the Hollywood Stars, the Angels' archrivals, when Bilko barreled into town. "It was just that Bilko was, no pun intended, too big to ignore. Here was this guy hitting all these home runs. You were just fascinated by him."

The first time Schulian saw Bilko play was on television. "I was probably sitting in my living room, eating a peanut butter and jelly sandwich. You weren't used to seeing ball players shaped like that."

Bob Case, eleven years old in 1956, wanted to look just like Bilko. So Bob and his friends stopped the Helms bakery truck every time it came through their neighborhood in the L.A. suburb of Glendale. "We ate as many donuts as we could because we were all trying to get fat. We honestly believed that all those homers came from being big."

Long before kids were emulating him in L.A., Bilko was being compared with home run–hitting greats Lou Gehrig, Jimmy Foxx, and Johnny Mize. His strength and power already were legendary.

In 1947 at the age of eighteen, he ripped twenty-nine home runs for Winston-Salem, North Carolina, in the Class C Carolina League. One of his home runs was a vicious line drive over the center-field fence at Winston-Salem. It supposedly shot into a large tree just outside the park, breaking off a limb, and plummeting a couple of youngsters to the ground.

The next year at Lynchburg, Virginia, he led the Class B Piedmont League in batting average (.333) and home runs (twenty). Legend has it he hit one ball so hard off the left-field fence at Lynchburg that the ball actually flattened out.

On seeing Bilko play for the first time, a Cardinals executive proclaimed, "There's a kid named Bilko, a great big kid who can really powder that ball. He's pretty crude, just a kid in Class C now, but remember the name, Bilko. You'll hear about him."[3]

Bing Devine, who transformed the Cardinals and New York Mets into World Series champions in the 1960s, was general manager of the Rochester Red Wings in 1949 when the 20-year-old Bilko belted 34 homers in the Class AAA International League. "Steve is the kind of a kid who can strike out on one pitch and the next time, when they think he's fooled again, he'll knock it out of the park," Devine said. "And he can hit it on his fists and still knock it out of the park. That's the kind of power he has."[4]

After Bilko socked four homers in a doubleheader, he was being called another Foxx. "Bilko, like the great Foxx of American League fame," the Associated Press reported, "is blasting home runs far and often and within a season or two should be terrorizing major league pitching."[5]

Not to be outdone, the United Press wire service described Bilko as a "giant" who is "built like, swings like and oft-times hits a ball as far as the mighty Jimmy Foxx."[6]

Cardinals owner Fred Saigh had great hopes for Bilko. "Gentlemen," he announced to baseball writers at spring training in 1950, "you are looking at one of the future great names in baseball."[7]

One of the names the former tax and corporate lawyer had in mind was Gehrig. "Bilko will make baseball fans forget Lou Gehrig."[8]

"He was our Mickey Mantle," said Schulian.

Case attended every Angels game he could in 1956.

After one game, he was sitting by himself in the parking lot near the Wrigley Field clubhouse door. The game had ended more than an hour earlier. It was almost midnight. Finally, the door opened. Bob jumped to his feet to greet Bilko and ask for his autograph. Bilko signed Bob's '56 Angels yearbook, patted him on the head and said, "Thanks for sticking around, kid."

Bob didn't wash his hair for a week. He still has the yearbook Bilko signed as well as a home uniform worn by Bilko during the 1956 season. Case bought the uniform from a collector forty-two years later. "He was like a god to me at that time in my life. All you heard was Steve Bilko, Steve Bilko, Steve Bilko."

Case grew up to become a business manager for Casey Stengel, the long-time Yankees manager, and represent movie actor Mickey Rooney and some thirty-five major league baseball players, including Warren Spahn, Rod Carew, and Tony Oliva. "Bilko is the only idol I ever had in sports," he said.

Schulian went on to be a sportswriter and share his boyhood memories of Bilko in numerous stories. "He was the first fat guy my friends and I ever had for a hero, the first fat guy we ever wanted to grow up to be."

Baseball players weren't supposed to be fat. They could be tall, short, or skinny but not fat. Few sports were as intolerant of excess flab as baseball.

Babe Ruth overcame criticism of his weight by becoming the greatest home run hitter of his generation. Mickey Lolich was an outstanding pitcher for the Detroit Tigers from 1963 to 1975, but just as much attention was focused on his potbelly as his left arm that notched 217 career victories.

Over the years, players have become bigger in size and teams more willing to accept a guy tipping the scales at 230 pounds plus.

The 1960s and 1970s gave us Frank "Hondo" Howard, six-foot-seven and 255 pounds; and John "Boog" Powell, six-four and 230 pounds. The 1980s and 1990s produced Cecil "Big Daddy" Fielder, six-three and 230; Frank "Big Hurt" Thomas, six-five and 240; and Jason Giambi, six-three and 250. More recent big boppers are David "Big Papi" Ortiz, six-four and 250; Ryan Howard, six-four and 240; Prince Fielder, five-eleven and 275; and Pablo "Kung Fu Panda" Sandoval, five-eleven and 240.

In the 1950s, Bilko was a freak of nature.

"His shoulders stretched six feet across," said Eldon "Rip" Repulski, a teammate at Rochester and St. Louis. "He was so huge that wherever he went, people would look at him and say, 'Oh-h-h, what a big guy that is!'"

"Steve was not fat," said Albie Pearson, the diminutive outfielder who played alongside Bilko with the major-league Angels in 1961–62. "He was one of the biggest boned men I've seen. His legs—you could put mine together and make one of his."

Bilko was twenty years old and weighed around 230 pounds when he made his major-league debut late in the 1949 season with the Cardinals battling the Dodgers for the National League pennant. The Cards lost five of their last eight games, but Bilko was impressive, reaching base ten of the twenty-two times he batted and recording a .294 average.

The Cards were expecting big things of Bilko in 1950. So when he showed up at spring training weighing 260 pounds, the baseball world was thrown off its axis.

The *Sporting News* devoted a full page to the subject. A banner headline proclaimed: CARDS GRIN AND GROAN OVER BEEFY BILKO. Sub-heads read: ROOKIE RATED AS PRIZE PROSPECT, BUT BATTLES SURPLUS FAT and WIFE'S MOM KEPT TABLE HEAPED FULL. Above a photo of Steve was another heading: CONTENDER FOR HEAVY-WEIGHT TITLE OF N.L.[9]

The story pounded away at the fat theme: "Bilko knew that he faced the opportunity to win a regular berth in 1950, yet he permitted himself to get super lardy over the off-season."[10]

Joe Garagiola was a catcher for the Cardinals at the time:

> They put a rubber suit on him and they made that poor fellow run around and sweat and sweat and sweat. And, then, they'd ask him to play nine innings after he was about dehydrated. He could hardly get the bat around. And he was still hitting the ball 400 feet in right-center field.

Bilko was back in Rochester after striking out ten times in ten games and hitting well under his weight. "It is hoped that he will there learn to decrease his weight and increase his batting average," one columnist wrote.[11]

Garagiola shook his head in dismay. "I'll never forget one day in St. Louis at the old ballpark, Sportsman's Park. He was sitting on the bench and looking out toward right-center field. Then he looked to left field. He said, 'You know, I guess I'm just a simple guy from Nanticoke, Pennsylvania, but I can hit a ball into the right-center field seats with my elbow and they want me to pull the ball where I hit long fly balls. I don't understand that.'"

Garagiola pinpointed two problems for Bilko with the Cardinals, and one of them, his weight, nagged him throughout his career. The other problem was the Cardinals' efforts to make Bilko a pull-hitter so he'd hit more home runs at Sportsman's Park.

Repulski was a rookie outfielder with the Cardinals in 1953 and, with Bilko and third baseman Ray Jablonski, formed the "Polish Falcons," a nickname they earned as stars at Rochester. Rip had good power himself, hitting 106 home runs in nine big league seasons.

"Sportsman's Park was a hard park to hit home runs in," Repulski said. "I hit nineteen home runs my second year [1954] but only three were in St. Louis."

The park was ideally suited for a left-handed hitter like Stan Musial because the right-field fence was only 310 feet from home plate. By comparison, it was 351 feet down the left-field foul line and 426 feet to center.

Cardinal managers—from Eddie Dyer in 1949 to Eddie "The Brat" Stanky in 1953—believed Bilko's natural power to left-center and right-center would be wasted and wanted him to pull the ball down the left-field line. Dyer believed Bilko could become the greatest hitter in baseball if he would only learn to pull the ball.

"Stanky always thought that if Steve would lose a little weight, he would pull the ball a little bit more," Repulski said. "He tried his best but he was just a big-boned guy and there was nothing he could do about his weight. Steve wasn't able to pull the ball that much either."

"He wasn't that type of hitter," explained George Freese, Bilko's best friend on the 1956 Angels. "I believe at that time some coach said, 'Oh, boy, here's a guy that's going to be great!' And they wanted to be able to say, 'I helped Steve do this.' I don't think Steve needed all that help."

In L.A., Bilko was left alone to hit as he pleased. Nobody bothered him about his weight.

Angels' manager Bob Scheffing told Bilko he wouldn't look at the scale if he promised to stay at 230 pounds.

"My best playing weight was 254 pounds," Bilko said, admitting that he got up to 270 pounds on occasion.

"I still feel that if everybody had left him alone and let him play his own way in the majors, he would've made it," Freese said. "Instead, everyone tried to change him and make him look like a Mr. America in tights."

Bilko was never able to rid himself of the "fat man" label.

"You don't hit the ball with your belly," Garagiola said. "I know some guys who are built like hitters and built like pitchers and all they do is look good in the hotel lobby."

Jim Brosnan, a scholarly pitcher who went on to become a best-selling author, was a seventeen-game winner for the 1955 Angels. He and Bilko were roommates during spring training.

"The bitch about Steve was that he was overweight, that he didn't look like a major league ball player, that he wasn't a good defensive ball player. I thought it was a lot of bullshit. In his own mind, Steve was sincere about wanting to be what his managers wanted him to be—slimmer."

Asked how much Bilko weighed when they played together in L.A., Brosnan joked, "Over a period of time, I think about 900 pounds. He must have lost that much, at least.

"The man was a great beer drinker. He had a wooden leg besides the two he was carrying which were huge—about the size of ale cans. I'm sure he kept a special tap in one knee in case he ran out."

Bilko's technique for losing weight was called a "steamer" and, naturally, involved beer.

"He'd take a six-pack of beer into the bathroom," Brosnan explained. "He'd seal off the door by putting towels against the bottom of the door, close the window and turn on the shower and the tap in the washbasin to hot. Then he'd sit on the edge of the bathtub while all this steam would rise and he'd drink a six-pack of beer—all six bottles. He said it helped him sweat. Of course, sweat meant you were losing weight. And this is how he'd do it.

"He was actually doing what he thought would help out—sweating a lot. I'm not crediting him with a helluva lot of common sense. But at least he had a lot of sincerity. You take a man with sincerity; put him in a major league uniform and that can pay off. I would've done it myself. But I've got a sense of humor and most managers don't have one."

Bilko started the '56 season with three personal goals: forty to fifty home runs, 200 runs batted in, and a .360 batting average.

He achieved two of them, hitting .360 and slugging fifty-five homers. He fell short of his RBI target, driving in 164 runs. He even stole four bases. For the second straight year, he was selected the PCL's Most Valuable Player.

Bilko was a notoriously slow starter but in 1956 he was hot from his very first at bat—a 380-foot homer over the right-field fence at San Diego's Lane Field. The pitcher was Eddie Erautt, a former Cardinals teammate, who during their time together in the majors sent Steve postcards, unsigned, with the name of Steve's favorite beer, *Kulmbacher*, written on it.

"Bilko actually hit it out of the park while falling away from a pitch," columnist Jack Murphy wrote in the *San Diego Union*. Steve went four-for-five in the opening game, prompting Murphy to suggest, "Nothing short of a rifle is going to stop him" for the rest of the season.[12]

Steve was hitting .500 with seven homers and twenty-one RBIs going into May when he belted sixteen homers, twelve in an eleven-game stretch. That gave him twenty-three in fifty games, a pace that soon had L.A. newspapers using a "Bilko Meter" and "Bilko Homerometer" to track his progress against the PCL's single-season record of sixty home runs set by Tony Lazzeri in 1925.

"Steve Bilko doesn't look like the same hitter he was a year ago," Bill Veeck said after a scouting mission for the Cleveland Indians. "Bilko is confident up there now. They're not pushing him back with the inside pitch and then getting him on the outside corner like they were last year."[13]

Bilko swatted the longest homer ever seen at Seattle's Sicks Stadium— a 550-foot shot that landed in the middle of a highway behind the left-field wall. "What is a man who can hit like that doing in this league when

Figure 6.1.   Steve Bilko became known as the "home pro" at Los Angeles' Wrigley Field, swatting monstrous home runs that had fans hanging homemade signs from the upper deck. *UCLA Charles E. Young Research Library Department of Special Collections, Los Angeles Times Photographic Archives.*

he should be hitting in the majors?" asked Elmer Singleton, a veteran Seattle pitcher.[14]

"He can outhit ninety percent of the batters in the majors," Scheffing raved.[15]

The Angels tore up Bilko's contract in July, giving him a new one for an estimated $14,000. In turn, Steve signed a waiver, granting him immunity from being drafted by the majors. "I figured that if a club wanted me bad enough to put a lot of money in me, they'd give me a good chance."

Bilko added eight homers in June and fourteen in July to give him forty-five heading into August.

"Whatever total Bilko has at the end of the season," James McGee said in the *San Francisco Call-Bulletin*, "they'll always claim one additional home run for him."[16]

In a game earlier in the year against Portland at Little Wrigley, Bilko belted a ball to deep right-center that was ruled a double by umpire Cece Carlucci. The Angels' Gene Mauch disagreed: "It goes as number twenty-six in my book."[17]

The next inning Portland outfielder Bob Borkowski told Carlucci, "The ball hit a fan right in the chest and came right back on the field."

"I couldn't do anything about it an inning later," said Carlucci. "But it could've happened."

Angels' president John Holland placed a $250,000 price tag on Bilko "if he breaks Tony Lazzeri's home run record." Otherwise, Holland said it would take $200,000 and "adequate playing replacements" for the Angels to deal him to a major-league team. "I'm not anxious to sell him, even for a quarter of a million. It's impossible to estimate how much he'll be worth for us at the gate next season, and perhaps the season after, as well."[18]

"That rates as a new high for minor league beef on the spike, amounting, as it does, to $833 a pound," *Sports Illustrated* calculated by dividing Steve's estimated 240 pounds into $200,000. The magazine declared, "This is a new Steve—more relaxed, more obese, and completely resigned to the fickleness of fate."[19]

Bilko was well on his way to a triple-crown season in early August when the DiMaggio brothers arrived in L.A. for an old-timers game at Little Wrigley. It was only the second time that Joe, Dom, and Vincent played in the same outfield together. "I can't wait to see him (Bilko)," Dom DiMaggio told one columnist before asking, "Has he lost any weight?"[20]

Dom was assured Bilko was twenty-five pounds lighter than the 260 he supposedly packed as a Cardinal rookie. "He must have found himself. I don't see how they'll be able to stop him when he goes up again."[21]

"The pressure going for a record is something terrific," Joe DiMaggio said, recalling his record fifty-six-game hitting streak. "Nobody would let me forget the fact that I was in the midst of a hitting streak. Everywhere I went I heard about it, read about it and it seemed like every time somebody recognized me they had to ask me about it."[22]

In early August the *Los Angeles Mirror-News* published a four-part series titled, "Bilko the Great."

"More people in L.A. today know Bilko than Marilyn Monroe," Scheffing rhapsodized.[23]

Bilko hit his fifty-first homer on August 27. He needed nine home runs in the Angels' last twenty-two games to tie Lazzeri's record.

Sacramento Solons manager Tommy Heath threatened his hurlers with a fine and removal from the game for throwing a strike to Bilko.

"Regardless of the situation, we were supposed to walk him," said Chet Johnson, the Solons' pitcher who mixed clowning with his curveball.

In one game, Johnson was pitching to Bilko and doing his usual showboat routine. "I threw the ball outside and then flexed my muscles. After two balls way outside, that big donkey reached across the plate and slapped one right down the line and just over the fence for a home run. But it wasn't a strike and Heath couldn't fine me."

Bilko hit four more homers to finish with fifty-five.

On the last day of the season, Steve Bilko Day, he told Angels fans, "I'm sorry . . .that I missed setting a new home-run record. But next year's coming." [24]

After the 1956 season, Bilko was rewarded with probably the richest contract in minor league history up to that point. The newspapers reported the contract was worth $15,000 but Bilko would later say, "It was a lot more than that. I made a whole lot on the side. I'd go to stores, stuff like that."

When Bilko said he could've matched the money paid many major leaguers, he wasn't bragging. It was fact. The minimum salary for major league players in 1957 was $6,000.

A brash young slugger named Dick Stuart joined the Hollywood Stars in 1957 and predicted that he would beat out Bilko for the PCL home run crown. The previous year Stuart blasted sixty-six home runs at Lincoln, Nebraska, in the Class A Western League. He would go on to hit 228 career homers in the majors.

"I like Stuart but he talks too much," Bilko said. "I can see him leading the league in one category—strikeouts. Nobody will even come close to him." [25]

The Angels returned to a predominantly night-game schedule in 1957 and PCL pitchers worked around Bilko more than ever, walking him a league-leading 108 times. He clouted fifty-six home runs anyway.

Stuart, meanwhile, lasted only twenty-three games at Hollywood before being demoted to Atlanta in the Class AA Southern Association. In seventy-two at bats with Hollywood, Stuart hit six home runs and struck out thirty-two times.

Steve defended his home run title in spectacular fashion and wherever he went in subsequent seasons, he was expected to repeat his glory years with the Angels. It didn't work out that way.

Bilko took a pay cut to play for the Cincinnati Redlegs of the National League in 1958. He was traded in mid-June to the Dodgers who were struggling through their first season in L.A. In seventy-eight games with both the Reds and Dodgers, he had a .234 average, eleven home runs, and thirty-five RBIs—a far cry from what was expected of him. It was back to the PCL in 1959, this time to the Dodgers' farm club in Spokane, Washington.

In a rare display of anger, Bilko threatened not to report to Spokane. He didn't expect the Dodgers to keep him as a first baseman as they still had Gil Hodges, but he thought he would be traded to another major league team.

"What does a guy have to do to get a shot up there? Here are a bunch of guys who hit .260 and .270 and they are up there as regulars. I hit over .300, drive in a lot of runs, set home-run records and they don't even want me. What kind of game is this, anyway?"[26]

Buzzie Bavasi was general manager of the Dodgers at the time, and Holland and Scheffing were guiding the Cubs. When Bilko played for them in L.A., they promised him a chance with the Cubs if they ever had the opportunity to get him.

"When the Dodgers sent me to Spokane, the Cubs could've bought me for the waiver price of $100," Bilko said. "I asked Buzzie: 'Doesn't somebody want me in the majors?' He said nobody was interested. I mentioned the Cubs because of what both Holland and Scheffing told me. So we got on the phone and I talked with Holland. He said: 'Whatever gave you the idea that we wanted you?' I wanted them to give me a shot with the Cubs—at least two or three weeks. And if I didn't do well in Wrigley Field, they could do what they wanted. I thought I really deserved a shot to go to Chicago and play a full season."

In 1960, Bilko returned to the majors with the Detroit Tigers. The highlight of an otherwise forgettable season (.207 batting average and nine homers) was a mighty blast he hit at Yankees Stadium.

"Bobby Shantz threw him a hanging curveball," said Ryne Duren, a pitcher for the Yankees at the time. "Did you ever see a guy swing as hard as he could and miss? Well, this time Bilko swung as hard he could and hit the ball. It went way up in the top deck and right up the exit hole. He just stood there and watched it, and gave the bat a flip."

Only three others had hit a ball into the upper deck at old Yankees Stadium.

"They told me it must have gone 600 feet," Bilko said. "Shantz threw his glove in the air. I told him I was paying him back for all the times he struck me out."

The birth of the major-league Angels gave Bilko one more opportunity. He made the most of it, playing part-time over the 1961–1962 seasons and, combined, hitting for a .282 average with twenty-eight home runs and ninety-seven RBIs.

For kids that idolized Bilko growing up in L.A, this raised the question of what he could have done in his prime playing every day for an entire season.

In 600 games in the majors, spread across ten seasons, Steve batted .249 with seventy-six homers and 276 RBIs. In 1,533 minor-league games, he hit .312, slugging 313 homers and driving in 854 runs.

"Bilko was not a bad major league ball player," Garagiola said. "Unfortunately, people think a guy is going to be as great in the major leagues as he was in the minors. That isn't necessarily the case. Big league baseball is a tough grind."

"Just because he was big doesn't mean he has to hit 50–60 home runs a year," pointed out Chuck Tanner, a major league manager for nineteen years who played with Bilko in L.A. in 1961–1962. "Bilko had a good career. Maybe he didn't do what other people thought he should do but he did what he was capable of doing."

Albie Pearson and Bilko were teammates on the 1961–1962 Angels. "Steve was constantly fighting a complex that everybody was against him. He didn't handle rejection very well."

Brosnan cited two reasons for the differences between Bilko's performance in the majors and minors.

"He could handle the ball, let's say eight inches out away from the inside corner—from the belt up, inside. In the major leagues, you've got to reduce that to about six inches from the inside corner. Steve could handle the fastball up and in that didn't move a lot in that slightly expanded area. When he got to the majors, he couldn't handle it and he couldn't lay off it. Maybe that's the key. He couldn't lay off the things that he didn't do well in the majors.

"The other part of it is that he was an introverted man. He was like Ferdinand the Bull. He was not quite sure of himself until he could prove himself to himself. And by not getting the same sort of applause and recognition in the majors that he had in the minors, he couldn't accept himself as a major leaguer."

Brosnan offered another theory:

"Psychologically, he had doubts about himself that were never resolved in major league competition. This was partly because he had such great success in the minor leagues. He was a genuine hero—an extraordinary performer. He couldn't really sustain that in the big leagues because he didn't have that kind of talent. He didn't have the arrogance either. All really good baseball players have a good deal of arrogance about them. He didn't have that. Steve had confidence but he was not an arrogant man. He was never an egotistical fellow, which is a necessity for success in professional sports."

Brosnan added this postscript in a letter:

"He [Steve] was a placid and ponderous man who might have been a major league legend had he been a bit more graceful and a lot more passionate. It seems to me that Stank [Eddie Stanky] and his other big league managers expected fervor and fire from a man who either didn't have those characteristics or didn't show them because they didn't feel right to him."

In October 1976, there was a barn-shaped bar, called the Tilbury Inn, on U.S. Highway 11 in West Nanticoke, Pennsylvania—across the Susquehanna River from Bilko's hometown of Nanticoke.

As Willie Nelson whined "Blue Eyes Crying in the Rain" on the jukebox, a man with a thick Irish accent sat down at the bar. He introduced himself as Pat and offered that he lived in nearby Wilkes-Barre. "What are you doing here on a Friday night?" he asked.

On hearing I was in town to see Bilko, Pat called out to a friend a few feet away. "Hey, Rich you heard of a baseball player, Steve Bilko?"

A large, pot-bellied man, Rich shouted, "Sure. I live right down the street from him. He hit fifty-six home runs one year on the Coast."

Rich picked up his beer from the bar and moved closer. "He stole four bases one year, too. He could really drink beer. He once walked into a bar over in Nanticoke and ordered a case to go. He paid for it and before he got his change, he'd drank three cans."

The yarn was almost identical to one in a *Time* magazine story in 1960: "Sportswriters fondly recall his beer-drinking exploits, like the time he hopped off a Cincinnati Reds bus during a brief stop to buy a case of cold brew, downed two bottles before getting his change." [27]

Pat was incredulous. "I'm going to have to ask my friends about this guy."

"Go over to Honey Pot and ask anyone about Bilko," Rich said. "They'll tell you."

Honey Pot is a section of Nanticoke so named because it sits like a bowl inside a hill. The neighborhood was a melting pot of Irish, Poles, and Slovaks who settled in Nanticoke around the turn of the twentieth century and worked the coal mines in the area until they were phased out in the 1950s.

Nanticoke is located in northeastern Pennsylvania's Wyoming Valley, about twenty-five miles southwest of Scranton. When coal was king, 26,000 people lived in Nanticoke. By 1976, that number had shrunk in half.

There's only one way in and out of the Honey Pot section. The road begins at the Nanticoke post office then snakes along the Susquehanna River past several businesses and an industrial park and, finally, past piles of coal.

A modern brick house among wood frame houses built by the coal companies in the early 1900s, the Bilko home stood out. Standing in the driveway, Steve made it even easier to spot. He was tanned and athletic-looking in a blue knit shirt, blue-and-gold plaid polyester slacks, and black loafers.

During his playing days, Steve was called "Lard Zeppelin" and "Big Boy Balloon." You'd expect him to be even bigger thirteen years into retirement. That wasn't the case. He looked fit enough to play again.

"I've been going to these old-timers games and people have been telling me, 'You look in better shape now than when you were playing,'" Steve said proudly.

The family room of the Bilko home was decorated mostly with trophies won by Bilko's sons, Steve Jr. and Tom, who led the Nanticoke Area High School to championships in football, baseball, and basketball in the late 1960s. They both played football at Villanova University. There were also color photographs of the boys in their high school football uniforms and his daughter, Sharon, in a cheerleader outfit.

Next to a desk was a life-sized, black-and-white cutout photo poster of a young Steve, looking grimly at the camera while fielding a ground ball. "A guy took that picture of me at Rochester and had it blown up."

The only other sign that this was the home of one of minor league baseball's greatest power hitters was the staircase going to the second floor. The banister was made of Louisville Sluggers baseball bats, accented with varnished baseballs at the top and bottom.

Steve grew up in a house one block away. His father was a coal miner, the last one in the area to use mules to transport coal cars underground.

"They had these tipples that would go down to about 1,900 feet and branch off into different directions," Steve said. "On Sundays I had to go into the mine by myself and feed the mules. I was scared as hell. The mules pinned me against the boards. I yelled at them: 'If you don't let me go and get out of here, I can't feed you.'"

Steve's dislike for the mines was as strong as his love for baseball. In a 1952 *Parade* magazine article, his mother, Elizabeth, wrote, "Almost as soon as Steve could walk my husband would put a baseball in Steve's hand . . . if I didn't keep tabs on him, the child would always be breaking glasses in the kitchen with his ball. He was always throwing a ball around somewhere, especially against the wall or the furniture. When he was a little older, I always knew where to call him when he was late for supper. He was down at a lot playing ball. . . ."[28]

When Steve wasn't playing baseball, he was playing football. He was a guard and fullback in high school, winning all-star honors the two years he played before signing a contract to play professional baseball in August 1945.

Steve was sixteen and about to begin his junior year in high school when Cardinals scout Benny Borgman signed him on a coal bank behind the Honey Pot ballpark after watching him wallop three mighty homers in a game.

The first one soared over the coal pile Borgman was standing on along the left-field fence. "It would have been out of Yankee Stadium," wrote

Jerry Izenberg, a *New York Post* columnist. "Yankee Stadium? Hell, it would have been out of the Grand Canyon."[29]

"I was convinced," Borgman told Izenberg, "that here was a guy who would one day hit sixty-five home runs in a single season."[30]

The Cards assigned Bilko to their Allentown, Pennsylvania, farm club in the Class B Inter-State League. He singled in his only at bat.

Ineligible to play high school sports, Steve left Nanticoke to play winter ball in Panama's Canal Zone. He finished school there.

Steve started the 1946 season at Allentown, and struck out in his only at bat. He finished the year at Salisbury, Maryland, in the Class D Eastern Shore League, batting .274, driving in ninety runs and hitting twelve home runs.

Steve had a big season (.338 average; twenty-nine home runs) at Winston-Salem in 1947, but he didn't receive much publicity until the next year.

"I had a good spring with Rochester. I don't know how many games I played [twelve] but when the Cardinals sent Rocky Nelson to Rochester, that meant I had to leave."

Nelson was a line-drive hitting first baseman who was highly regarded by the Cardinals.

"They asked me where I wanted to go. Nelson had been at Lynchburg and led the league in hitting [.371 in 1947]. I said I'd like to go there and see what I could do. I thought it would give me some idea if this guy was that much better a ball player. I figured if I didn't have a good year, I'd get out of the Cardinal organization. I led the league in hitting, home runs and doubles."

The Cardinals were a perennial National League power in the 1940s, winning four pennants and finishing second five times. They slipped to fifth in 1950 and placed third the next three years.

Musial was the Cardinals' first baseman until Vernal "Nippy" Jones took over in 1948; Musial returned to his natural position in the outfield. Jones and Nelson shared first in 1949 and then, from 1950 to 1952, eight different players, including Bilko, tried the position. Musial wound up playing the most games at first base because the Cardinals couldn't find any other consistent performer.

"I always had Musial hanging over my head," Steve explained. "Like if I went oh-for-four or oh-for-ten . . . first thing you know Stan comes in and plays first. A guy like that you just don't move."

Based on his clutch debut with the Cardinals in the heat of the 1949 pennant race, he seemed to have first base clinched for 1950. In January, though, Steve married his high school sweetheart, Mary Sunder, and immediately began to gain weight. The added pounds meant trouble at spring training.

"I got on the scale and I think I was 260 pounds. They said, 'No, you can't be that much,' so I lost forty pounds in six weeks."

Steve's parents came to see him play in Philadelphia. "I went up to my mother and said, 'Hi, Mom.' She said, 'I don't know you.' I was forty pounds lighter, you see. I said, 'Well, I'm your son.' She said, 'No, you're not.' I said, 'Yeah, I just lost some weight.' That was early in the year. After four or five innings, I was tired out.

"That's when the weight thing started. No matter where I went, they said, 'Get on the scale! Get on the scale!' When I went to Los Angeles, I asked them, 'Do I worry about being Mr. America or do I play ball?' They said: 'We want you to play ball.' I said, 'Okay, I don't want to hear nothing about weight. I'm tired of it.' So when the writers asked me what I weighed, I told them, 'Between 200 and 300 pounds. If I say I weigh 230, you say I weigh 250 or whatever you want to put in the paper. You just take your choice and we'll keep everybody guessing.' I didn't get on the scale after that."

Marty Marion, a slick-fielding shortstop on three world championship Cardinal teams, replaced Dyer as the Cardinals' manager in 1951. Steve played in twenty-one games, batting .222 and hitting two home runs, before being sent to Columbus, Ohio, for a brief stint and, then, back to Rochester.

Marion and Bilko clashed.

"I was never known as a great fielder; Marty Marion was a great fielder. We were playing at Philadelphia. A guy hit one off the end of the bat. They are hard to get. They spin, go one way and then a different way. I bobbled the ball for an error. When I walked into the dugout, he said something about it. I said, 'My name is Bilko; it's not Marion. I'm not noted for being the greatest shortstop alive.' A couple of days later I was gone."

Marion also was gone the next season, with Stanky taking over as manager. But Steve had other problems. After playing in twenty games, batting .264 with one homer, he broke his right arm. It was an embarrassing injury because the story made the rounds that Steve tripped on a blade of grass.

"I was running from first base to the bench at Sportsman's Park. They were resodding the field and hadn't finished yet. I hit the higher part where they were resodding and, trying to break my fall, I broke my arm."

Bilko finished the 1952 season at Rochester, hitting .322 with twelve homers and fifty-five RBIs in eighty-two games. Steve and two other Rochester stars, Repulski and Jablonski, joined the Cardinals in 1953. Each won starting assignments—Bilko at first base, Jablonski at third base and Repulski in centerfield—and became mainstays in a Cardinal lineup that included Musial, Enos Slaughter, and Red Schoendienst.

"We were only a game or something out of first place at the all-star break," Steve said. "Stanky told us, 'When the Money Men start hitting, we'll be okay. You guys carried us the first part of the season.'"

The Cardinals finished in a third-place tie with Philadelphia, twenty-two games behind the first-place Dodgers. A season-ending slump dropped Steve's batting average some twenty points to .251, but he still had twenty-one homers and eighty-four RBIs.

The Cardinals' patience with Bilko was finally paying off and it appeared that he was going to be their first baseman for a long time.

The unexpected happened during the off-season as Steve celebrated his twenty-fifth birthday. The Cardinals paid $100,000 for Thomas Edison Alston, a black, left-handed hitting first baseman who hit .297 and twenty-three home runs in 1953 for San Diego in the PCL. The Cards were under pressure to field their first black star.

Bilko reported to training camp in 1954 "a quarter pound over what I was supposed to be." Stanky threatened to fine Bilko five dollars for every pound that he was overweight. So he charged Steve five dollars.

"If you were a big guy, he'd drive you right in the ground," Cardinal pitcher Eddie Erautt said of Stanky. "He harassed Steve all the time."

"I had a fabulous spring training," Steve said. "I was told to stay in shape. As soon as they got a chance, they'd send Alston out. The next thing I knew I was sold to the Cubs."

The Cardinals actually wanted to trade Bilko to Cleveland in the American League, but first they had to obtain waivers from other National League teams. A $60,000 price tag reportedly was placed on him to discourage any takers. The Cubs refused to waive Bilko and the Cardinals eventually settled for $12,500.

"I couldn't see what Chicago wanted with me," Steve said. "If I'd gone to Cleveland, I'd probably been there until I finished my career. The Indians didn't have an established first baseman and that's what they wanted me for. I wouldn't have had a Musial there. I wouldn't have had any big name to buck. For the first time in my life, I'd be going into a town where there was nobody there and I'd have a good shot at it. If I could do the job, somebody would have to knock me out of it."

Steve paused. "In St. Louis, I always had Stan standing over me. Wherever I went, I always had a first baseman there before me who'd had a good year."

Steve's competition with the Cubs, Dee Fondy, batted over .300 the previous two seasons. With Cincinnati in 1958, he battled George Crowe who hit a career-high thirty-one homers the year before. Gil Hodges was with the Dodgers when Steve joined them. Norm Cash, newly acquired from the Chicago White Sox, challenged Steve in Detroit in 1960 and Ted Kluszewski had 264 major league homers when the Angels drafted him and Bilko in 1961.

"When I went to the Cubs, I didn't believe it. The only thing I found out there was how many different ways you could lose a game."

It was past noon. Mary Bilko served lunch. Steve had a lunchmeat sandwich, a small piece of cake, and a cup of coffee. "That's more than I usually eat," he offered. I have a piece of toast and a cup of coffee in the morning. I have another cup of coffee on my break at work. For lunch, I have a sandwich and cake. I don't eat again until I get home about 5:30."

Steve's appetite once was the butt of countless jokes.

In 1962, the Angels gave players bicycles to ride around Palm Springs during spring training. Danny Thomas, a television comedian and actor, quipped, "When Bilko got his, instead of riding it, he sprinkled it with ketchup and started eating."[31]

We finished lunch and went for a drive in Steve's 1972 Buick LeSabre. "This was my Dad's," Steve said as we started. "He gave it to me before he died—the last thing I got of his."

In Nanticoke, we stopped at a red light on the corner of Main and Market Streets. "This is the only light in town," Steve chuckled.

We went to a bar named Yeager's.

A poster behind the bar made it clear that Bilko was a celebrity here. Promoting Rochester's annual old-timers game, the Commissioner's Classic, the poster featured drawings of Bilko, George "Specs" Toporcer, Tom Poholsky, Joe Altobelli, and Luke Easter. Bilko and Easter were teammates in Rochester in 1963, Steve's last season in pro ball.

A half-dozen men were watching the bar's lone television showing a football game between Ohio State and UCLA.

Yeager's is named after Albert Yeager, more commonly known as Pug.

"If he's there, you'll see why," Steve said.

Pug wasn't around. His wife was tending bar, and she quickly served us eight-ounce glasses of draft beer for twenty cents apiece.

"It was fifteen cents until a couple of weeks ago," Steve said.

Two beers later, Pug's wife slapped a black plastic token on the bar. "That's good for ten cents off on your next beer," she explained.

A few minutes later, another token was placed in front of me. "This is on Frank," she said.

Frank Higgins was quietly watching the football game until a man dressed in Wrangler jeans, denim shirt, and a faded Phillies baseball cap walked in carrying an ice chest. The man opened the cooler to reveal a bass weighing about five pounds.

"That man is a bass fisherman," Frank said. "Other guys tell you how big a bass they catch. He shows you."

Steve introduced Joe Maday, a stocky, dark-haired man with an engaging smile.

"This is my legacy," Joe said, pointing to the bass. "The lakes in this area aren't fished out. You don't have to go to New York or Florida for instant action. It's here in our backyard—the mountains. Here, a man walks into a bar with a five-pound bass, that's proof."

When Joe found out Steve was being interviewed for a book, he began a testimonial that lasted for most of an hour.

"He has been our representative in the major leagues," Joe said. "We've grown up with this man. We were Stan Musial fans but we were looking for Bilko's name in the box score. We looked every day. What he'd do—oh-for-four, one-for-three, two-for-four?

Steve stared quietly at the TV. "We're all Steve's friends. But we're still in awe of him. He can give you an insight into baseball nobody else can.

"He's the only one to plant one from Lincoln School into the stadium. Did he tell you about that? Well, the ball went more than 400 feet. No one has come close to that.

"He played football in high school. He made all-scholastic team in Wyoming Valley as a freshman. Did he tell you that?

"He won't tell you what he is. We'll tell you what he is."

Joe described himself as Steve's number one fan and explained that every year he gives the Steve Bilko Award to the best baseball player in the Nanticoke school system.

"I was in Tampa, Florida, two years ago," Joe continued. "Moose Skowron asked me to relay a message to Steve: 'Ask Bunky if he can remember a home run he hit off Bobby Shantz?' He hit the ball into the upper deck of Yankee Stadium where Mantle and Maris never came near."

Frank Higgins was listening intently.

"The sad part is he backed up so many big-name first basemen for so many years," Frank said.

Joe wanted to talk some more about Bilko.

"Did Steve tell you about the softball game? It was in the Hanover section of Nanticoke—a company-sponsored game. He planted one over the pavilion. Over 300 feet. That is called a plant around here. That means you hit it out of sight."

Joe told of a dart game for the Athletic Club of Nanticoke championship when an opponent tried to disrupt Steve's concentration.

"Steve told the guy, 'You know, Charlie, I batted in front of 50,000 people with the bases loaded and they never shook me up. Believe me, you'll never shake me up.' He threw a seven—two points less than perfect. And we won the championship."

Pug replaced his wife behind the bar and Joe asked him about a softball game involving Steve.

"They had a game in Honey Pot," Pug said. "They brought Bilko into the game and it was over. The other team quit."

Suddenly, Joe was silent.

"I've just been knocked out of the box with the Richie Allen thing," he said. "For the money they paid baseball players in the 1940s and 1950s, they put out twofold for what they put out today."

Figure 6.2. Steve Bilko didn't become the big league star many expected, but his 389 home runs in the minors and majors combined made him a hero at places like Sivick's Café in his hometown of Nanticoke, Pennsylvania. Bilko was forty-seven when this photo was taken in October 1976. *Photo by author.*

The week before, Allen, who was making $250,000 for the 1976 season, walked out on the Phillies after they clinched the National League East title. He refused to play in the playoffs or World Series unless his pal, forty-year-old infielder Tony Taylor, was placed on the team's roster for postseason play.

Frank spoke up: "We, of Nanticoke, feel that the money paid to Bilko during his era, compared to the players today, was unfair."

Joe asked Steve, "What were you expected to hit in the majors to stay there?"

"[A batting average of] .300," Steve replied.

"Today, you only have to hit .240," Joe said. "You're the greatest if you hit .300."

We left Nanticoke for nearby Mountain Top and the Dana Perfume Company plant, where Steve worked as an inspector of raw materials. Twenty years earlier, Bilko was a celebrity in L.A., as big as any athlete or movie star.

"I didn't want to be a big celebrity. I was satisfied with doing a good job, being with my family and stuff like that. When I was done playing ball, I was content to go home and be with my kids. We went to shows but they were shows like *Lawrence Welk*. I used to go see *Roller Derby*. But other than that, we never went anywhere."

The shy Bilko and gaudy L.A. made for an odd couple.

"I mixed with a couple of movie stars like John Wayne, but they were really baseball fans. They were like we were. If I went anywhere, it was always with the type of people who live around here."

Steve stopped the car outside the Dana plant.

"That's our big D," he said, pointing out a huge script-style letter "D" for Dana outside the main entrance.

Steve was asked if he planned on working until he was sixty-five years old, when he'd be eligible for Social Security.

"Gee, I don't know," he said. "If anybody is going to quit work, it'll be my wife. I can take my baseball pension when I'm fifty—a little more than two years from now. I figure that if I take the pension, she can quit working."

Steve's response seemed insignificant at the time. But as it did so many times during his baseball career, fate would throw Steve a curve.

On March 7, 1978—nearly eight months before his fiftieth birthday— Steve died at a Wilkes-Barre hospital from a heart attack he suffered a few hours before at home.

Sports Illustrated reported Steve's death matter-of-factly in the back of the magazine:

> DIED: STEVE BILKO, 49, major league first baseman for ten years for six teams; of an undisclosed illness; in Wilkes-Barre, Pa. Bilko, a minor league player of exceptional promise who once hit 56 home runs for Los Angeles of the Pacific Coast League, found the majors a struggle and retired with a career batting average of .249 and 76 home runs.[32]

On the cover of the same issue was the face of a smiling, young baseball player, Clint Hurdle of the Kansas City Royals. The headline proclaimed, THIS YEAR'S PHENOM. The photo could have been of Steve Bilko in one of several seasons with the Cardinals.

In the 1970s, Hallmark published a greeting card booklet titled *What Makes This Country So Great?* The booklet features *Peanuts* comic strip characters and opens with Linus saying, "Just think of all the people who have made this country great!" He lists George Washington, Benjamin Franklin, Thomas Jefferson, Abe Lincoln, and Simon and Garfunkel, among others. Lucy suggests Betty Friedan, Kate Millett, Rona Barrett, and other women activists of the era. Sally chips in with movie actresses Arlene Dahl, Elizabeth Taylor, Zsa Zsa Gabor, Mitzi Gaynor, and the wrestler, Gorgeous George. Schroeder recommends Van Cliburn and several other musicians.

"Not to mention Bill Haley and the Comets!" says Snoopy.

"And Willie Mays, Ty Cobb, Babe Ruth, Steve Bilko, and Sandy Koufax," reminds Peppermint Patty.

"And let's not forget Lassie, Rinny, Bullet . . . and Alan Shepard," adds Snoopy.

Suddenly, Charlie Brown has a revelation and declares, "You! You're what makes this country so great!"

Peppermint Patty has a parting thought: "Steve Bilko couldn't have said it more beautifully."[33]

The writer of the Hallmark booklet wasn't the only one with a special affinity for Bilko.

"I could just as well have been Corporal Hodges or Private First Class Musial," Phil Silvers said of his adopting the name Sgt. Bilko for his television role instead of the names of perennial all-stars, Gil Hodges and Stan Musial. "I gave it to a guy who needed it."[34]

Steve Bilko was never the superstar he was supposed to be, but for one summer in 1956, he was as mighty as Babe Ruth and as magnificent as Mickey Mantle.

"He really had everything," Borgman, the scout, said after hearing of Bilko's death. "Scouts dream about finding that kind of guy. No matter how it ended I know one thing. On one August afternoon in Honey Pot, he was beautiful."[35]

NOTES

1. *New York Herald Tribune*, March 14, 1950, 23.
2. *Los Angeles Times*, July 27, 1961, C1.
3. *New York Herald Tribune*, March 14, 1950, 23.
4. *Charleston Daily Mail*, February 14, 1950, 14.
5. *Salamanca Republican-Press*, August 15, 1949, 6.
6. *Charleston Daily Mail*, February 14, 1950, 14.
7. *Auburn Citizen-Advertiser*, May 3, 1952, 6.
8. *New York Times*, May 12, 1950, 46.
9. *The Sporting News*, April 5, 1950, 5.
10. Ibid.
11. *New York Times*, May 12, 1950, 46.
12. *San Diego Union*, April 11, 1956, A19.
13. *Los Angeles Mirror-News*, May 31, 1956, Part III, 2.
14. *Seattle Post-Intelligencer*, July 1, 1956, 20.
15. *Los Angeles Examiner*, July 30, 1956, Section 3, 2.

16. *San Francisco Call-Bulletin*, August 2, 1956, 34.
17. *Los Angeles Mirror-News*, June 14, 1956, Part III, 3.
18. *Los Angeles Examiner*, August 2, 1956, Section 3, 2.
19. *Sports Illustrated*, August 20, 1956, 15.
20. *Los Angeles Herald-Express*, August 4, 1956, A10.
21. Ibid. August 6, 1956, B1.
22. Ibid., B1.
23. *Los Angeles Mirror-News*, August 1, 1956, Part III, 2.
24. *Los Angeles Times*, September 17, 1956, A2.
25. *Los Angeles Herald-Express*, April 24, 1957, D3.
26. *The Oregonian*, April 14, 1959, Section 2, 1.
27. *Time*, May 30, 1960, 62.
28. *Parade*, June 29, 1952, 7.
29. *New York Post*, March 9, 1978, 66.
30. Ibid.
31. *Los Angeles Times*, April 3, 1962, B3.
32. *Sports Illustrated*, March 20, 1978, 79.
33. Charles Schulz, *What Makes This Country So Great?*
34. *Seattle Times*, March 18, 1958, 28.
35. *New York Post*, March 9, 1978, 66.

SEVEN

Gangbuster Gene and Gang

"Mauch has been a perennial favorite villain among Seattle fans. Now that he has become a menace with the bat as well as in the field and on the bases, the villainy is compounded." —Lenny Anderson, *Seattle Times*, June 29, 1956

Gene Mauch was one of those players that fans of opposing teams loved to taunt or, if you were a kid, use his baseball card for target practice with your BB gun. Across town in Hollywood, Carlos Bernier of the Stars stirred the same passion.

The Stars and Angels were bitter rivals and from 1954 to 1956, Mauch and Bernier played the role of villains as well as any actor in the nearby movie studios.

"The Hollywood fans hated the Angels and the Angel fans hated the Stars," Bernier said. "The fans of the Angels hated Carlos Bernier and all of the Stars. Same way with the Hollywood fans. They hated Gene Mauch and the Angels. Everybody hated each other."

The animosity extended into the radio booth where the announcers, Bob Kelley of the Angels and Mark Scott of the Stars, didn't speak to each other. The rivalry divided ministers and long-time friends, like my father and Rev. Eugene Robinson. En route to a Stars–Angels game in Hollywood, Dad asked Gene, a diehard Stars fan, "How can you be a Christian and pull against the Angels?"

He was joking but you could never be sure when it came to Angels and Stars loyalists.

Irv Kaze was public relations director for the Stars and George Goodale for the Angels. Irv often needled George about the home-run-friendly confines of Little Wrigley compared to the Stars' more spacious Gilmore Field.

"If one of their guys hit a fly ball to right or left field at Gilmore and we'd catch it in front of the fence, I would look at George and say, 'Home run at Wrigley!' He'd be smoking a cigar and I could see the smoke going up."

Whether it was sneaking quick puffs on a cigarette in a corner of the dugout or blowing on the flames of enmity between the Angels and Stars, Mauch left his own trail of smoke.

In 1954, he tangled with Bernier in one of the rivalry's signature brawls. The first punch was thrown by L.A. shortstop Bud Hardin after a hard tag on Bernier, who was attempting to steal second base.

"I jump up to throw a punch at him," Bernier recalled. "Gene Mauch came in behind me and I turn around and punch him. What happened is everybody fight and I sit on the bench. I don't know how I got on the bench. I think the umpire take and sit me on the bench. I tried to get up but the policemen wouldn't let me."

Mauch got in a few punches at Bernier before the fisticuffs ended and his favorite sparring mate ejected.

"Most fun I ever had playing ball," Mauch said of his three seasons with the Angels.

Prior to joining L.A. in 1954, Mauch bounced around pro baseball for eleven years with twelve teams, five in the majors, where he batted .222 mostly in substitute roles.

"Aside from having a good seat on the bench and learning a lot of inside baseball, the only benefits I obtained during that stretch was the time accruing on my baseball pension," Mauch said.[1]

Playing every day, Mauch endeared himself to L.A. fans with a scrappiness that inspired one local sportswriter to call him "Gangbuster Gene."

Mauch was well on his way to becoming known as the "Little General," the nickname he earned managing twenty-six years in the big leagues.

Infielder Johnny Goryl played twelve games for the '56 Angels and was a coach for the Minnesota Twins in 1980, when he succeeded Mauch as manager.

"His ambition was to become a major-league manager," Goryl said. "Everybody knew that."

The infield was a formidable gang with Mauch at second, Steve Bilko at first, Casey Wise at shortstop, and George Freese at third. It also was an improbable gang.

Bilko once was described as looking like "a deep sleep going someplace to wake up."[2]

Mauch was "as intense as a light bulb, as explosive as six sticks of dynamite in a bouncing truck," wrote Jim Murray, a *Los Angeles Times* sports columnist. "He smolders a lot, seethes."[3]

Freese and Bilko were kindred spirits, while Wise, the youngest of the group, was a loner. "Ballpark and home, those were most important to me."

"He was a cocky guy," Wise said of Mauch. "I didn't like him at first. He was my competition because I was primarily a second baseman. But then as things progressed and I established myself, I regarded him as a good friend."

Freese played for the Stars before joining the Angels in 1956.

"When I played against him at Hollywood, I hated him. But when I played with him on the same team, I could understand that he wanted to win at all costs."

Wise signed with the Cubs in 1952 after a workout arranged by Mauch. By the time he joined the Angels in 1956, he had a bachelor's degree in mechanical engineering from the University of Florida and was considered a top major league prospect at second base—the same position that Mauch played the previous two seasons in L.A.

"I just figured that we were going to compete," Wise said. "And I was naive enough to think that I was going to make it."

Angels' manager Bob Scheffing had other ideas. He didn't have a shortstop on the roster, and there was no assurance his counterpart with the Cubs, Stan Hack, was going to send Richie Myers or Ed Winceniak, seasoned shortstops that were competing for the right to back up Ernie Banks, the Cubs biggest star.

"You need to get a bigger glove if you're going to play shortstop," Scheffing told Wise during spring training.

Scheffing was so ecstatic over Casey's play to start the season that he gushed, "If Ernie Banks or Pee Wee Reese would be sent here right now, Wise would still be my shortstop."[4]

"I always thought that Casey's and Mauch's greatest asset was their ability to think," said Gale Wade. "They knew where guys were going to hit the ball. And they played accordingly. You can be the fastest shortstop in the world and if you don't play smart, you may not accomplish what you're supposed to do."

"I don't think anyone was a magician," Wise said. "We were solid."

The Angels were counting on Freese to replace the aging Buzz Clarkson at third and display the power that produced ten homers in seventy-nine games for the Stars the year before.

"I was surprised I even stayed because I started off the season oh-for-thirty or something," Freese said.

Freese had three hits in his first thirty-three at bats as he was recovering from a broken index finger on his right hand and couldn't get a good grip on the bat.

Soon after Clarkson spotted a flaw in his batting stance, Freese got three hits in a game and started hitting Buzz-like home runs. "Scheffing stuck with me and when I started hitting, everything just fell in place."

"Steve Bilko was obviously the big threat," said Bob Anderson, a pitcher for the Angels. "But considering everybody else, I felt that George was number two. He was not the fastest guy in the world but he had tremendous reflexes. He always got a good piece of the ball."

By the end of the season, Freese had an entirely different view of Mauch.

"When I played against Gene at Hollywood I tried everything to knock him down or spike him. There was something about him that I didn't like. But when I got on the same team with him, holy mackerel, it was just unreal. You had to appreciate and respect everything he did."

Freese remained skeptical about the battles between the Stars and the Angels.

"It was a *big* rivalry. You expected a donnybrook almost every game. Something was going to happen. But I always thought that some of those fights were staged. Especially Carlos Bernier. He was always the one starting them."

The mother of Stars–Angels free-for-alls took place in 1953—a year before Mauch arrived on the scene. *Life* magazine made the melee famous with three pages of photographs.

The fight took place during the first game of a Sunday afternoon doubleheader at Hollywood's Gilmore Field before an overflow crowd that spilled onto the outfield. Only a rope separated the fans from the players.

The headliners were Frank "Mousey" Kelleher and two guys who were as quiet as a mouse—Ted Beard and Joe Hatten.

The Stars' Kelleher and Beard were as mild-mannered as choir boys, never saying as much as "boo" to an umpire, let alone get kicked out of a game. The Angels' Hatten was a veteran left-handed pitcher better known for a sharp-breaking curve than a left hook. But Kelleher was fighting mad after a Hatten curveball hit him in the stomach.

Cece Carlucci was the home plate umpire.

"Like a dummy, I went to pick up the ball," Carlucci said. "I look up and here's Kelleher starting out for Hatten. He runs and hits him. He threw a haymaker. I thought it was Rocky Marciano. Geez, he knocked him ten or twelve feet. Hit him in the chest. Now the battle is on."

The first round ended with Carlucci ejecting Kelleher for starting the battle. Stars manager Bobby Bragan argued Hatten should also be given the heave-ho.

"I said, 'No way. Hatten didn't fight. He didn't do anything.'"

Bragan claimed later that Carlucci could've prevented further trouble if he'd tossed Hatten.

"What did Hatten do?" Carlucci asked. "He was just trying to keep Kelleher loose. I'd do the same thing. If anything, he [Hatten] was chicken. He didn't even swing back."

The speedy Beard, often referred to as "Little Teddy" because he was five-foot-eight-inches tall, entered the game as a pinch-runner for Kelleher.

"He never said anything except 'yes' and 'no,'" explained his roommate, Tommy Saffell.

Beard was on a mission of his own. Earlier in the week-long series, Stars shortstop Jack Phillips suffered a knee injury on a "footballish take out" by an Angel runner trying to break up a double play at second base. "When somebody gets hurt in the knees, it's not good," Beard said. "I really got mad."

First pitch, Beard took off for second. "I was going to cut up the shortstop covering the bag, but I didn't get the chance," he chuckled.

On the next pitch, Beard streaked for third.

"They got him by ten-to-fifteen feet," Carlucci said.

Beard's spikes were flying high when he rammed into third baseman Murray "Moe" Franklin, a former teammate playing in his first game for the Angels.

"That's when the shit hit the fan!" Carlucci said.

"You've got to hit anybody that's close to you," Beard explained.

He was already wrestling with Franklin.

"Moe and Teddy were really going after each other," Carlucci said. "By that time everybody is in on it. I was down a couple of times."

At one point, Bragan asked Carlucci, "How you doing?"

The fighting went on for about fifteen minutes, with players flailing away at each other everywhere Carlucci looked. "We couldn't stop it," he said. "Now, I'm concerned about the 5,000 people on the field."

William Parker, L.A.'s chief of police, also feared fans joining the fisticuffs. He and his wife had returned home from the beach just in time to turn on the TV and watch Kelleher tee off on Hatten. As Mrs. Parker provided a blow-by-blow account of the brawl, Chief Parker called for the riot squad. "Three extra squad cars and eleven motorcycle policemen" immediately rushed to Gilmore Field.[5]

"They were coming from every angle," Carlucci said. "I think we ended up with fifty-five of them."

They showed up with a warning from Chief Parker "that any additional incident would result in stoppage of play and the booking of offenders for disturbing the peace."[6]

Beard and Franklin were booted from the game. "Even though they fought like hell," Carlucci said, "I never saw anybody like they wanted to kill each other—except maybe Teddy Beard and Moe Franklin. That fight was a mean one."

The rest of the doubleheader was played with policemen manning both dugouts. Only coaches and players participating in the game were allowed to sit on the bench. Everybody else was banished to the clubhouse. "If they wanted a pinch hitter or something, they could send for them," Carlucci said.

There was no more trouble on the field, but a battered Franklin was itching for a rematch.

"If Beard ever wants to challenge me again, I'll meet him under the stands any time," Franklin fumed. "The pictures show he was out to spike me and he did. I clouted him for it and my hand is so swollen I won't be able to play."[7]

Franklin had chest cuts and numerous spike wounds on his left arm. Beard jammed an ankle. Several other players sustained face and leg cuts. One Angel had to be revived with ammonia after being flattened by Kelleher.

"I've been thrown at lots of times," Kelleher said, "but this time it just struck me wrong."[8]

The police asked Hatten if he wanted to file assault charges against Kelleher but he declined, saying, "I wasn't trying to hit him."[9]

Beard said nothing about the fight until prodded a half-century later: "The only thing I know is that one time they played a little rough and, then, the next time we met, I played a little rough with them."

Chief Parker "promised ample guards on hand" the next time the teams squared off, but one wag proposed instead that Red Cross nurses be stationed in the dugouts.[10]

The fight was declared the worst in PCL history. Imagine what might've happened if those favorite villains, Mauch and Bernier, had been around to duke it out.

Mauch was player-manager for the Crackers in Atlanta.

"I was in Pittsburgh," Bernier said. "I'm glad I wasn't there in Hollywood."

Don Swanson, a twenty-three-year-old left-hander, was the winning pitcher in relief against the Vancouver Mounties on May 5, 1956—his last appearance for the Angels even though he had a 2–0 record and fine 2.79 ERA.

Leading by three runs, Swanson was close to walking the opposing pitcher, Chuck Locke, when Mauch called time out to tell Swanson: "This son-of-a-bitch can hit. He's a pitcher but don't put the ball too close. Go for the corner."

Locke slammed Swanson's next pitch for a home run—the longest hit at Vancouver's Capilano Stadium at that time. "The drive cleared the left-center field fence near the 415-foot mark and was still rising," the *Sporting News* reported.[11]

"Gene Mauch never talked to me after that, ever," Swanson said. "That's how he was. He thought of nothing but winning the game."

Mauch was the head and heart of the Angels as much as Bilko was the beef and brawn. What the five-foot-ten, 165-pound Mauch lacked in size, he made up for with guile and guts.

"There are a lot of teams with outstanding talent," said Richie Myers, an all-star shortstop with Sacramento before joining L.A. in 1956. "But for some reason they don't have the cohesiveness to pull that talent together. They had the players like Mauch who could keep it together."

Mauch used his encyclopedic knowledge of opposing players to instruct the team's young pitchers, position the defense, and counsel his manager on strategy.

"He could read batters," said Myers. "He could tell you the pitch, watch the catcher's sign and if they were going to get a curveball, he damn near knew where they were going to hit it. He always had that little advantage, that little jump that you need. The first few steps you make in the infield or outfield, wherever you are out there on defense, that's the difference between the good ball players and the mediocre ones."

He kept umpires on their toes with his ability to cite the most obscure baseball rules.

"He knew the rules," said Cece Carlucci. "He studied that rule book."

He was a master at stealing a catcher's signs when he was on base and alerting teammates what type of pitch was coming.

"He was good at it," Freese said. "But one time he said a curveball was coming and I got a fastball. Man, I went ass over tin cups. 'That's it, Gene,' I yelled. 'No more.'"

He insulted and harassed opposing players.

"I remember him challenging pitchers from the dugout, ready to fight," said Wise.

He slowed runners on their way from first to third by stepping in front of them long enough to make them hesitate to avoid a collision but not long enough to be called for obstruction.

He once threw a handful of dirt in the face of the Stars' Bernier sliding into second base to trigger his famous temper and get him thrown out of the game. Of course, the feisty Mauch was always ready to fight Bernier or anybody else.

"He had kind of a history of being a little guy that never knew when he was licked," said Wise.

"He was a fighter," added Carlucci. "He wouldn't take any crap from I don't give a damn who it was."

Carlucci was the first base umpire in a game when Bob Murphy, a young pitcher for Oakland, whizzed one past Mauch's head.

"I hear Mauch holler at the pitcher: 'Another close one and I'm coming out there.'"

The next pitch was inside but only chest-high.

"He throws his bat and is running toward the pitcher. He throws a right and I get him from behind. He never did get it off. We're both down and the guys were all around. The umpires are all there with the players so nobody is going to jump on because I'm down there."

Carlucci got up and said, "Mauch, you're gone!"

"What about Murphy?"

"Nope, you threw your bat and you went out after him. You go."

Carlucci chuckled as he recounted the story.

"Fiery as hell. He battled everybody."

The '56 Angels yearbook devoted a full page to Mr. Angel—Arnold "Jigger" Statz, who played nearly 3,000 games for L.A. over eighteen seasons. Statz hit the first home run at Little Wrigley but he was best known for his all-out hustle, stealing sixty-one bases one season and hitting as many as eighteen triples and sixty-eight doubles in another.

At five-foot-seven, 150 pounds, Statz was not much bigger than many of the kids who came to see him fly around the bases and in centerfield where he made acrobatic catches virtually barehanded. He cut out the palm out of his glove so he could feel the ball better.

On opening day of the 1942 season, the sixteen-year-old Mauch ditched school to watch Statz play.

"I saw Jigger hit two home runs opening day and not another home run the rest of the season," Mauch said. "I got a kick out of Jigger because he was about my size. And I liked the way he played."

The summer of '42, Mauch was the third baseman and catcher for the L.A. team that won the American Legion Junior national championship. Thirteen of the team's fifteen players went on to play pro ball.

"We were a cocky bunch of ball players," Mauch said. "We started every game saying we were five runs behind. That's the way we played."[12]

Mauch never lost that cockiness.

"He was a puffed up, cocky little guy that really was not that good a ball player," said Eddie Basinski, a teammate when Mauch, then eighteen, broke in with the Dodgers in 1944 and two years later at St. Paul where his sixty-four errors topped International League shortstops.

"Gene wasn't a likely looking athlete," Wise said. "He was kind of stocky with short, stubby fingers. But he was a determined, smart guy."

Bobby Usher played against Mauch in Legion ball and later in the majors when Usher was with the Redlegs and Mauch the Braves. The two teams were traveling together in North Carolina when their bus came to a halt at a low bridge underpass. The bus driver questioned whether there was enough room to drive safely under the bridge.

"Gene very smartly said, 'Lower the air pressure in the tires; we'll get under it,'" Usher recalled. "And we did."

Mauch took the same cerebral approach on the field, devising trick plays to surprise opponents and provide the one run that often decided a game.

"He was always thinking, always moving, always coming up with some scheme," said Carlucci.

In a game against Oakland's Tom Borland, a pitcher fresh out of college, Mauch stole home to give the Angels a 4–3 victory.

"The idea was for Mauch to break just as the pitcher began to bring the ball down after stretching," Scheffing explained. "He's required to make a full-second stop. The natural reaction of a kid—or even a veteran—is to throw home without pausing when he sees the runner coming in and thus balk. That's what Borland did. Only the umpire never called the balk. Anyway, we won."[13]

Scheffing pretty much let Mauch do as he pleased.

In a game against Seattle, Mauch was batting against Larry Jansen, a former New York Giants pitching star. Scheffing was sending Gene signals.

Mauch said,

> We've got the winning run on third base. Bob takes the palm of his hand and moves it up and down like, "Make him get the ball up! Make him get the ball up!' Because you want to hit a fly ball and get the run in from third base.
>
> And I started laughing. I went down to the third-base coaching box and I said, "Grump, we hit against this guy five years in the National League and he doesn't throw the ball *up*." He said, "I know it. I was just kidding. Get 'em!" He threw me a low slider and I got the ball between third and short.

Mauch never discussed his role on the team with Scheffing. "We just understood each other."

Scheffing turned the defense over to him.

"We had plays that nobody ever used before," Mauch said. "With a bunt situation—an obvious mortal-lock bunt situation—Steve would play back at first base and I would charge all the way from second base and field bunts. And we made countless double plays."

"Gene was a serious player," Wise said. "And Bob wasn't anybody to fiddle around with either. They set the tone for the team."

Going into the 1956 season, Mauch was thirty years old. He had never hit higher than .324 or hit more than eleven home runs in a season.

By mid-June, he was hitting .376 with nine homers. He had a .359 average and eighteen home runs in August when Giants scout Dutch Reuther declared him the best player in the Coast League: "Gene Mauch ought to be playing in the majors right now."[14]

"I feel more like a ball player at thirty than I ever did before," Mauch said. "I'm at the degree of productivity now that I should have been at twenty-five."[15]

Mauch attributed his performance to controlling his temper.

"I stopped umpiring. For years, every time I went to bat I was so concerned with the merits of each pitch; I didn't concentrate on my swing. I was too busy helpin' the plate ump call balls and strikes."[16]

Mauch's numbers for the season (.348 batting average, twenty home runs, and eighty-four RBIs) are dismissed by some as a fluke and cited as an example of the steroids-like effect that Little Wrigley had on the team's performance.

"There's one guy that hit twenty home runs that wouldn't have in an ordinary park and that was me," said Mauch. "But we would've won just as many games."

"He was a good player who came into his own with the Angels," said Usher. "He was manager material from the get-go."

Shortly before Mauch was sold to the Boston Red Sox in September, Scheffing predicted he "would hit for a higher average in the majors than any other player on my club."[17]

Scheffing was right. Mauch hit .320 in seven games for the Red Sox in 1956 and .270 in sixty-five games in 1957, his last as a full-time player.

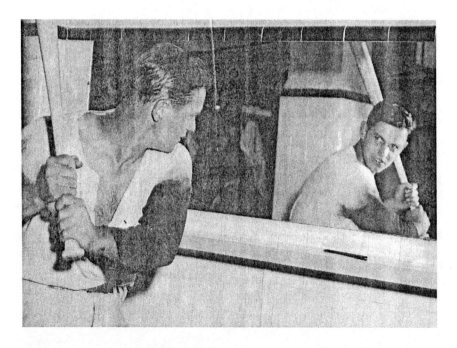

Figure 7.1.   Gene Mauch checks the batting stance that helped him to career highs in 1956. *Author's collection.*

"I was physically done. My body was worn out. I dove head first too many times."

Mauch managed the Minneapolis Millers in 1958–1959, guiding the Red Sox affiliate to two straight American Association postseason playoff titles and Junior World Series appearances. The Millers swept Montreal in the 1958 Series, with Mauch's .444 hitting leading the way, before losing the next year to Havana in seven games.

Wise was playing for Louisville in 1959 when he and Mauch faced each other for the first time since they were teammates in L.A.

With the Angels, they talked hours about baseball and such things as the hit-and-run when the runner on first takes off for second while the batter hits the ball to right field, enabling the runner to reach third on a single. Wise and Mauch executed the play perfectly many times. When Casey used it against the Millers, he got an earful from Mauch standing in the dugout.

Casey laughed and yelled back, "You taught me that."

As roommates go, they were an odd couple.

Casey Wise was a college graduate with three years of pro baseball experience; Gene Mauch turned pro directly out of high school and already had twelve years under his belt.

Casey was intense but rarely lost his cool; Gene was a hothead. Casey was a nonsmoker, Gene a chain smoker. Gene was nearly seven years older than Casey. Gene wanted to be a major league manager; Casey was determined to do more with his engineering degree than his father, Hughie, a former player, manager, general manager, scout, and builder of ballparks.

Hughie and his wife, Virginia, had two sons—Hugh Jr. and Kendall Cole, whose initials K.C. led to the nickname Casey.

Hughie was a catcher who said, in jest, that "anybody was crazy to stand up there and let someone throw at you for nine innings."

He caught two games in the majors for the Detroit Tigers in 1930 and spent the rest of his playing career in the lower minors.

Hughie started managing in 1936 at Portageville, Missouri, and moved the franchise and his family to Owensboro, Kentucky in the middle of the season. He owned the team until a corporation was formed the following spring.

At Owensboro, Hughie did everything from selling advertising space on the outfield fences to using his engineering degree from Purdue University to oversee the building of a new ballpark.

Hughie went on to manage teams in Pawtucket, Rhode Island, and Eau Claire, Wisconsin, and design and build a complex of fields in the Florida cities of Fort Lauderdale and Sarasota used by the New York Yankees and Chicago White Sox for spring training. He built a minor league training camp for the Boston Braves in Myrtle Beach, South Carolina, and he transformed an old airfield into a baseball diamond in Way-cross, Georgia.

"Dad did all that plus scouting," Casey said. "His whole frame of reference was baseball. He thoroughly enjoyed what he did. Money wasn't important to him. What was important to him was the project at hand."

Hughie also raised his own crop of ball players.

Hugh Jr. signed with the Milwaukee Braves as an outfielder and played four seasons in the minors.

Casey, two years younger than his brother, was playing baseball at the University of Texas when the Cubs signed him in 1952.

That's when Casey met Mauch.

Hughie was scouting for the Braves, based in Boston at the time, and Gene was playing for their triple-A team, the Milwaukee Brewers. Casey, then nineteen, was playing semipro ball in Iowa, so his father lined up workouts for him with the Chicago White Sox and the Brewers.

"I was going to take a little infield practice and a few swings in the batting cage and have them look at me," Casey said. "I wasn't ready to sign."

When the White Sox tryout was rained out, Casey headed to Milwaukee to practice with the Brewers and Mauch.

"I'm going to drive down to Chicago and visit my sister," Gene told Casey after the workout. "Just ride with me."

Mauch's sister happened to be married to Cub shortstop Roy Smalley. Gene got Casey a tryout with the Cubs, who were so impressed that they offered him a contract for $26,000. In today's dollars, that's about $222,000.

Casey signed but with a caveat: "I'm not going to spring training and screw up college. I've got my engineering degree I'm going to get."

He transferred from Texas to Florida and for the next three years, 1953–1955, attended classes until June.

Casey played ninety-eight games each of the first two years, hitting .297 for Sioux Falls, South Dakota, and .284 for Des Moines, Iowa.

"When I got to L.A. in 1955, Gene was not friendly," Casey said. "I don't know if it was the competitive thing or not."

Scheffing wasn't warm and fuzzy either.

"I'm a young guy out of college coming to this veteran team and Chicago is saying this guy has great potential and da-da-da. So when I got there, Scheffing was very skeptical about me. I could sense it."

Mauch moved to third base so Casey could play second. He started three games, going one-for-nine.

"I was terrible. I think Scheffing jumped on it. 'Hey, I'm not going to play this guy very much. You might as well get him somewhere where he can play because he's only playing three months out of the year.' He talked them into sending me to Beaumont."

Casey batted .276 in seventy-three games at Beaumont to earn another chance with the Angels.

This time he joined the team for spring training.

"I was optimistic but I don't know what's going to happen. Gene was a fixture and they had gotten Richie Myers."

Myers was still with the Cubs along with Winceniak. They were rated one-two among Coast League shortstops the year before, and Scheffing was counting on one of them coming to L.A.

Meanwhile, he put Casey at shortstop, a position he played in high school but never as a pro.

"He hit me a bunch of ground balls. I made the plays and he was impressed. I was getting a lot of hits in spring training. I convinced him and me that I could do it."

Scheffing shrewdly put Casey and Gene together as roommates on road trips.

Casey was a batboy for his father's teams and often traveled with them.

"I'm very observant. I watched all the ball players at Owensboro, Pawtucket and Eau Claire and just absorbed what they did."

At first, Casey wondered why he was being paired with Gene, and then he realized it was Scheffing's way of teaching him the intricacies of baseball and playing the infield.

"He kind of turned me over to Gene. He wasn't like a tutor; he didn't have the patience to sit around. But if you had your antennae up, listened and drew him out a little bit, you almost by osmosis gathered insight into the game. Being around him, you had to absorb a lot."

Casey hit safely in twenty-one of the Angels' first twenty-five games and was batting .276 with ten doubles and eleven RBIs when Myers joined the team in mid-May. By July, he was batting .293 with twenty-one doubles. Myers got into only fifteen games before health problems ended his season.

"I felt pretty confident that nobody was going to be taking me out of the picture. They were going to have to prove it. I just kept getting my hits and playing well."

Casey played in every one of the Angels' 168 games, batting .287 with seven home runs and sixty RBIs. He led the league in at bats (705) and was among the league leaders in hits (202), doubles (36), and runs scored (122).

"After that '56 season, I thought I could play," Casey said. "I wasn't lacking for confidence. For all I knew, I was going to the Hall of Fame."

The stars were shining brightly and perfectly aligned for Casey in 1957.

He wasn't going to the Hall of Fame in Cooperstown, New York, but he was bound for Chicago with Scheffing, the Cubs' new manager, and John Holland, the architect of the Des Moines and L.A. teams Casey played on, and now Grand Poobah of the Cubs front office. They were his biggest boosters.

The March 1957 edition of *Baseball Digest* featured a smiling Casey on the cover while, inside, a story titled, "Wondrous Wise," quoted Holland: "We thought his fielding had been great at short, but it was simply out of this world at second."[18]

Casey was even making believers of the Chicago media, highly critical of the eleven players Holland and Scheffing brought with them from L.A.

As spring training was ending, the *Sporting News* wrote, "Wise probably never will inspire any new recitations of the immortal poem *Casey at the Bat*, but he will be a good man to have around and perhaps an even better one to play second base or shortstop for the Cubs."[19]

Scheffing praised Casey's defensive abilities, citing a fielding record he set at Des Moines and a consecutive streak of 204 chances without an error. "He isn't a great hitter, although he may be that later, but he gets his hits."[20]

"Everything was positive," Casey said. "Everything was there for me to take."

Casey was relaxing on his fifty-three-foot yacht, called *Owl*, docked near the Naples, Florida, condo where he and his wife, Joan, lived in 2001. It was a sunny and warm December day, far different than the cold and wet weather in Chicago opening day of the 1957 season.

"We were playing the Braves; Warren Spahn was the pitcher. I hit a line bee bee right to the left-fielder. He didn't even have to move. I thought, 'This is going to be great! Wow!' I didn't get anything close to a hit after that."

The Cubs were 3–8 going into a game against the Phillies at Connie Mack Stadium in Philadelphia. Casey was batting .160—less than his weight of 170 pounds.

Light snow was blowing in the frigid night air. The fans were half-frozen, making them better off than Casey.

"My forte was fielding and I made four errors—tied a major-league record."

The errors came in the first five innings.

"I remember chasing a foul ball down the right field line and getting there and it just hit me in the glove. My eyes were almost frozen over at the time. Nothing works when you're cold. Your hands are stiff, you're not fluid. It was just awful.

"I booted a ball—a wrist burger. It jumped up and hit me. I knocked it down, picked it up and threw it into left field. That was two more errors.

"I forget what the other one was. I used to say, 'Hit me the ball, I'll take care of it.' Now I'm thinking, 'God I hope another one doesn't come out here.'"

Casey had two hits in the game, but nothing could ease the embarrassment of the four errors.

"I was so upset that I threw on my clothes and walked back through a bad neighborhood at night to the hotel a mile or two away. I kind of wished some guy had tried to mug me because I would've probably taken him down."

Casey started nine more games, lifting his batting average to .220, before the Cubs acquired Bobby Morgan, a journeyman infielder, from the Phillies. Morgan had ten hits in his first six games, sending Casey to the bench and, eventually, back to the Coast League.

"They thought that I had become overwhelmed with the major leagues."

Casey pleaded with Holland, "Hang in there with me just a little longer."

"We've already decided and we'd like for you to go to Portland and get yourself organized," Holland said.

Morgan wound up hitting .207. After batting .246 at Portland, Casey returned to the Cubs, finishing the season with a .179 average.

"I knew that they knew I could play. But the team was floundering and Bob and John were under a lot of pressure with this L.A. thing and their fair-haired boys. A lot of times the moves they make in the major leagues are to show the public that they are doing something."

In one game, Casey went from being a prized prospect to trade bait.

The Milwaukee Braves, the 1957 world champions, tapped him to be the utility infielder they needed. He got two shots with the Braves, the second one in 1959 starting with a *Milwaukee Journal* columnist asking, "What is it that happens any way, to these young fellows of such good promise in the minors who get their chance and then fail to live up to all they've showed?"[21]

A month later, Casey was on his way back to the minors, ensuring his place among the biggest big-league busts with a base-running blunder that turned a hit into a rally-ending double play. "I can tolerate physical errors, but a thing like that was inexcusable," fumed Braves manager Fred Haney. "It wasn't major league. As a matter of fact, it wasn't even minor league."[22]

It was more of the same at Detroit in 1960, where Casey hit a rock-bottom .147. He decided it was time to do something with his engineering degree after pinch running in a game at Yankees Stadium. He tried to score from second on a line-drive single to the Yankees right-fielder, Roger Maris.

"Maris had a gun for a throwing arm," Casey said. "He fielded the ball on one hop, fired it to home plate and, hell, I was out by six feet. I just knew, as I was sitting there, tagged out, that they were going to make a move on me. And they did. That's when I said: 'Damn it, I'm not going to fail like this anymore. I'm going to go do something that I can succeed at.'"

Casey finished the season with Denver in the American Association before leaving baseball to work for a chemical company in the area of industrial waste management.

> You have high expectations and then you don't make it. You're young, your ego and your pride, and everything are so involved that you feel like you failed.
>
> As I got older and got away from it, I came to the conclusion that the only way you can be immune from these inequities that happen is to be so much better than your competition that they can't deny you. You've got to be Henry Aaron, Ernie Banks or somebody that is just so much better that you can goof up and it still doesn't matter. Those of us that weren't that good, it was just the luck of the draw sometimes.

Casey soon found his new job of convincing companies to treat their manufacturing waste properly tougher than hitting .200 in the majors. "What problem?" they asked as the river outside the plant was covered with thick foam from the waste flowing into it.

One night at a truck stop, Casey was having a cup of coffee, mulling over what to do with his mechanical engineering degree. He recalled the braces his brother had as a kid and how they operated. He started thinking about the biomechanical aspects of orthodontics.

"I'm going to dental school," Casey resolved to himself. "I don't care what it takes or how long. I'm going to do it."

In 1962–1963, he combined dental school and baseball, playing for the Jacksonville Suns, a Cleveland Indians farm team, in the International League.

"The first year was close to being as good a year as L.A. because we won everything."

He was a player-coach in 1963 when Suns manager Ben Geraghty died of a heart attack in the middle of the season. Casey took over as manager, inheriting a losing team with "guys that were over-the-hill, all pissed off and fightin' in the clubhouse."

The pitching staff had a lot of potential with promising youngsters like Tommy John, Sam McDowell, Sonny Siebert, and Mike Cuellar. They needed more opportunities to pitch, so Casey got rid of several veterans.

"They deserved to have a chance. They had talent and I stood up for them."

This upset Ed Donnelly, a veteran left-hander who was winless and pitching poorly. When he refused to mop up in a game the Suns were losing, John volunteered.

"We were getting killed. Somebody had to pitch."

Donnelly went ballistic, accusing Casey of jeopardizing John's career and ruining his own. He challenged him to a fight after the game.

Donnelly was waiting for Casey in the clubhouse.

"Look, Ed, I don't want to fight with you."

"Well, you're going to," the pitcher screamed, taking a swing.

Casey punched back. The fighting continued until Walt Bond, a six-foot-seven, 228-pound outfielder, picked Casey up from behind and carried him to the manager's cubicle.

Donnelly was released the next day. John made his major-league debut with the Indians later in the season.

Before John left for Cleveland, Casey had a talk with him. "You're going to see guys with better fastballs, better curveballs. Just remember one thing. You've got a Tommy John fastball and a Tommy John curveball. Go up there and just be Tommy John. You've got enough stuff. You can pitch up there and win." [23]

The advice was based on Casey's own experience.

"I know that I tried too hard. I was giving him a little confidence, just telling him, 'Don't press too hard cause it won't work. Just go out and pitch your game and see what happens.'"

John pitched twenty-six years in the majors, winning 288 games. Cuellar won 185, McDowell 141, and Siebert 140.

Casey found his field of dreams in Naples, Florida, as an orthodontist—the city's first.

He moved to Naples in 1968 and almost every day for twenty-three years, he looked into the mouths of kids and snatched victory from the jaws of defeat.

Nobody cared about the four errors he made in a game or the time he was thrown out at home plate. If you asked Casey about striking out against the Yankees' hard-throwing Ryne Duren in the 1958 World Series, he mentioned the single he got off Duren in the 1956 PCL all-star game and a comment afterward by a scout for a major-league team.

"If you can hit guys like that," the scout told Casey, "you're going to make it in the big leagues."

Casey died in 2007 of complications following heart surgery. The obituary in the *Naples Daily News* focused on his career as an orthodontist and contributions to the community.

"Getting into orthodontics in a town that was fresh and growing was the best thing that ever happened to me," Casey said.

Cooperstown's loss was Naples' gain.

The last players to leave Little Wrigley after a day game were George Freese and Steve Bilko.

When the game was over, they immediately headed for the two hot tubs in the Angels clubhouse, where they talked and guzzled bottles of beer until Angels trainer Joe Liscio got leg cramps delivering them. It was a task better suited for a beer truck.

"Steve could drink beer like there was no tomorrow," said Bob Anderson. "And he never seemed any different."

"Steve loved his beer," George said. "I couldn't keep up with him. We'd drink the beer and sweat it out. Get some more and sweat it out."

This continued until rush hour traffic cleared and they went home.

George played for Hollywood in 1955, hitting a home run in the decisive fifth game to beat the Angels in their season-ending playoff series.

Over the winter, the Stars demoted Freese to a team in the lower minors because "he can't play any position well enough for us to keep him." The Angels thought otherwise and selected him in the minor league draft. "If we couldn't beat him, we'd join him," Scheffing said.[24]

"I was surprised as hell when I found out they were going to send me to double-A ball because I had a good half-year in Hollywood," George said.

He hit .302 for the Stars after batting .257 in fifty-one games for the Pittsburgh Pirates. During the winter of 1955–1956, he was a big gun in the Puerto Rican League before he ended up with a broken finger.

Never mind that George was damaged goods, doubtful if he could play. Angels president John Holland called George's release by the Stars "typical Hollywood gratitude" and predicted he would outperform his replacement with the Stars and hit as many balls out of Little Wrigley as Bilko.[25]

It was rough going for a while.

In mid-May he was hitting a paltry .218 with one homer and thirteen RBIs. By the end of July, he had raised his average to .288 and had nineteen home runs and ninety-three RBIs, including eight in a single game.

George finished with a .291 average, twenty-two home runs and his 113 RBIs were forty-one more than anybody with the Stars. He outplayed his younger brother, Gene, the Stars' third baseman the last half of the season. Gene hit .274 with eleven homers.

Freese and Bilko, roommates on the road, set a goal of combining to hit more than sixty home runs, the Holy Grail, because it was the single-season record in both the PCL and majors. They teamed to blast seventy-seven.

The sluggers were brother in arms. They had similar backgrounds, both growing up in coal-mining towns and achieving stardom at an early age.

At eighteen, Freese was the starting quarterback for the University of Pittsburgh. He also played at West Virginia University, receiving All-America honorable mention in 1946. He turned down an offer from the Pittsburgh Steelers to play pro baseball for the Brooklyn Dodgers.

George had the reputation of a good-hit, no-field third baseman by the time he reached L.A.

"My fielding was questionable," Freese said. "That's what kept me out of the big leagues. I knew I could hit."

Figure 7.2. Dumped by the Hollywood Stars, George Freese found that the halo and wings of an angel fit perfectly as he slammed twenty-two homers and batted in 113 runs. *Courtesy George Freese.*

Freese had a career batting average of .303. In 1954 at New Orleans in the Southern Association, he hit .324 with twenty-three home runs and 104 RBIs.

"He was one of two players that I ran into in thirteen years of minor league baseball that could hit the curveball better than the fastball," said

Marland "Duke" Doolittle, a catcher in 1954 for Memphis in the Southern Association.

"He was a guy you always had a lot of fear of, particularly in the L.A. ballpark," said Bill Werle, a pitcher for the Portland Beavers.

Bobby Bragan managed both Freese brothers, George in Hollywood and Gene with the Pirates.

"Gene had a little more flash to him but George was more stable. He was soft-spoken and did the job every day."

This applied to Bilko as well.

"He was not a big quotable guy," said Irv Kaze, the Stars' publicist. "It was, 'Give me a bat and let me take my four swings a day and see what happens.'"

"Publicity was the furthest thing from his mind," George said. "He never talked about it. He never thought about it."

Bilko, of course, was a huge star in L.A.

"We used to say that if he ran for mayor, he'd win," said George Goodale, the Angels' PR man. "Of course that was an exaggeration but he was very popular."

Steve preferred the hot tub to the spotlight, a bottle of beer over a glass of the finest California wine, and watching TV rather than hobnobbing with celebrities at a Hollywood party.

When Bilko was asked to attend a press reception with the actor Phil Silvers to promote the TV show featuring Silvers as Sgt. Bilko, Steve balked: "I won't go unless George goes."

George borrowed a sports coat from Steve and they went to the party.

"The coat fit me like a blanket," George joked.

"We met Phil Silvers and had a really nice time," Bilko explained. "If I could've gotten a couple of days off, I could've gone with him to Las Vegas and been in his act. I guess it would've been to show his gratitude for using my name. It was my name or Kluszewski's. Bilko is a lot easier to say than Kluszewski."

"I have a picture of Steve, Phil Silvers and myself," said George. "Boy, do I treasure it."

On the final day of the 1956 season, the entire Angels infield was honored at Little Wrigley for being named to *Look* magazine's PCL all-star team.

Prior to the award ceremony, the emcee, Chuck Connors, a ball player-turned actor, took George aside to coach him on what to say on receiving the award.

George stepped to the microphone on the pitcher's mound and delivered the line Connors gave him: "I want to thank the Hollywood Stars for making this possible."

For Angels fans, George's one-liner was a grand slam, one of the biggest hits of the season.

Figure 7.3. Left to right: George Freese, Phil Silvers, and Steve Bilko are all smiles at a CBS television press reception in 1956 to promote the show, *You'll Never Get Rich*, starring Silvers as Sgt. Bilko. *Courtesy George Freese.*

The turnstile was clicking at the Cubs spring training camp in Mesa, Arizona.

Players were coming and going so fast that their uniforms should have had "hello" on the front and "goodbye" on the back. Few were around long enough to even be on a first-name basis. George was dismissed before spring training ended.

"It surprised the heck out of me," Freese said. "I knew that I wasn't the greatest fielder but I had a hellacious spring training."

John Holland, a Cubs vice president, broke the news to him.

"George, you had a really good year against Portland," Holland said. "They really want you. So we're going to send you to Portland."

"Hell, I didn't come here to make the Portland ball club," George snapped.

With the Angels, Freese hammered Portland pitching for a .381 average, ten home runs, and thirty-two RBIs in eighteen games.

"Freese had great power—pull power," said Eddie Basinski, a Portland infielder.

Multnomah Stadium in Portland was tailor-made for Freese, a right-handed pull-hitter. Down the left-field line, 305 feet from home plate was "Home Run Meadows," the name for the bleacher area where a twenty-foot-high fence protected fans from annihilation. It was 389 to center and 335 to right.

Going to Portland was a blessing in disguise. Just as his beer-drinking buddy, Bilko, was a legend in L.A., Freese became one in Portland, where he moved from his hometown of Wheeling, West Virginia.

The first year was forgettable as he hit .261 and eleven homers, missing half the season with a wrist injury. "I started out real good and then, I swung at a ball and missed it and tore about every tendon in my left wrist."

George rebounded in 1958 to hit .305, a career-high thirty-five home runs, and drive in eighty-one runs. The next year he hit .319 with twenty-one homers and eighty RBIs, followed in 1960 by a .255 average with twenty-five homers and eighty-seven RBIs. He even made it back to the majors briefly in 1961 as a pinch-hitter for the Cubs. From 1962 to 1974, he managed in the low minors, mostly in the Cubs organization.

In 2008, George was inducted into the Oregon Sports Hall of Fame for his outstanding career with the Portland Beavers.

George didn't need help with his Hall of Fame remarks.

He told about a home run he hit in a 1958 exhibition game against the St. Louis Cardinals. George was playing third base for the Beavers. His brother, Gene, was at shortstop for the Cardinals.

When George came to bat in the eighth inning, Gene called time out and motioned for the outfielders to come in close.

"I didn't pay much attention to it but I was a little mad."

The pitcher was Lindy McDaniel, older brother of Von, another Cardinals pitcher. He knew what it was like to be upstaged by a younger brother. George hit 198 homers in his career but only three in the big leagues. Gene had 115 homers in the majors.

George swung with all his might on a pitch from Lindy. The ball shot off the bat, soaring into Home Run Meadows in left field.

As George rounded second base, Gene dropped to the ground like he was fainting in astonishment.

"He fell down," George said. "I don't know why I didn't stop and kick him in the butt."

It wasn't necessary. His bat already did it for him.

Gene Mauch won 1,902 games as a major-league manager, twelfth best in baseball history. He transformed the Philadelphia Phillies from a last-place team in 1960 to a pennant contender in 1964. The Montreal Expos, an expansion team, went from fifty-two to seventy-three wins their first two years under Mauch. The Minnesota Twins improved by nine games his first season as manager in 1976, and he guided the California Angels to a division title in 1982, after they finished last the year before.

He was a gutsy, innovative manager who got the most out of the talent on his teams. But when Mauch died of lung cancer in 2005, the headline of his obituary in the *New York Times* read GENE MAUCH, 79, MANAGER OF NEAR MISSES. [26]

With twelve games to play in 1964, the Phillies lost ten straight games to blow a six-and-a-half game lead. In 1982, the Angels blew a 2–0 lead against the Milwaukee Brewers in the best-of-five championship playoff series. The Angels were one strike away from the World Series in 1986 when a home run by Dave Henderson rallied the Red Sox to three consecutive wins and the American League championship.

"If it's true you learn from adversity, then I must be the smartest SOB in the world," Gene said. [27]

Ironically, Mauch won three games less than Casey Stengel, the legendary Yankees manager who managed in ten World Series.

Bob Case was friends with both managers.

His grandmother played poker with Casey and his wife, Edna. He got to know Casey as a kid and grew up to be his business manager.

"He never had children of his own so he kind of took me under his wing," Bob said. "He was the number one guy in my life. He helped me, gave me self-esteem."

Case was a sports marketing executive in the 1980s, helping several Angels players secure endorsements and speaking engagements.

"I used to go down to the field early and talk to him," Case said. "Gene would sit in the dugout and watch the opposing team take batting practice. He had piercing kind of eyes. He watched every move.

"Other than Casey Stengel, Gene Mauch was the most brilliant manager in baseball. He'd take a seventh-place team and make it a fifth-place team; a fifth-place team became a third-place team."

"He knew what it took to make a player better," said Johnny Goryl, a Twins coach under Mauch. "It was unfortunate what happened to him in Philadelphia but he always believed in going with the horses that made the club good. That's what he lived by and that's how he managed."

Mauch was criticized for starting his best pitchers, Chris Short and Jim Bunning, thirteen times in the Phillies' final twenty games in 1964. He was bashed for pitching Tommy John and Bruce Kison on three days' rest in the 1982 playoff series. And he was second-guessed for pitching changes he made in the fifth game of the 1986 playoffs.

In each case, Mauch ran with his horses.

"If a guy was going good," Goryl said, "he was the guy who was going to be out there playing for him."

Reggie Jackson played three years for Mauch's Angels. "If I had an editorial for Gene Mauch," Jackson said, "it would just be in one short sentence: You have my respect and I'm proud to know you and proud that when you talked about me, that you called me your friend more than a good baseball player." [28]

Behind a tough-guy exterior, there was a big heart.

Bilko and Mauch were one-two in hitting throughout the 1956 season.

"This comes from the bottom of my heart," Mauch said. "This isn't feigned. I wanted Steve to lead the league in hitting. I wanted him to lead the league in home runs. I called pitches for him. I called them from first base. I called them from second base. When I called pitches for him, his eyes got big as saucers. We never told anybody. It was just him and me."

One day Bob Case was telling Gene about plans to organize a reunion of the '56 Angels—the Bilko Athletic Club.

"Bob," Gene said, "how can we have a reunion without Bilko being there?"

NOTES

1. *The Sporting News*, August 15, 1956, 27.
2. *San Francisco Chronicle*, August 5, 1956, 5H.
3. *Los Angeles Times*, October 5, 1986, Section III, 1.
4. *Los Angeles Examiner*, September 11, 1956, Section 3, 2.
5. *Los Angeles Mirror*, August 3, 1953, 51.
6. *Los Angeles Times*, August 3, 1953, Part I, 1.
7. *Los Angeles Herald-Express*, August 3, 1953, 1.
8. *Los Angeles Mirror*, August 3, 1953, 51.
9. Ibid.
10. *Los Angeles Herald-Express*, August 3, 1953, 1; and *Los Angeles Mirror*, August 3, 1953, Part III, 1.
11. *The Sporting News*, May 16, 1956, 32.
12. *Los Angeles Times*, August 9, 1992, C3.
13. *Los Angeles Mirror-News*, July 15, 1955, Part IV, 3.
14. *The Sporting News*, August 15, 1956, 27.
15. Ibid.
16. *Los Angeles Herald-Express*, August 13, 1956, B1.
17. *Los Angeles Times*, September 5, 1956, Part II, 2.
18. *Baseball Digest*, March 1957, 52.
19. *The Sporting News*, April 3, 1957, 17.
20. Ibid.
21. *Milwaukee Journal*, June 2, 1959, Part 2, 14.
22. *Milwaukee Journal*, July 6, 1959, Part 2, 11.
23. Tommy John with Dan Valenti, *T. J.: My 26 Years in Baseball* (New York: Bantam Books, 1991), 77.
24. *Los Angeles Times*, April 16, 1956, IV, 3.
25. *Los Angeles Times*, April 13, 1956, C1.
26. *New York Times*, August 9, 2005, A16.
27. *Los Angeles Times*, August 10, 2005, D2.
28. *Los Angeles Times*, August 15, 2005, D12.

EIGHT

Windy

"Gale Wade, fleet Los Angeles centerfielder, made an over-the-shoulder catch of [Harry] Elliott's tremendous 426-foot drive in the sixth inning and an instant after he caught the ball he crashed through the low fence in front of the scoreboard. Wade slammed through a bolted gate in the fence and disappeared behind the barrier, coming to rest on top of a lawn mower and several other pieces of equipment used in repairing the diamond." —From article in the *San Diego Union,* August 20, 1956

Mounted on the basement wall of Gale "Windy" Wade's home in Dysartsville, North Carolina, is a photo poster of Ray Nitschke, the legendary linebacker for the Green Bay Packers in the 1960s.

"I always wanted to meet him," Windy said. "There was a friend of mine who was living in Green Bay. They belonged to the same golf course. Ray was by the pool. I told him: 'By golly you were the guy that, to me, meant football.' That picture of him with mud on his face and no teeth."

On the same wall are pictures of Wade's two sons in football uniforms—Scott, a linebacker at the University of South Carolina in the late 1970s, and Michael, a defensive end at Western Carolina. "Both of them had football scholarships."

Windy always wanted to play football for Notre Dame. In 1946 he was a star halfback for the Bremerton, Washington, high school team. The quarterback was Don Heinrich, later a quarterback for the New York Giants and Dallas Cowboys in the National Football League. "I got a call from almost every college in the country. If I'd got one call from Notre Dame, I would've never seen a baseball."

He accepted a football scholarship from Texas Christian University, but changed his mind when a Brooklyn Dodgers scout offered him $5,000 to play baseball. "That was a million dollars to me. You could go to college for $1,000 a year back then. I figured $5,000 will get me through college. That wasn't good math. But I was seventeen years old and that was my thinking."

One of several baseball photos on the wall shows Windy in a Chicago Cubs uniform with outfielders Walt Moryn and Hank Sauer. "Moryn never would shift; Sauer never would shift. They got married to the lines and stayed there."

Windy likes to brag about the 1956 Angels' outfield with Bob Speake in left, Windy in center and Jim Bolger in right. "The centerfielder always shifts the outfield. I studied hitters and catalogued them. I knew what every one of them hit and when they hit. We might shift forty feet on one count—from a two-and-one count to a two-and-two. When I moved, they moved right with me. That's what made it a great unit."

Windy paused in front of the next photo. "Now this is what I got in trouble for. This is what I loved to try."

In the photo, Windy is flying in the air, his body slamming against the chest of the second baseman. "He wound up in left-centerfield," Windy said proudly.

"The biggest kick I got out of baseball was breaking up a double play at second base. I'd rather do that than hit a home run. Winning one ballgame to me was a whole season. If it meant taking a catcher out at home plate or knocking out the second baseman with a rolling block, I did it. I sacrificed my body to win ballgames."

In 1948 at spring training with the Dodgers, Windy aimed one of his cross-body blocks at Jackie Robinson in an intrasquad game. "He's starting to turn a little bit toward first to make the double play, that's when I got him. Oh, man, he came up off the ground and we went at it. Right there about twenty feet behind second base."

Another rolling block in a game in Venezuela in 1955 started a riot and a near international incident. Windy barreled into Chico Carrasquel, a star shortstop for the Cleveland Indians and a national idol. Chico was knocked unconscious and removed from the game.

Windy recounted the brawl:

> I'm sitting on the bench. Norm Larker was up. He hit a line drive past the first baseman down the right field line. I'm watching it, but I see something out of the left corner of my eye and I turned. Chico had got dressed, went around and come back through our dugout. He was going to blindside me. He had started to swing; I pulled back. He swung just past me. When he did, I was on him. Right down to the floor of the dugout I took him. I've got him there in the corner.
>
> All at once, there comes the whole bunch out of the third base dugout. They come over and start hitting me in the back. I had Chico down underneath me in the corner, but I couldn't come out of there because there was nowhere to go. These guys were really working me

Figure 8.1.   Gale "Windy" Wade, the Angels centerfielder from 1955 to 1957, played with a reckless abandon. *Courtesy Gale Wade.*

over. Suddenly, it stopped. Somebody had me by the back of my jersey. I thought, 'Oh-h-h God, it's one of them.' I hung on but he kept on pulling.

Pulling on Windy's jersey was his teammate, Larker. He rushed to the dugout to rescue Wade. They played the rest of the game—which was stopped after eleven innings with the score tied—and were safely escorted out of the ballpark by a lieutenant colonel in the Venezuelan army.

"I took them all out. And they all knew it when they got near second base. They knew that they were fair game. Of course they tried to low-bridge me. That was part of it."

The six-foot-one, 195-pounder feared no man or outfield wall.

With three games to go in the 1955 season and the Angels fighting for first place, Windy banged into the left-field wall at Seattle's Sicks Stadium, suffering a bruised hip and ending his season.

"Gale would run through a brick wall to catch a ball," said Dave Hillman, a pitcher for the 1956 Angels.

Dave was at San Diego's Lane Field when Windy busted through a bolted gate in the wood fence and landed on top of lawn-mowing equipment stored there. For Gene Mauch, the Angels' second-baseman, the crash epitomized Windy's daring style of play: "You see these guys on

TV riding those bucking broncos and those steers and you can picture ol' Windy. He was one of those kind of guys."

"I can see him going through that fence," Dave recalled years later. "He wasn't trotting either, Buddy. He was free-wheeling. We thought he was hurt badly, maybe even killed."

"I remember the guy that hit the ball—Harry Elliott," Windy said. "I caught the ball just as I made contact with the gate. Of course, the thing flew apart and I went through and landed on top of some dadgum mowing equipment."

"We were all wondering how in the world he ever got out of that without getting cut to pieces," Dave added. "There must've been six or seven sharp blades on that thing."

"We were afraid," Dwight "Red" Adams said. "We thought, 'Oh, geez, he's got his head wedged between the discs on the mower.' We ran out there and he was still down."

"I got up and went back into the ballpark," Windy said. "I don't think I ever turned loose of the ball. The umpire ruled it a home run because I left the ballpark with the ball. Scheffing [Angels' manager Bob Scheffing] argued the call and played the game under protest. The league president wound up changing the home run to a ground-rule double."

Windy was a football player in a baseball uniform.

"Football was really my sport. Baseball was a very difficult game for me. I chose the wrong direction when I went into professional baseball. I should've stuck with football. The very nature of a football player is different. And my feeling was when I went on the field was to always go all out. Ol' Man Rickey [Branch Rickey, president of the Brooklyn Dodgers] instilled that in all of his players, but I already had it instilled in me when I signed with the Dodgers."

Playing any kind of sport was far from Windy's mind growing up on a farm in Turkey Creek, near Branson in the Missouri Ozarks.

Wade's father, Charlie, was a hard-working man who had no use for then–U.S. president Franklin D. Roosevelt and the Works Progress Administration (WPA), the ambitious jobs creation program of the 1930s. "He hated the WPA—'We Piddle Around,' he called it. He couldn't stand to see somebody standing around. We worked. We went from 4:30 in the morning to dark."

Charlie Wade expected his four boys and daughter to work as hard as he did on their forty-acre farm, where they raised cattle, hogs, tomatoes, and everything needed to be self-sufficient. "Listen real close because I'm only going to tell you once," Charlie warned Gale.

"If you didn't hear him good, you were in trouble," Gale said.

And trouble meant whippings. "If we were outside, Dad would whip us with a hickory. Inside the house, you'd always get it with a razor strap."

Charlie's temper was as intimidating as his size—six-foot-three and 220 pounds. One bitterly cold winter night he locked his wife, Willie Mae, out of the house and ordered the kids not to let her inside. Willie Mae spent the night in the barn. "My dad was cruel to mom. We begged her to leave."

Willie Mae divorced Charlie in 1939 and moved to St. Joe, Arkansas, about sixty miles away. That left Gale at home with his sister, Cleta, who was three years older than Gale, and brother, Loren, who was three years younger. Cleta worked in the fields plus did all the cooking, washing, and ironing.

The Wade farm was on the highest ridge in southern Missouri and at night, Gale could see the lights of Hollister and Branson, five and seven miles away, respectively. But the house didn't have electricity, requiring Cleta to use an iron heated on a wood-burning stove.

Charlie went into Hollister every Saturday night. "He always wore a white shirt when he went to town. And the collar had to be starched. When you iron a starched collar with them old irons, they'll glisten."

One Saturday night, Charlie was getting dressed when he saw a shiny spot on his shirt. "He was mad. And he never cut us any slack."

Gale and Cleta, then twelve and fifteen, knew another whipping was coming. They were in the kitchen when Charlie walked in and headed for his razor strap. As he reached for it, Gale grabbed a 32-20 Winchester rifle hanging over the door of his bedroom nearby. "I pointed it straight at him. He was about ten feet away and just starting to hit her with the first lick. He saw me and stopped. And without saying one word, he hung that razor strap back up, put the shirt on and got in his car and left for town. I'm sure I would've pulled the trigger if he'd hit her."

Gale was scared. "I don't know what we're going to do," he told Cleta. "I think he'll kill me."

Two weeks later, they ran away to Arkansas, where they lived briefly with their mother, Willie Mae, until Charlie came to get them. Before leaving, Gale told Willie Mae, "If you don't come get us, we're going to run away again."

Willie Mae soon returned to Missouri, where she was awarded custody of both Gale and Cleta. Together, they headed to Bremerton, Washington, to start a new life.

Gale was thirteen in January 1942 when he showed up at Bremerton High School wearing overalls and a white shirt, his go-to-church clothes in Missouri.

"I ain't goin' back," Gale announced to his mother after the first day of school. "They laughed at me."

"Do you know why they were laughing at you?"

"I think it's my overalls."

With money from her job washing dishes at a restaurant, Willie Mae bought her son corduroy pants so he could blend in with the rest of the boys at school. But there was no hiding muscles that one Angel teammate likened to cords of rope.

"I was a big, strong kid," Gale said. "I weighed about 170 pounds as a sophomore in high school."

The football coach, Dwight Scheyer, noticed. "I went to practice and he put me on the line. I didn't go back the next day because I didn't want to be a lineman."

"What would you like to play? Coach Scheyer asked.

"I saw these guys running with that football," Windy replied. "I can run that thing.

"I didn't know anything about the game but as far as running and shifting and moving, my God, I'd run cows and hogs and everything else. I could turn on a dime. Running came natural and all I had to do was take the ball and go and dare anybody to hit me."

By his senior year, Windy was 190 pounds and running over defenders while Heinrich, the quarterback, was piling up passing yardage that earned him a scholarship to the University of Washington. "After all these years," Heinrich said well into his pro career, "I still have to say I never saw anybody start faster on a quick-opening handoff than Wade. If he had decided to go into professional football, he would have made somebody take notice." [1]

But Notre Dame never called Windy. That opened the door for a Dodgers scout, who saw him playing American Legion baseball, to sign him as a pitcher. "On the farm, I threw a lot of rocks. I didn't have a curveball or anything but I could throw hard."

Windy hurt his throwing arm the first season. But he could still run fast. "Ol' Man Rickey loved speed. If you could run, he loved you."

"Would you like to be an outfielder?" Rickey asked Windy.

"I don't know anything about it."

"We'll take care of that."

Duke Snider, the great Dodgers centerfielder, was assigned to teaching Windy how to play the outfield while Pete Reiser, the National League batting champion in 1941, provided hitting instructions. "I've always said Duke did a better job than Pete."

Windy split the 1948 season between Ponca City, Oklahoma, and Cambridge, Maryland, both Class D teams—as low as you could go in the minor leagues in those days. "I was having a good year, stealing a lot of bases."

The last game of the season Rickey shows up in Cambridge. When the game was over, Windy was told: "Mr. Rickey wants to see you in the general manager's office."

"I thought it was the end of the world. You know what he wanted? He wanted to know if I wanted to play football."

Rickey had purchased the Brooklyn Dodgers football team in the All-America Football Conference. He offered Windy $4,000. "Buddy, that was my dream. I took off the next day for training camp.

The year before Windy played junior college football in Independence, Kansas. He promised the coach he'd return for the 1948 season.

Windy's roommate with the Dodgers was Bulldog Williams. "That was back in the days when they didn't wear face masks. None of them had any front teeth."

During the first practice, Windy, running out of the tailback position in the single wing formation, took a handoff, saw a "streak of daylight," and "I knew that I was through it and gone. All at once, I got hit from here, and I got hit from here and there were silver stars everywhere."

Windy was still seeing stars when he returned to the huddle. "I was leaning over, looked up and the ol' big linemen were all grinning at me. That's the way they initiated me."

He played one game against the Buffalo Bisons, and then the football coach from the junior college in Independence called.

"Gale, you promised me that you would come back. I didn't go out and recruit anybody for tailback."

"I was on my way the next day. I didn't tell the coach. I didn't tell Bulldog Williams. I didn't tell anybody."

Windy left behind his dream of playing pro football, but he felt obligated to the coach in Independence. "That's one thing to this day that's very important to me. By God, you give your word, you stand behind it."

Over the years, Speake and Wade became good friends.

"Gale's word is as good as his bond. To give up the opportunity to play professional football, the money, and the glory to fulfill a commitment to a coach says a whole lot about a guy."

Wade was dreading spring training in Vero Beach in 1949.

He had not heard from Rickey since leaving the football Dodgers. The 1948 season was the team's last but, of course, nobody knew that at the time.

"You know what? When I saw him in spring training, he came up to me and said, 'You doing, okay?' Boy, was I glad he didn't say any more."

Windy steadily improved in the field and at bat. The one constant was his speed. By the end of 1953, he had 296 stolen bases, or nearly fifty per season.

The Cleveland Indians were looking for someone to groom as a replacement for Larry Doby, their aging all-star centerfielder. So they acquired Windy's contract from the Dodgers for $60,000 and two players.

These were the days before agents. Players negotiated their own contracts with shrewd general managers like the Indians' Hank Greenberg.

"I had in mind what I wanted—$15,000. They were out $60,000 and two players and couldn't get it back. So I had some leverage."

At a meeting in Greenberg's office, Windy was presented a contract to sign. It was for the major league minimum of $6,000. "I was so disappointed. Here I was getting ready to ask for more than double that amount."

"To tell you the truth, I think I'm worth more than that," Windy told Greenberg.

"Well, what are you thinking, son?"

"Ten thousand dollars," Windy said, picking something in between.

"He couldn't get his secretary in there fast enough to change the contract and have me sign it. That was the worst financial mistake I ever made. I could've got $15,000."

The speed that attracted the Indians to Windy wasn't all that blinding after he injured his left foot in a benefit game in Joplin, Missouri, organized by Mickey Mantle.

"Mickey was pitching. I hit one down in the right-field corner and I was going for three all the way. The first step past second the inside cleat on my left foot caught a rock dead center."

By spring training, Windy could hardly run because of bone spurs in the foot. "I tried to make the club really on one leg. I absolutely could not run."

The Indians sent him to Indianapolis, their top minor league farm club in the American Association. Wearing a shoe on his left foot two sizes larger than normal to allow for an inch-thick sponge, Windy played through the hurt to hit .273 and help lead Indianapolis to the pennant.

On December 1, 1954, Windy received a Western Union telegram from Wid Matthews, personnel director for the Chicago Cubs and one of his biggest supporters from their time together in the Dodgers organization: "We are happy to inform you that the Chicago National League ball club has purchased your contract from Cleveland. To reestablish our friendship and to acquire a hustling ball player of your type we feel is a great thing."

The Cubs traded slugging outfielder, Ralph Kiner, to the Indians for Windy, pitcher Sad Sam Jones, and $60,000.

Windy Wade was on his way to Chicago—the Windy City.

The 1955, 1956, and 1957 baseball seasons were a tale of two cities for Wade.

You might think a player nicknamed Windy would feel right at home in a place called the Windy City. That wasn't the case.

Meanwhile in Los Angeles, Windy was embraced with open arms.

If Steve Bilko was bulky, Windy was chiseled and as tough as a gunslinger in a Western movie. "He was sort of the good-looking wild child," one Angels fan recalled.

It's no coincidence that Windy hung out with Chuck Connors, the baseball player turned *The Rifleman* on TV; posed for publicity photos with singers Pat Boone and Shirley Jones; or was friendly enough with Gorgeous George, the flamboyant pro wrestler, to call him GG.

The Windy City was a different story. "I never felt comfortable in Chicago."

The Cubs last won a World Series in 1908. They haven't appeared in a World Series since 1945, when Andy Pafko patrolled centerfield. Almost as elusive as the Cubs quest for a National League and World Series title is their search for a centerfielder.

Phil Rogers of the *Chicago Tribune* wrote in 2011, "You can blame scouts. You can blame goats. You can blame brick walls. I blame Leo Durocher, who threw Wrigley Field off its axis when he proclaimed Adolfo Phillips could be the 'next Willie Mays.'" [2]

You could almost fill Wrigley Field's bleachers with players who have paraded through centerfield since Pafko vacated the position in 1951.

The 1955 season is typical of the musical chairs played in center. Wade started the first three games before Bolger took over for a game. Lloyd Merriman started ten of the next eleven games, and then Bolger returned to the lineup. Eddie Miksis, primarily an infielder, started playing center when Wade was farmed out in early May.

The player Wade replaced in Chicago and later in L.A. was Bob Talbot. The year before Talbot was labeled "the Cub greyhound" and assigned the task of playing between Hank Sauer in left and Kiner in right. "We used to say it was like playing between two donkeys," Talbot said. "You just heard when the ball was in the air: 'Go get it, Bob.'"

Talbot started the 1954 season weighing 160 pounds; he finished at 138. "I tell everybody that they ran me right out of the big leagues."

Kiner was gone in 1955, but the lumbering Sauer was still around.

Windy, Talbot, Bolger, and another speedster, Solly Drake, took turns playing centerfield during spring training. Never one to hold back, Windy protested, "Every fourth game isn't enough work for me. I need plenty of hitting practice." [3]

Cub manager Stan Hack decided to begin the season with the left-handed-hitting Wade playing against right-handed pitchers and Bolger versus lefties. He abandoned the plan after the third game against the Cincinnati Redlegs at Crosley Field in Cincinnati.

"Nothing now, it seems, will beat the Cubs except more and worse fielding by Gale Wade," was the lead sentence in the *Chicago Sun-Times* story on the game. [4]

Windy dropped a wind-blown fly ball that enabled the Reds to score two runs and tie the score in the seventh inning of a game eventually won by the Cubs.

"The wind was blowing out *hard*," Windy recalled. "Big Bob Thurman hit one nine country miles high to short center. I'm thinking about the wind and I'm coming under it and I know that ball has to go out. But I keep cat-walking in, cat-walking in and I thought, 'God, I can't let the thing drop in front of me.' Well, it got about twenty feet over my head and that's when the wind got it. I went back on my back—flat on my back. The ball was in the web of my glove when I hit the ground. And, then, it fell out. I'm lying there flat on my back."

To make matters worse, Windy had only one hit in twelve at bats. He was soon back in the minors, first to Toledo and then Los Angeles.

When Windy hit Tinseltown in 1955, the Angels were in seventh place with a 31–36 won-loss record. They went 60–45 the rest of the way to tie for third with Hollywood and four games behind the first-place Seattle Rainiers. "Best of them all at the finish were the Angels," wrote Charlie Park in the *Los Angeles Mirror-News*.[5]

In his first forty games as an Angel, Windy hit .306 and stole fifteen bases with daring head-first slides. He earned $400 from the PCL for his "hustle" in three categories: reaching first base the most times during the month, most putouts for an outfielder, and most stolen bases.

"Give you all he had all the time," said Bobby Bragan, who managed Wade at Fort Worth in 1952 and Spokane in 1958. "He played hard, he slid hard, and he was never out. You knew he was there—down the hall, in the pool room, off the field."

In mid-July, Windy scolded Los Angeles newspapers for not giving PCL baseball adequate coverage. "You fellows will probably want my blood now. But it doesn't make any difference to me. I don't care what you guys or the fans think of me, only what the Cubs think of me. That's all."[6]

The *Mirror-News* made Windy a correspondent and for the next two months he was writing about Angels games. "I wrote what I thought."

"After the game he'd write out the stories in longhand and take 'em down to Western Union," Scheffing explained. "The first time he handed the operator a mess of papers the guy said, 'I can't send that stuff.'"

"'The hell you can't,' Wade told him, 'that's your business, isn't it.'"[7]

Windy posted a batting average of .310 and twenty-three stolen bases for the Angels—good enough for the Cubs to give him another shot in 1956.

"Gale looked bad with the Cubs a year ago but with Los Angeles he was an entirely different player," Scheffing said in a May 1956 *Baseball Digest* story. "He made our ball club. We started moving when he joined us and climbed from the second division to third place.

"I'll say without reservation that Wade, playing like he did for me with the Angels, is a better centerfielder than any the Cubs have had since I've been around the team—and that covers a span of fourteen years.

"I believe he had a touch of 'big-league-itis' last spring. He lacked confidence and couldn't do himself justice. After the good year he had with the Angels, he has the self-assurance he needs."[8]

Unfortunately for Windy, 1956 was a rerun of his first fling with the Cubs. "I believe I would just throw the book at Wade, not attempt to teach him anything," Matthews, the personnel director, wrote in a report assessing the team's players. "He will give you a disastrous thrill but then he also will give you many game-winning thrills."[9]

In announcing Wade as the opening day starter, Hack stressed he hadn't clinched the job. "It's still an elimination contest as far as I'm concerned. I have not counted Solly Drake out of it yet. And I want to see more Pete Whisenant out there."[10]

Matthews, meantime, was on a centerfielder safari: "Somewhere there must be a centerfielder we can get. I don't know what we'll have to give to get a topflight centerfielder. But I'm ready to go high for one—and Mr. Wrigley [owner P. K.] will back me to the limit."[11]

In the season opener against the Milwaukee Braves, Windy thrilled Cubs fans with a leaping backhand grab of a line drive near the left-centerfield fence. He came within inches of robbing Joe Adcock of a home run, jumping to touch the ball before it cleared the centerfield fence. The next game he provided the "disastrous thrill" Matthews referred to in his preseason report.

"Wade's football gallop knocked the ball from Moryn's hands for a three base error," the *Chicago Tribune* reported.[12]

The *Chicago Sun-Times* carried a similar account titled: ERROR BY WADE OPENS WAY FOR 2-RUN 7th.[13]

"I couldn't believe what I read," said Windy, who maintained Moryn ran into him as he was about to make the catch.

> I didn't blame Walt. That was no big deal.
>
> But the next day I went to take outfield practice and the fans in the left-field bleachers started getting on me. The lineup was already made up; it was in the dugout. I was leading off, playing center. I go back into the clubhouse and I happened to glance again and the lineup had changed. Solly Drake was playing center. I was out of the lineup just like that.

And just like that Windy was back in L.A., playing center for Scheffing again.

"When Hack made that change that day, I was under pressure to try and show something. But if you don't get another chance to do it, that's it.

"I knew that no one could out-run me. No one knew base stealing as well as I did. I knew how to play the game. I could throw. And I could field. I had some errors that were charged to me, which I never complained about because I didn't care about what I fielded. If I fielded .970, that was fine with me. But I tried to make every catch. If I had any chance at all, I'd go after it. A lot of times you got errors for taking chances. Some guys knew how to field 1.000. For me, that wasn't the big thing. If you're on a winner, that's the fun of it. You could hit .400 and be on a loser, what fun is that?"

Windy reported to the Angels in late May with catcher Elvin Tappe and picked up where he left off the year before. "Gale Wade and Elvin Tappe came back yesterday," Bob Hunter wrote in the *Los Angeles Examiner*. "And so did the Angels."[14]

The Angels had lost five of their previous six games and were trailing the Padres 10–2 in the seventh inning when Wade and Tappe hit "monumental three-run homers" to spark an eight-run inning and set the stage for Bilko and Speake to hit game-winning back-to-back homers the next inning.

Windy was back. And so were the Angels. They reeled off nine straight victories to improve their record to 33–16 and solidify their position in first place.

In his first twenty-five games in L.A., Windy hit .330 with eight homers, equaling his output for the entire 1955 season. He was running the bases with abandon, stealing home in two straight games—a rare feat.

He put his troubles with the Cubs behind him but not his displeasure with Hack: "Hack doesn't have the courage to be a good major league manager. When the Cubs cut me, Hack wasn't even man enough to tell me himself. He sent the message with the clubhouse boy."[15]

Windy wound up with a .292 batting average, a team-high sixteen stolen bases and twenty home runs—twice his previous best for a single season.

Perhaps Wade's greatest contribution was his hustle and leadership in the outfield.

"Gale knew your game, and where you should be at all the times," Speake said. "If Jim in right field or I in left didn't move to where he wanted us, he wasn't above calling time out and coming over and putting an X on the ground. He had that kind of leadership.

"You didn't loaf on him. You ran out to your position, you ran to the bench because that's what Gale did. And Gale's driving force was to win the ballgame of today."

"L.A. was kind of like a rocking chair in 1956," Windy said. "Everybody was so relaxed. If you're relaxed and got the confidence, that's the key. It's like playing golf or bowling. That relaxed feeling makes all the difference in the world."

While the Angels were being hailed by local media as one of the greatest minor-league teams in baseball history, the Cubs were cleaning house in Chicago. Hack and Matthews were out; Scheffing and Angels president John Holland were in.

On being named Cubs manager, Scheffing said, "I had three fellows at Los Angeles this year I believe can help the Cubs in 1957—outfielders Bob Speake, Jim Bolger, and Gale Wade." [16]

Windy welcomed the news by saying, "I think Bob Scheffing will give me the best chance I've had yet. I've always respected Bob as a man and a manager." [17]

A *Chicago Tribune* headline in mid-February summed up Windy's situation: 2 STRIKES ON CUBS' WADE—WAITS FOR BIG ONE. [18]

"He may fool a lot of people," Scheffing said. [19]

Scheffing believed Wade was ready for the majors and publicly voiced his confidence despite a wobbly start in spring training. "He was the same last year with Los Angeles. Wade didn't look good in the spring, but he got progressively better as the season wore on and he was a good player." [20]

Strike three for Wade came in late March, when he was traded to the Dodgers, the organization he broke in with ten years earlier. He was going back to Los Angeles, now affiliated with the Dodgers, who had already announced they would move from Brooklyn to L.A. the following year.

When the news broke, Wade was nowhere to be found. "We've been looking for him for two days," Holland told newsmen. "He tells us now he has been out on the desert prospecting." [21]

"Somebody made that up," Windy explained. "I was at Bob Scheffing's house." Scheffing had a home near the Cubs training camp in Mesa, Arizona.

"I was really disappointed when they said I was going to be sent down. I always thought that Scheffing was a square shooter. I continue to think so. It wasn't his fault; it was my fault I was going down. He had really pulled hard for me. He wanted me to make it so badly."

Wade played five more years in the minors. In the end, Scheffing was right when he said, on sending him down in 1957, "I guess Gale is just a minor league ball player." [22]

Getting hit in the head by a baseball traveling ninety miles per hour is something every batter thinks about—but not for long.

Hitting requires total concentration. Any thoughts about being brushed back or knocked down gives the pitcher the advantage he wants over a hitter.

"I don't think pitchers throw at the real good hitters," Wade said. "They are usually throwing at guys like me."

In Venezuela in 1955, Windy was leading the league in home runs. "That put me on the list to be thrown at."

The night before the game when Wade flattened Carrasquel at second base with a rolling block, he overheard a conversation detailing plans to knock him down. "I went to our manager and told him what I overhead and said, 'You might be able to defuse this thing.'"

First time up, Windy was hit on the first pitch. "It wasn't just a knockdown. He was going for the head. I spun around and it went off my shoulder."

In his next at bat, the first pitch was high and tight. The second pitch hit him in the ribs. "I didn't tell anybody but I had my mind made up. If he hit me again, somebody was going to pay the freight."

Wade went to first base. On the first pitch, he broke for second. "I didn't want to steal it because I wanted the ball to get there. I wasn't thinking about Chico because I like Chico. It just happened that he was covering second base and had the ball, waiting. I took him right into left field and it knocked him out. He was totally out."

Knockdown pitches were a part of the game. He knew that if he was swinging a hot bat, he was likely to be a target.

In 1961, Wade was thirty-two and in his second season with the Dallas–Fort Worth Rangers in the American Association. He regained the competitive fire that he lost briefly after his third and last failed attempt to make the Cubs. He had two more solid years in the PCL with Spokane and Seattle before joining the Rangers in 1960 and hitting .270.

"Every year I played, I always started out slow. In 1961, I started out fast."

"He loved to be right in the heart of any baseball," said Jack Hannah, a Rangers pitcher and younger brother of Joe, a catcher for the 1956 Angels. "He was writing a newspaper column. And he was having a good year."

And, then, on May 30, Gale's wife, Billie, died from colon cancer. She was thirty-three.

On the basement wall of Gale's home in Dysartsville is a photo of their three children in 1961. Dawn was seven years old; Michael, five; and Scott, three.

He lingered by the photo as he talked about what happened next.

"Walker Cooper was the manager. He put me in the lineup as soon as I got back. But I didn't do a darn thing. So I asked him to take me out—first time I ever asked to be taken out of a lineup in my life."

"I'll let you know when I'm ready," Wade told Cooper.

"I was at a Mexican restaurant one night after a ballgame. Sitting by myself. I went into seclusion, you might say. This lady came over and sat down. She knew me; I never did know her name."

"Do you mind if I give you some good advice?" the woman asked.

Gale said, "No."

"Quit draggin' around. Get out and get with people."

On his way back to his apartment that evening, Gale thought about that.

"'Now, wait a minute, this ol' draggin' around, that's exactly what I'm doing.' I went out to the ballpark the next night and started hitting line drives in batting practice. I went to Cooper and told him to put me in."

Gale went on a roll against the Louisville Colonels in a seven-game series in Fort Worth. In one game, he got two key hits off of pitcher Moe Drabowsky, a former Cubs teammate.

Three days later in Louisville the two faced off again in the first game of a twilight doubleheader.

Gale expected to get knocked down because he was on a hitting streak. But Moe also knew Gale had lost his wife two months earlier. And Moe was a friend.

> I thought, "Moe won't knock me down. He won't knock me down."
> When you know you're going to get knocked down, you stay loose. You're going to turn your shoulder into the ball and take it. You're not going to attack the ball.
> Being a fastball hitter, I didn't want to have him throw one in there and not be swinging at it. I'm ready to attack the ball.

The sun was setting over the left-field wall. Gale lost track of the ball in mid-flight and as soon as he did, he started to turn away. It was too late. Wham! The pitch shattered his right cheekbone, just below the temple.

"It would've killed him if it had hit in the temple," said Jack Hannah. "We were all brokenhearted over it. And so was Drabowsky. He wasn't trying to brush him back. It was a total accident—the ball just got away from him. That was the end of Gale Wade's baseball career right there."

Wade woke up in the hospital, his head packed in ice and his vision forever impaired. Over the next several days, members of the Louisville team stopped by the hospital to express their concern and wish him a speedy recovery. Drabowksy never showed up or called.

Cubs owner P. K. Wrigley called. "He wanted to know if I'd be interested in managing in the minor leagues."

Windy declined.

"Tell me why," Wrigley asked.

"Mr. Wrigley, on opening day I wouldn't have nine men to put on the field."

Wade saw a different type of player entering the game: "a bunch of guys thinking only about themselves, not the team. There's no way in the world that I could manage those types of players."

Gale thanked Wrigley and got on with the rest of his life.

Windy was reminiscing about the golden year of 1956 with Angel teammates, Bob Speake and Dave Hillman.

"Remember Gorgeous George, the ol' wrestler?" Windy began. "He was the calmest, nicest man you'd ever see. We called him GG."

"He embarrassed the living heck out of me one time. He wanted to know if I would go to downtown L.A. with him. I said, 'Yeah, I'll go.'"

"He was the only guy on the ball club that's associating with a guy named Gorgeous George," Bob said to Dave.

"He always drove a pink Cadillac. His hair was not long but it was real stringy and blonde. We went down to Seventh Avenue — right down in the middle of L.A. We went to this store and then back to where his car was parked. We start across the street and all at once he reared back and threw his arms up in the air. He stopped traffic. It struck me that GG is going into one of those show deals."

"You were holding the ropes," Bob said.

"People recognized him. Lord, they even got out of their cars. He had this one person kneel down right in the middle of the street and take the oath — the Georgie Pin oath. He had this gold-plated bobby pin called a Georgie Pin. You'd solemnly swear that you'll always do this and do that with a Georgie Pin."

Bob looked at a team picture of the 1956 Angels and noticed that Windy was a late addition. "They pasted your head in. You were out all night and missed the picture session."

Dave piled on: "Did GG get a hold of you that night?"

"You were running with GG," Bob concluded. "Boy, you came down a notch, running with GG."

"I tell you what, GG was tough."

But no tougher than Gale Wade.

"With the Cubs, I never paid a whole lot of attention to Gale," Speake said. "I'm the quiet type. And Gale speaks his mind. Plus the fact he's hard-nosed and strong-jawed. I didn't want to mouth off to him. I was afraid he would hit me. So it took a long time for me to get through the barrier that the guy is real."

After the death of his wife and the bean ball that ended his baseball career, Windy returned to the 425-acre farm in Dysartsville he purchased with his baseball earnings. He remarried, went to work in management for a rural electric cooperative, and raised his three children.

At age eighty-five, he and his wife, Barbara, divide their time between Dysartsville and Sebring, Florida, where they bought a retirement home in 1985.

Gale starts each day with his own version of the breakfast of champions — corn flakes topped with fruit cocktail and drowned in whole milk in a large bowl.

He has a dent in his right cheekbone from getting hit in the head by Drabowsky's fastball but otherwise, he shows few of the effects of running into fences and bulldozing infielders. In fact, Gale looks like he could still charge into centerfield and play both ends of a doubleheader.

Gale can describe in vivid detail how he almost shot his father, Charlie, when his sister, Cleta, was about to get whipped again with a razor strap. "He was across the kitchen table from me when I came through that bedroom door with my gun. I leveled it right across that table. I never said a word. I would've pulled the trigger."

The last time Gale saw Charlie was in 1956, when he stopped by the family farm en route to L.A. from Chicago, where he was the opening day centerfielder for the Cubs. Charlie had lung cancer.

"He called me Rusty because my hands were always dirty."

They walked around the farm for a while, then headed back to the house where their near-deadly showdown occurred fifteen years earlier.

"Rusty," Charlie said, "if I had it all to do over again, I think I'd done a couple of things different."

That was as close as Charlie ever came to apologizing for the physical abuse he heaped on his wife and children.

Gale was bear hunting in Alaska when Charlie died at the end of the 1956 season. With the passage of time, Charlie's cruelty has been softened by other memories. Charlie never harmed Loren, the younger brother left behind, and he shared with young Gale some advice his son always remembered.

"We had a little heatin' stove in the corner of the front room and Dad read the Bible every night. I was sittin' on the other side of the stove readin' a children's book, *Run Dick Run!* I was having a hard time figurin' that one out."

Gale looked at his father and said, "I'd sure hate to have to read that one."

Charlie closed the Bible. "If you can do three things in life, you may not have to read this book."

"What?"

"Believe in God. Be honest. Be a good neighbor."

Gale reflected for a moment on his dad's advice.

"I tried to live like that. It hasn't always turned out that way, but at least I always tried and it's the way I still live."

NOTES

1. *Seattle Times*, April 27, 1959, 18.
2. *Chicago Tribune*, March 23, 2011 Section 2, 3.
3. *Asheville Citizen-Times*, March 27, 1955, 2B.
4. *Chicago Sun-Times*, April 15, 1955, 8T.
5. *Los Angeles Mirror-News*, September 13, 1955, Part III, 3.
6. *Los Angeles Mirror-News*, July 20, 1955, Part III, 1.
7. *Los Angeles Mirror-News*, August 31, 1955, Part III, 1.
8. *Baseball Digest*, May 1956, 85.
9. *The Sporting News*, February 22, 1956, 8.
10. *Chicago Sun-Times*, April 16, 1956, 72.
11. *The Sporting News*, April 25, 1956, 17.
12. *Chicago Tribune*, April 20, 1956, 1 (Sports).
13. *Chicago Sun-Times*, April 20, 1956, 73.

14. *Los Angeles Examiner*, May 25, 1956, Section IV, 2.
15. *Los Angeles Mirror-News*, June 21, 1956, Part III, 1.
16. *Chicago Sun-Times*, October 13, 1956, 52.
17. *The Sporting News*, March 13, 1957, 28.
18. *Chicago Tribune*, February 15, 1957, B4.
19. Ibid.
20. *The Sporting News*, March 27, 1957, 18.
21. *The Sporting News*, April 10, 1957, 24.
22. Ibid.

NINE

In Stout Steve's Shadow

"Bolger and Speake are somewhat in the position of the man who has a million dollars but who pals around with a fellow who has ten million. They are overshadowed by a large Angel named Bilko, Steve, hitter extraordinary." —Dick Hyland, *Los Angeles Times*, August 17, 1956

Jim Bolger and Bob Speake arrived in Los Angeles in 1956 with a common goal: prove they belonged in the major leagues where they spent the previous season with the Chicago Cubs. They succeeded with career years, earning another shot in 1957.

Bolger posted a .328 batting average with twenty-eight home runs, thirty-seven doubles, and 147 runs batted in. His home run and RBI numbers were second in the league to Steve Bilko.

Speake was almost as impressive with a .300 average, twenty-five home runs, twenty-nine doubles and 111 RBIs. Playing left field, he tied for the league lead in most double plays by an outfielder—six. Bolger, the right fielder, was in on four double plays.

"Put either Bolger or Speake on any club in the league and he is that team's top star, defensively as well as offensively," wrote Dick Hyland, a columnist for the *Los Angeles Times*.[1]

"You know who was probably the best player on the team?" asked Gene Mauch. "Jim Bolger. Steve and I would eat up the ordinary pitchers. And Bolger would beat all the tough ones. He hit all of the good pitchers."

One of the pitchers that Bolger beat up on was Ryne Duren, a pitcher who wore eyeglasses so thick a teammate once suggested he use tripods to hold them up.

"I've never seen anybody hit Ryne Duren like Bolger did," said Speake. "Most of us were scared to death. How Bolger hit him is beyond me."

Figure 9.1.   Jim Bolger compiled a .326 average with 147 RBIs and twenty-eight home runs by beating up on the league's best pitchers. *Author's collection.*

The few occasions that Bilko couldn't play, Bolger and Speake picked up the slack. In a mid-August game against Sacramento, Bolger took over Bilko's cleanup spot in the batting order and ripped three hits, including two doubles, to drive in three runs. Speake replaced Steve at first base and walloped a Bilko-like home run.

"Everybody looked to Steve," said Dave Hillman. "But if he was having a bad day, somebody else would step up and take care of it."

Bolger's defensive play even wowed his teammates. "He was something," said George Freese. "He could play right field. I've seen him dive after a ball and slide head-on into a brick wall. He'd get up and just shake his head."

The six-foot-two-inch, 180-pound Bolger played the outfield with the same tenacity that made him a star running back at Cincinnati Purcell High School and earned college football scholarship offers from Notre Dame, Ohio State, Wisconsin, and many others.

In making a catch at Portland's Multnomah Stadium, Bolger was spiked in a collision with Speake, playing centerfield. A gash in his left leg, requiring six stitches, forced him out of the game. He was back in the lineup the next day, slashing three hits, including a homer, and batting in three runs. "It just gashed the skin right along the bone," Bolger said. "Hell, I was going good. I didn't want to get out of the lineup."

The twenty-four-year-old Bolger was seldom satisfied with his performance. In fact, his not-so-sunny disposition earned the nickname "Sunny Jim."

"He was always complaining," said Freese, who roomed with Bolger early in the season when Freese was mired in a hitting slump. "He'd go three-for-four and he'd come in the room and say, 'Boy, I just can't have a good day.' So I told Scheffing, 'Get me out of there or I'm going to throw him out the window.'"

Adams also roomed with Sunny Jim: "He was kind of a grumpy guy. He wouldn't be happy with a couple of hits. He'd want three or four."

The Cubs sent Speake to L.A. to recover from a wrist injury he suffered in St. Louis at the end of the 1955 season. He crashed into the left-field wall at Sportsman's Park while making a game-saving catch.

The bases were loaded with two outs in the bottom of the eleventh when the Cardinals' Alex Grammas hit a ball to deep left-center field. "We were playing him straight away, which meant we were giving the big part of the park behind us," Speake recalled.

As Speake raced toward the concrete wall in left field, he could hear Gale Wade, the centerfielder, running behind him and hollering, "Plenty of room! Plenty of room!"

"You keep saying plenty of room as long as the guy can catch the ball and not get killed," Gale explained. "If you can catch the ball and only hit the wall, so what? I kept telling him, 'Plenty of room!' He went back and caught it and then he hit the fence."

"I went sideways into it," Bob added. "And in trying to protect myself, I got my hand trapped between my body and the concrete wall. It was just a split second. It was the wrong place to have your hand."

Speake was carried off the field on a stretcher with a severely dislocated left wrist. "I could scratch my elbow."

Over the years, the play has become the subject of good-natured bantering between the two Missourians and long-time friends.

"He always said that I ran him into the wall," Gale said. "Heck, just a broken wrist for one out, that ain't bad!"

"I had teeth marks on that wall," Bob said.

"Oh, he made a great catch—a heckuva catch."

"There's only one problem," Bob pointed out. "He dislocated his wrist!"

"I know and I wasn't concerned about that," Gale deadpanned. "That's secondary."

Bob turned serious: "That's how I wound up in Los Angeles."

Ironically, Speake was responsible for Bilko winding up in L.A. the year before.

Speake reported to the Cubs spring training camp as a first baseman, the only position he had played in five years as a professional. He was a rookie trying to make the big jump from Class A to the majors so he was given little chance of displacing Bilko as the backup to Dee Fondy, the starter.

"I had a hot spring in 1955, and Bilko had sort of bounced from pillar to post. So the tossup was either me or Bilko. They kept me."

The Cubs used Speake exclusively as a pinch-hitter the first seventeen games of the season. In nine pinch-hit appearances, he delivered four hits and a walk.

On arriving in Philadelphia May 1 to play the Phillies in a doubleheader, Bob Scheffing, a Cubs coach at the time, asked Speake if he had ever played the outfield.

"Yes, I played one game in the service."

"Get a finger mitt and go out there and get some fungoes," Scheffing said.

Bob borrowed a glove from a Cubs pitcher and chased fly balls in the outfield. "I must've looked like an idiot with those wind currents from the double deck."

The next morning he went to a Philadelphia library and read a book by Terry Moore, an outstanding defensive center fielder for the Cardinals in the 1930s and 1940s.

"It's the only place I knew to find out how to play the outfield. He talks about the convex and concave walls, getting in front of the ball and hitting the cutoff—things that you learn in spring training. That's the only outfield education I had. I was in the lineup that night."

Speake replaced slumping Hank Sauer, the Cubs' home run–hitting left fielder. He went hitless in three at bats but turned in a defensive gem by doubling up a runner at first base after catching a fly ball.

Sauer was still taking what was described as a "rest cure" the next game when Speake slammed a bases-loaded triple to spark another Cubs victory. In his third start, Speake hit a home run against the New York Giants that soared over the Polo Grounds' two-story roof in right field.

The home run was the first of ten Speake hit in May. By the end of the month, Cubs fans were chanting "Speake to me" each time he came to bat. "Speake up" was the watchword at Wrigley Field—"things will be all right with the Cubs whether they're behind or not."[2]

With the popular "Mayor of Wrigley Field" riding the bench, packs of Beech-Nut chewing tobacco that previously showered on Sauer by bleacher fans, now peppered Speake after he hit a home run. "He was MVP," Speake says of Sauer, the National League's Most Valuable Player in 1952 and coming off his most productive home run year (forty-one) the season before. "I'd come into the dugout and I'd have tobacco pouches and I'd dump them in Sauer's lap. He'd say, 'Boy, now take one.' I said, 'I don't want 'em.'"

The twenty-four-year-old native of Springfield, Missouri, dubbed "Wonder Boy of the Ozarks," was the toast of Chicago and the talk of the baseball world.

"Bob went like a house afire for the month of May after he replaced Hank Sauer in left field," recalled Wid Matthews, personnel director of the Cubs. "He was the hottest thing in the National League. Every time we needed a timely hit he came through and he was socking homers as if he were another Babe Ruth."[3]

The most dramatic home run by Speake was a game-winning two-run shot against the Milwaukee Braves in the tenth inning off of future Hall of Fame pitcher Warren Spahn. "You don't mind getting beat, but it hurts more when a busher beats you with a homer," Braves general manager John Quinn reportedly said after the game.[4]

"We'll see who's a busher," Speake said. "I'm from Missouri and we just don't talk that way down there. We may think it, but we never say it."[5]

On May 25, Speake hit a line-drive homer onto the right-field catwalk at Wrigley Field to beat the Cardinals. He hit home runs in each of the next two games, including another one against Quinn's Braves.

In the Cubs' doubleheader sweep of the Cardinals on May 30, Speake homered in both games, inspiring a *Chicago Tribune* story titled CUBS SPEAK(E) WOE FOR CARDS. *The Chicago Sun-Times* featured a box score headline that read, BOB-BOB-BOBBIN' ALONG.[6]

"I never saw anybody have a greater single month than Speake did," said Cubs manager Stan Hack. "Whenever we needed a run to win he came through for us."[7]

The year before—1954—the six-foot-one-inch, 180-pound Speake hit .264 with twenty home runs and eighty-two RBIs at Des Moines in the Western League.

"How does he do it his first year in the majors?" a sportswriter asked Rogers Hornsby, the Cubs hitting instructor and one of the greatest hitters of all time.

"It's easier to hit major league pitching if you've got any guts," Hornsby said. "Speake's got it, too. You can tell by the way he stands up at the plate. No one who was ever scared of a pitcher was ever a good hitter."[8]

On June 3 against the Giants, Speake homered again—his eleventh of the season and eighth in fourteen games, increasing his RBI total to thirty-two.

On June 7 the *Tribune's* Edward Prell wrote "The best left fielder in the league as time for the July 12 All-Star spectacle in Milwaukee nears is twenty-four-year-old Bob Speake of the Cubs. Not even his most rabid followers will class the Missouri Ozarkian with either Mays or Musial. But this All-Star game should reward current great play."[9]

Speake began June hitting .304; he ended the month with a .252 average—only seven hits in forty-seven at bats. By mid-June, Speake was on the bench and Sauer back in left field. "The second swing through, they were trying to beef up the hitting and motivation so Sauer went back in," Speake explained. "I was relegated to pinch-hitting. Sauer didn't revive anything."

The Cubs started June in second place, six games behind the league-leading Brooklyn Dodgers. Over the next two months, they won only twenty-three games while losing thirty-nine. At one point, they lost nine straight games and fifteen of sixteen. They finished sixth, twenty-six games behind the pennant-winning Dodgers.

The scuttlebutt in the league, Speake said, was "Wait 'til the second swing. I didn't know what they meant. What it meant was that the Cubs start good but in the second swing, they go into the tank. And, boy, we did. We were in second place and then all of a sudden, it didn't matter whether you won or lost. If you won, great! But you were expecting to lose."

Speake hit only one more home run to finish with twelve, along with forty-three RBIs and a .218 batting average. Sauer wound up with almost identical numbers: twelve homers, twenty-eight RBIs, and a .211 average.

"They classified an out as a slump," Speake said. "You go oh-for-five, you're in a slump. They had me in extra hitting practice as if there was a problem."

Matthews, the Cubs personnel director, said after the season, "Bob Speake is an outstanding example of a player who can profit tremendously by special instruction."

He went on to say, "The pitchers caught up with him. They found he had a weakness for the inside pitch above the belt. Bob thought those inside pitches were balls."[10]

Speake said,

A slump isn't something that physically happens to you—fatigue or anything. A slump is self-induced because I'm not picking it up at the point of release out of a pitcher's hand. That's a slump.

We were standing around the batting cage in St. Louis. Stan Musial is standing there. Not a bad hitter himself. Hank Sauer asked Stan, "How do you hit?"

"Boys, all I can tell you, if it's coming through that little window, I swing." The only way Stan could see the ball was in this little window. You concentrate on picking the ball up right out of the pitcher's hand. Hitting isn't done at home plate. It's done at the mound.

The turning point in Jim Bolger's career came late in the 1952 season at Burlington, Iowa, in the Class B Three-I League when he decided to wear glasses. Suddenly, he was catching fly balls that had been falling untouched around him. And he started hitting line drives like he was expected to on signing with the Cincinnati Reds at age eighteen out of high school.

The Reds promoted Bolger to their Columbia, South Carolina, affiliate in the Class A Sally League in 1953, where he posted a team-best .301 batting average and set a league record for most putouts in the outfield. "One of the finest young outfield prospects in baseball," raved Ernie White, the Columbia manager.[11]

In one game, the story goes, Bolger made three spectacular catches. On the first catch he bounced off the left-centerfield wall, and then, on the second, the rightfield wall. On the third catch, he knocked himself out running into the centerfield wall. White rushed to the outfield to check on Bolger.

"Are you all right, Jim?"

"Yeah," Jim replied, "but you better see how that pitcher is before he gets someone killed."

The Cubs acquired Bolger from the Redlegs after the 1954 season, when his .311 batting average and sixteen triples at Tulsa earned him a spot on the Class AA Texas League all-star team, and a shot at playing centerfield for the Cubs in 1955.

Bolger saw limited action, starting forty-four games in center and hitting .206 as the Cubs shuffled him in and out of the lineup with Eddie Miksis, a converted infielder, and Lloyd Merriman. "You've got to produce right away," Bolger said. "They won't hang with you that long."

On reporting to the Angels for spring training in 1956, Bolger faced a skeptical manager in Scheffing, who told him, "A guy with glasses can't play center field."

"There was a bias in those years against anybody who wore glasses," Bolger said.

Despite the success of Dom DiMaggio, a centerfielder for the Boston Red Sox, and several infielders and pitchers, including Duren, there was a common saying that big league scouts "seldom make passes at players who wear glasses."

Scheffing later acknowledged that he didn't think Bolger would make the team in spring training. He tried Sam Brown, an All-America running back at UCLA the previous fall, and Don Eaddy, a third baseman, in center before deciding on Bolger.

"I wasn't hitting that well," Bolger said. "What really turned it around—I started turning my head more toward the pitcher. Not my body, just my head. I felt you had to hit with both eyes facing the pitcher. A lot of guys kind of peek around. They turn their bodies and shoulders so far in that they are actually hitting with one eye. I started picking the ball up real good, real fast. I just took off."

"He would turn his head about ninety degrees to his shoulders," Casey Wise marveled. "I didn't know how he could twist his neck that far. He just practiced and practiced."

"What Bolger was doing, unknowingly, was centering his eyes to the glass lens," Speake explained.

> When he got into the batter's box, he put his chin onto his left shoulder, centering his eye ball to the lens. High, low, inside or out, it didn't matter because the baseball stayed inside the rims of his glasses. Most hitters want the ball down, hitting with leverage so pitchers would throw to high strikers. That was Jim's wheelhouse, resulting in line drives. At Little Wrigley, his line drives went for home runs. Greatest high-strike hitter I've ever played with. And he had great strike zone control."

Bolger opened the season in centerfield, switching to right field when Wade arrived in late May.

In the fourth game of the season, the Angels faced Duren and the Vancouver Mounties, managed by Lefty O'Doul, a character every bit as colorful as Duren.

"Guys were saying, 'With your stuff, just throw it over,'" Duren said. "'You've got great stuff. They're not going to hit you.' Everybody assumed that the reason I didn't throw it over was because of being afraid to be hit. And trying too hard. I just didn't have a sense of touch.

"Lefty's philosophy was to throw it high and tight, and low and away—two extremes. I developed a feel or a touch for what I had to do to at least adjust if I missed."

One day Duren was warming up on the sideline before a game at Vancouver's Capilano Stadium.

"Throw one high and tight," Lefty ordered.

"The higher I'd throw it, he'd say, 'No, high and tight. Up here.' So I finally threw one right out of the stadium and he said, 'now, you've got it.'"

Duren credits O'Doul for his success as a relief pitcher with the championship New York Yankees teams from 1958 to 1961.

After throwing 100-mile-per-hour warm-up pitches past home plate and halfway up the backstop, Duren would yell to Yankees catcher Yogi Berra, "You're going to have to give me the outside signs. I can't see your fingers."

"He had such movement and velocity on his fastball, he didn't have to throw anything else," said Albie Pearson, who faced Duren in the minors and majors. "His glasses looked like Coke bottles. Mix that with a little alcohol and you're talking about a threat."

Duren was a heavy drinker until he conquered his alcoholism later in life. Poor vision alone made hitters fear for their lives. "If he could see better," wrote Jim Murray of the *Los Angeles Times*, "He'd be just another guy with a fastball. This way, he's a one-man war-of-nerves."[12]

Bolger was a man-of-steel against Duren.

"Jim hit Ryne like he owned him," Speake said.

"Jim would rather hit against Ryne Duren than eat," Hillman added. "When Ryne started pitching, his bat started jumping."

"I had a pretty good season against him," Bolger said. "I had faced him before in A and double-A ball. When you've seen a pitcher, you can be ready for what's coming."

Duren won three of five games he started against the Angels, striking out forty.

In the first game, he whiffed nine. Bolger had two hits. Bilko doubled and struck out three times. "God, I used to strike Bilko out," Duren said. "If a guy popped a ball pretty good, he could get it by Steve. Steve could hit the off-speed and the lesser fastballs."

In their second meeting, the Angels won, chasing Duren after three innings. Bilko was hitless but Bolger touched Duren for two more hits, including a triple.

Duren didn't get a decision in the Mounties' 18–13 win as he left the game in the fifth inning after giving up two mighty home runs to Bilko. Bolger hit a double.

He rebounded in the next game to blank Bilko and strike out seventeen. Bolger had three hits.

Duren struck out nine in his third victory over the Angels, limiting Bolger to one hit. Bilko sat out the game.

"Bolger was tough," Duren said. "He was just quick with the bat."

"I felt confident that I was always going to get a piece of the ball," Bolger explained. "He wasn't going to strike me out like he did a lot of people. Even though he threw extremely fast, I could pick the ball up pretty easy. It was a matter of seeing the ball real quickly — right out his hand."

Bolger was also at his best against the Hollywood Stars, the Angels' long-time nemesis. He batted a sizzling .388 with four home runs.

In a four-game series with the Stars the last week of the season, Bolger had six straight hits in a doubleheader and in another game ripped a bases-loaded double.

"He was a deceptive guy," Adams said of the quiet, introverted Bolger. "The more you were around him and saw him play, the more you appreciated the ability he had."

"I was intense," Bolger said. "I kept it all in but I sure liked to win. If I had a couple of hits, I thought maybe that I should've had one or two more."

That intensity is what his Angels teammates remember most about Sunny Jim.

"He used to practice his swing all the time," Wise said. "In the hotel lobby. In his room. Everywhere. He would turn his head and hold his bat up. And he would practice over and over mentally his swing."

"Ask Bolger how many glasses he went through during the 1956 season," said Johnny Briggs, a pitcher and teammate with the Angels as well as the Cubs the next two years.

"Probably three or four, I don't know," Bolger replied.

Briggs laughed. "Bolger was something else. He struck out one night and he came in and set them on the concrete of the dugout and busted them with a bat. Throw them away and tell the clubhouse boy, 'Go get me another pair of glasses.' He had a backup pair."

"That was with the Cubs in 1957," Bolger said, flashing a rare smile. "I liked Johnny. He was my kind of guy. He was a red-ass. He'd get mad if somebody would get a hit off him."

Bob Speake, the "Wonder Boy of the Ozarks," was coming to Los Angeles and Angels' manager Bob Scheffing was elated. "This fellow will hit over .300 and collect twenty-five home runs," he said prophetically.[13]

Speake wasn't happy to be leaving the big leagues, but he was looking forward to playing every day under Scheffing who was a mentor of sorts and instrumental in his becoming an outfielder in Chicago. He was also eager to test his left wrist injured at the end of the 1955 season. "When I would swing, boy, it was like your fillings were going to come out. But it was getting better."

Speake joined the Angels eleven games into the season. He replaced Bob Coats in left field and batted in eleven runs with his first eleven hits. "Bilko was the bell cow last year," Scheffing said. "He still is. But if he happens to have an off day or so I've got other guys in there who can knock in runs."[14]

Just as he did with the Cubs the previous May, Speake went on a home run tear, slamming eight. Bolger hit five in the same period and Bilko a whopping sixteen. With Bilko hot, everybody else was getting good pitches to hit.

"The electricity off of Bilko caught us all," Speake said. "We became his greatest rooting section. When he hit one, we all became electrified and wanted to do as well as we could. We wanted to be part of his domain."

Part of Bilko's domain was the whirlpool in the Angels clubhouse. "Bilko and Freese always had a six-pack after every game. So I sat down, opened a beer and took a couple of swallows. I never liked the stuff and reaffirmed at that point that I didn't."

The magic potion for Speake was winning.

The Angels stumbled in June to briefly drop out of first place but bounced back in July to post a 26–9 record. By the PCL all-star break in mid-August the Angels were twelve-and-a-half games up on second-place Seattle with Bilko, Bolger, Freese, and Speake the top four run producers in the league. They finished the season that way.

"Bilko was the shining star—the 'pede' on the pedestal. He brought us all along and caused each of us to have a good year. We were all confident—especially me.

"Ball players of that era, as a rule, never got close to each other," Speake added. "There was a saying: One-a-comin', one-a-playin' and one-a-goin' because we were chattel mortgage. We were under the reserve clause. It was dangerous to become close."

Chuck Connors, the baseball player-turned-actor, often charged into the Angels clubhouse after a home game shouting, "Sweat, sweat, you slaves, sweat!" and asking: "Which one of you is not going to be here next week?"

"Here comes Dog Food Man!" the players yelled back, referring to the dog food commercials that got Connors started in his acting career.

"The chemistry of the 1956 Angels was such that it didn't really matter who you were with," Speake said. "The camaraderie was there. We moved as a unit. When ball players root for each other and have the talent that was on that team, you're going to have a winner."

The players were loose. The big four of Bilko, Bolger, Freese, and Speake were belting home runs and Scheffing was letting the team do its thing—win.

"He was a handler of men, not ball players. If any one of us was having a down time, he let us work through it. All of a sudden, you're back and hitting the ball pretty good and he'd say, 'Why don't you take a day off?'"

On numerous occasions during the season, Scheffing told Speake, "You didn't get your top wrist in it."

"Bob was a soft-spoken guy. I wished I had stopped and said to Scheff: 'Explain what you mean?' In retrospect, I think what he was saying was that the swing and the bat speed created by my top wrist in 1956, was not as great as 1955 prior to the injury. Physically, was I babying that thing? I don't know."

Speake learned to hit after he retired from baseball and began teaching hitting at a baseball camp and playing fast-pitch, triple-A softball. He hit sixteen home runs one year against world-class pitchers.

"I'm looking at the pitcher and I can tell you whether he needs a shave or not. When you pull that trigger in fast-pitch softball, you've got to have bat speed. That's when I realized what Scheffing meant when he was telling me I wasn't getting my top wrist in the swing. The top wrist releases the built up energy against a locked front leg, which drives the ball. It's called bat speed."

Every so often Speake wonders how many more home runs he might've hit with the Angels, and the next three years with the Cubs and San Francisco Giants. And, then, he remembers that 1956 was a great year—the best of his career.

Speake and Bolger were back with the Cubs in 1957, this time with Scheffing as their manager. Hopes were high—until the season started.

The Cubs lost twelve of their first fifteen games. They didn't win a home game until five weeks into the season. By the second week, they were in last place where they finished tied with the Pittsburgh Pirates.

The parade in center field continued as Speake and Bolger shared playing time with five others. Speake also played left field and first base against left-handed pitching. Bolger played the other two outfield positions as well as three games at third base.

Speake improved on his 1955 numbers, batting .232 with sixteen home runs and fifty RBIs. Bolger hit a respectable .275 with five home runs and twenty-nine RBIs. He batted .354 as a pinch-hitter, delivering a league high seventeen in forty-eight at bats.

The pinch hit he's proudest of came against Jack Sanford, a tough right-handed pitcher who won nineteen games for the Philadelphia Phillies in 1957.

Bolger batted for Ernie Banks, the slugging shortstop known as Mr. Cub in recognition of his outstanding career with the Cubs. Banks suffered a muscle strain in the back earlier in the game and couldn't bat. "I jumped on the first pitch and hit a home run. I might be the only guy to ever pinch hit for Ernie Banks."

Bolger might as well have the words "pinch hitter" stenciled on his forehead. "I got categorized as a pinch hitter."

After starting a game and going four-for-four, the next day he was back in his customary role of pinch hitter in waiting.

"How come Bolger is not playing today?" Jim remembers a writer asking Scheffing. "He had four hits yesterday."

"Well, they were all singles," Scheffing replied.

> Pinch hitting is do-or-die. I developed kind of an 'I don't care' attitude whether I succeeded or not. That relaxed me. I knew I had one shot.

And I knew there were guys who were better hitters than me that were playing every day and striking out two or three times a game. I figured if I struck out, that was it—can't worry about it.

The numbers catch up with you sooner or later. There were a lot of times I hit a ball right on the nose that was caught—line drives. In the newspaper the next day they look like any other out. But you did your job. You hit the ball hard.

The numbers caught up with Bolger in 1958. He batted .225 for the Cubs before being traded to the Cleveland Indians who, in turn, sent him to the Phillies. Appearing primarily as a pinch hitter with the two teams in 1959, he managed only four hits in fifty-five at bats for a .073 average.

Bolger returned to the Pacific Coast League (PCL) in 1960, batting .279 for Sacramento. He hit over .300 the next two years, playing for San Diego, then in the PCL, and Louisville of the American Association. Twelve years had passed since Bolger made his major league debut with the Redlegs—the 1,000th player to appear in a Cincinnati uniform. He was now thirty.

"They sold my contract to Oklahoma City. I asked for more money and they said I was getting paid as much as triple-A ball players get paid."

The Oklahoma City 89ers were affiliated with the Houston Colt .45's, one of two teams added by the National League in 1962.

"Go out and have a good spring and we'll bring you up to the major league club," Bolger was told.

"'I don't have to prove I can hit triple-A ball,' he said. '"I've hit .300 three times in triple-A ball and I don't have to prove that.' So I just hung it up."

Dwight "Red" Adams was going over a list of his Angels teammates.

"Gentleman Bob," he said on seeing Speake's name. "He was a gentleman—a quiet guy who could go any place in the world and get along with anybody. He could've been a preacher, a lawyer, or any damn thing he wanted to be."

In 1965, five years after leaving baseball, Speake and several business colleagues started American Investors Life Insurance in Topeka, Kansas. The company merged with Amerus in 1997 and then was acquired by Aviva Life in 2006.

"Our capitalization at that time was a million dollars. Counting all of its operations around the world, Aviva is worth $400 billion."

Speake could only imagine such lofty numbers in 1957 with the Cubs. The best he could do was his .375 batting average as a pinch hitter—second best in the league.

He opened the season in left field, moved to first base and then center-field where he started more games than anybody else. Like Bolger, he became one of the league's top pinch hitters.

That got the attention of the Giants and their manager, Bill Rigney.

Speake was a Giant-killer in 1957. In fifty-eight at bats against the Giants, he had seventeen hits, including three home runs and a triple, for a solid .293 average.

So the following spring the Giants acquired Speake in a trade for outfielder Bobby Thomson, who swatted the epic home run called "shot heard around the world" to beat the Dodgers and capture the 1951 National League pennant. The Cubs and Giants were playing in Mesa, Arizona, the next day. "We walked across the field and traded uniforms. I became a Giant; he became a Cub."

Rigney explained the trade to Speake.

"Bob, let me tell you why we want you. You're killing us as a pinch hitter. We want you to kill the other guys. We've got this kid coming up but we don't think he's going to make it. So we want you to play first base."

"Who is this kid?" Speake inquired.

"Orlando Cepeda."

"I played against him in winter baseball. He's just a kid but I'm telling you, he's going to be something."

Cepeda, a native of Puerto Rico, proved Speake right, winning National League Rookie of the Years honors as a twenty-year-old and going on to be inducted into the Hall of Fame.

"The Giants put me on waivers twice in 1958. And the Cubs claimed me twice. So the Giants pulled me back both times. They never put me up again."

Speake was used almost exclusively as a pinch hitter. And just as it did for Bolger, the numbers caught up with him. In fifty-two appearances, he managed seven hits and eleven walks. Overall, he batted .211 with three home runs.

The 1959 season was more of the same.

"I'm twenty-eight years old and I'm sitting there wondering when I'm going to get to play. First base? Not a fat chance. Willie Mays was in center so that's taken care of. Their farm system had blossomed. They had Leon Wagner, Willie Kirkland, and Felipe Alou in the outfield—all good, young players."

After appearing in thirteen games as a pinch hitter, Speake was sent to Phoenix, the Giants' farm club in the Coast League. He hit twenty home runs in 101 games and got a glimpse of another future Hall of Famer—first baseman Willie McCovey. By the end of the season, McCovey was playing for the Giants and tearing up the league with a .354 batting average. Cepeda was now in left field—the other position Speake played.

"The writing on the wall was there for me as far as the big leagues and playing every day."

Speake returned home to Springfield and teamed with friends to open a sixteen-lane bowling establishment. "I told the group if you want to talk baseball, I can talk all night. But if you want to talk business, you're going to have to talk slow. And sometimes twice."

He became a hitting instructor at a baseball camp run by Mickey Owen, a former major league catcher, and he started playing fast-pitch softball.

He soon realized that a small bowling alley wasn't going to cut it. He tried to incorporate three other bowling houses in Springfield into a multirecreational operation but that didn't work out.

Speake learned a valuable lesson from bowling that helped him succeed in the insurance business. "If you're going to sell something, whether it's a product or service, you have to create a relationship. That's true in the bowling business as well as the insurance business with mom and dad at the kitchen table.

"In the insurance business, it's not only the relationship but it's also service. It was mandatory that our employees recognized that the agents were independent and could act so. Our service had to be supreme. That's the bottom-line to our success."

A team picture on Speake's office wall reminds him of the success the 1956 Angels enjoyed.

"This group of guys knew what they were there to do. They weren't going anywhere in the immediate future. The Cubs weren't having a year in 1956 any better than we did in 1955 nor any better than we did in 1957."

He paused to reflect before adding a final thought: "We were like a family. There was such a tight camaraderie around Bilko. We became Bilko's Boys."

NOTES

1. *Los Angeles Times*, August 17, 1956, A2.
2. *Chicago Sun-Times*, June 2, 1955, 92.
3. *The Sporting News*, November 23, 1955, 9.
4. *The Sporting News*, June 8, 1955, 14.
5. Ibid.
6. *Chicago Tribune*, May 31, 1955, Part 3, 1; and *Chicago Sun-Times*, May 31, 1955, 64.
7. *The Sporting News*, October 26, 1955, 21.
8. *Chicago Sun-Times*, June 1, 1955, 59.
9. *Chicago Tribune*, June 7, 1955, Part 4, 1.
10. *The Sporting News*, November 23, 1955, 9.
11. *The Sporting News*, January 20, 1954, 16.
12. *Los Angeles Times*, May 14, 1961, H1.
13. *Los Angeles Times*, August 17, 1956, A2.
14. *Los Angeles Times*, May 2, 1956, C2.

TEN

The Singing Catcher

"The cowboy was a hero. The baseball player was a hero. He was a hero because of the image he conveyed by virtue of the fact that he was loyal to his teammates." —Jack Hannah, former minor league pitcher and younger brother of Joe Hannah, catcher, 1956 Los Angeles Angels

The upbeat cowboy music coming from the stage of the Smith Family Theatre in Pigeon Forge, Tennessee, was the kind often heard on the radio in the 1930s and 1940s.

"We're the Hannah boys from San Joaquin Valley, California," the burly bass player announced. "Two hundred miles north of Los Angeles, thank God. And 220 miles south of San Francisco. And I want to thank Him again. And I want to thank Him that we can be here with you in Pigeon Forge."

"As old as we are, we're thankful to be anywhere, Joe. I'm his favorite brother, Jack. He's the only one. This is my nephew, Lon. I'm his uncle."

And so the Sons of the San Joaquin opened another concert filled with the airtight, three-part harmonies they learned growing up in the foothills of the Sierra Nevada Mountains east of Visalia, California.

"Cowboys would drive cattle in front of our school," said Joe. "They had their chaps on; they were real cowboys. Shoot, we were just cowboys."

That's where Joe and Jack Hannah began their romance with cowboys and music as well as their journey into professional baseball.

Joe was five and Jack three when their father, Lon, moved the family from Missouri to California in 1937, bringing with them a love for baseball. "It was Jesus first and the St. Louis Cardinals second," explained Jack.

The elder Hannah dreamed of Joe and Jack playing major league baseball. Neither made it. But they came close.

Joe was a catcher for thirteen years in the minor leagues, seven at the highest level—triple-A and open classifications.

Jack, two years younger than Joe, was a pitcher for seven years in the Milwaukee Braves and Los Angeles Angels organizations.

On opening day of the Angels' 1956 season, Joe caught both games of a day-night doubleheader and became the father of a baby boy—Lon Jr. The season concluded with Joe singing and strumming "Empty Saddles in the Oat Bin" as part of an impromptu show that the Angels players staged for fans. The significance of these two seemingly unrelated events wouldn't be apparent until many years later.

"We knew he could sing a little, but, I at least, had no idea he had this exceptional talent," said Dwight "Red" Adams, a pitcher for the 1956 Angels.

At a family reunion in 1987 to celebrate their father's eighty-fifth birthday, Joe and Jack teamed with young Lon to sing Western classics like "Cool Water" and "Tumbling Tumbleweeds" made famous in the 1930s by the Sons of the Pioneers.

"We just loved their songs," Joe recalled. "They were of the outdoors. They were of cowboys."

"We were inundated in our home with music," Jack said. "Our mother was a fine pianist. We learned to harmonize singing in church. And we were always in church. We'd drive fifteen miles into town to go to church. We'd sing to and from church. We'd sing in the truck. We'd sing driving the horses. We'd sing working on the ranch. Singing was just a way of life for our family."

The songfests led to the creation of the Sons of the San Joaquin in 1989 and the blending of two great American traditions.

"It was baseball and cowboys," Jack said of their childhood. "And there's a great parallel there."

The Hannah brothers were inspired by the famous baseball players and cowboys of their time—from Bob Feller and brothers Mort and Walker Cooper in baseball to cowboys such as Roy Rogers and the Lone Ranger.

"It had to do with a way of life and the character that was built in me through playing the game and mimicking these guys, impersonating them," added Jack.

"The physical skills that are needed to be a good cowboy are amazing. The sixth sense in handling a horse is the same thing as knowing how to run the bases. Baseball is a game that happens instantly. You're out there on the field and there's a myriad of things that can take place at an instant. The same is true in cowboying."

The mystique that surrounded the cowboy also permeated baseball for the Hannah boys.

"There was something in it that called up courage, challenge and focus on the thrill of competition," said Jack. "Money was a secondary thing, even though a mature person realized that you had to make a living. But it was not an obsession. General [Douglas] MacArthur said in his last speech, 'It's The Corps, and The Corps, and The Corps.' It was the same in baseball then. It was The Game, and The Game, and The Game."

"Did you know that Joe was an All-America football player in high school?" asked Jack. "Joe was an awesome football player. He could've played college football anywhere he wanted—USC, Notre Dame, UCLA. If he'd played for USC, he would've never played baseball. He would've been a pro football player. He'll never say it. Joe is extremely humble."

All Joe will say is "I was supposed to have been a very good football player."

"Dad was a provincial man," explained Jack. "He had a seventh grade education. He always wanted us to be good boys and major league ball players. Getting Joe into professional baseball—the first Hannah—was very important to Dad. I don't think Dad assessed the significance of a formal education simply because it was not within the scope of his experience. He saw Joe and me, even with a high school education, as having a far better education than he did."

Joe was eighteen and a new high school graduate when the Angels, then in the Pacific Coast League, signed him in 1950.

Before Joe signed the contract, his father told Jack Fournier, the Angels scout, "I want you to look at Joe's hand."

Fournier looked at the index finger on Joe's right throwing hand. The tip was missing—blown off by a plastic dynamite cap when Joe was eleven years old. "Damn, does the ball sail when you throw it?"

Joe was a pitcher before he started catching. Any questions about the velocity and accuracy of his throws were answered when he appeared in two games for the Angels near the end of the 1950 season. "You won't find it in the box scores but I threw out two of the league's fastest runners trying to steal second."

After standout years at Janesville, Wisconsin, in 1951, and Topeka, Kansas, in 1952, Joe went into the military for two years. He returned to L.A. late in the 1954 season, hitting .286 in seven games and earning a shot with the Chicago Cubs.

Going into spring training in 1955, Cubs manager Stan Hack compared Joe with Harry Chiti, another highly regarded prospect. "I have talked to a number of people who saw him catch in the Army and they tell me it won't be Chiti who will be our number one catcher, but Hannah. They say he's ready for the majors."[1]

Despite an impressive spring showing, Joe was sent to L.A. and then Macon, Georgia, in the South Atlantic (Sally) League.

The manager at Macon was the colorful Pepper Martin, a big country music fan. One of the pitchers, Ottis "Jake" Jacobs, played the guitar and teamed with Joe to sing Hank Williams's tunes between Sunday doubleheader games at home. "We didn't have a real good ball club," Jake said. "But we kept the fans well entertained."

On bus trips to Charlotte, Jacksonville, and other Sally League cities, Joe and Jake sang while Pepper accompanied them on the harmonica he took wherever he went. "It was an old school bus," Jake noted. "You could hardly hear it was rattling so badly."

The ballpark in Montgomery, Alabama, was next to the cemetery where Williams, a country music icon, is buried. "It was right behind the left-field fence," Jake added. "We'd go there after night games and sit on a bench and sing all the songs carved on his monument."

Joe appeared in eighty-seven games at Macon, batting .264. "Joe was a good catcher," explained Jake. "He called a good ballgame."

Spring training with the Cubs in 1956 was a rerun of the year before with the same result. Joe wound up in L.A. with Jim Fanning, a veteran catcher who spent much of the 1955 season with the Angels.

Joe's batting average ranked among the top ten in the league during the first month of the 1956 season. He was hitting .362 after two weeks, .322 after three, and .316 after four. He was still hitting around .300 and doing a solid job defensively when Elvin Tappe arrived from Chicago in late May and immediately replaced Joe in the lineup.

"It came as a jolt to me because I was one of these guys that had this impression that a person had to win his job," Joe said. "Don't get me wrong. I was never angry about it. But I was hurt. I was doing well. The pitchers were pitching good to me. The team was winning. And all of a sudden, I'm playing the second game of doubleheaders. I really was brokenhearted."

Joe didn't show his disappointment.

"I can picture him now," said Adams. "Every time you looked at him, he was grinning. He saw the humor in everything. You couldn't find a better guy for the role he played."

Tappe was a familiar face in L.A., playing for the Angels from 1953 to 1955. One of the first things Bob Scheffing did on becoming manager of the Angels in 1955 was to arrange for Tappe to join him. "He really knows how to handle the pitchers," Scheffing said.[2]

Tappe batted an anemic .121 but received a lot of the credit for the Angels late-season drive from the second division to a third-place tie.

Elvin celebrated his return to the Angels with a three-run homer that got L.A. started on a nine-game winning streak. He went on to surprise everyone by hitting .267. That was well above his lifetime average of .216 coming into the season. And Elvin's three home runs were just two shy of his output over nine previous years in pro ball.

Behind the plate, Tappe was the maestro that Scheffing, a former catcher, expected him to be.

"For us younger pitchers, Elvin really took on the role of a coach," said Bob Anderson, the Angels' twenty-year-old stopper. "He knew our strong points, our weak points and where we needed help."

"Elvin was very astute catching," explained Ray "Moe" Bauer, the Angels' left-handed relief specialist. "He didn't like you to shake him off."

Bauer recalled the time Scheffing complained to Tappe about how he called a game.

"The game was called all right," Tappe objected. "Why don't you call the next game?"

"That's what we're going to do," Scheffing agreed.

"It's a nip-and-tuck game," Bauer continued. "The bases are loaded with two outs. The count goes to three-and-two. Elvin looks over for the sign. Scheffing spreads open his hands as if to say, 'You call it.' Elvin called the pitch."

After the game, Tappe told Bauer, "He's never going to do that to me again."

"Elvin knew his limitations," added Bauer. "He was a good, smart catcher. And he was a baseball man."

According to conditioning tests conducted for the Cubs by a University of Illinois doctor, Tappe's "reflexes were below normal, his muscles were somewhat too dense and his hand strength not adequate."[3]

Tappe did not have a particularly strong throwing arm, but he had a quick release and was extremely accurate.

"His mechanics as a catcher were super," said Fanning, who was shipped out to make room for Tappe.

Joe wound up playing in ninety-three of the Angels' 168 games, batting .272 with one home run and thirty-three RBIs.

"Joe was a fantastic catcher," said Gene Fodge, another Angels pitcher. "If I had a choice of who I wanted to throw to, it was Joe. We were on the same track. Tappe probably was right ninety-nine percent of the time but there were a lot of times we didn't think alike. I just wish Joe had gone farther than what he did. But baseball is baseball."

And in the 1950s, baseball players had two choices: go where the management of their teams told them, or quit.

"When I was playing in Los Angeles, I was not a major league ball player," Joe said. "However, there were major league ball players—catchers—that were not as good as me."

Joe was on the Cubs winter roster for the 1957 season but not for long. He was sent back to the Angels who, in turn, shipped him to Memphis. He split the season between Memphis and Fort Worth. By year end, Havana purchased his contract and then sold it to the Toronto Maple Leafs in the International League.

Joe played for Toronto all or parts of the next four seasons. In 1962, he joined the Hawaii Islanders in the PCL.

At Hawaii, Joe was reunited with Eddie Haas, a talented young out-fielder for the 1956 Angels. On the very same day Joe was relegated to the Angels bench in favor of Tappe, Eddie was replaced by Gale Wade and sent to the lower minors despite a respectable .275 batting average.

"I never hit with power," Joe lamented, "and I should have. I was so strong. I fisted a lot of balls. I didn't hit the ball on the sweet spot. Man, I was almost in tears. Here I was thirty years old and my big dream was to be a major leaguer."

Joe told Eddie, "The ball doesn't fool me. I think I'm going to hit the ball and it ends up on my fist."

"Get your front arm out straight when you start your swing," Eddie suggested. "That makes the head of the bat come around faster and you'll get out in front of the ball."

"That made all the difference," Joe said. "I could hit the inside pitch much better. I started hitting balls on the sweet spot. I ended up having the best year of my career."

Playing in ninety-six games, he batted .298 with eight home runs and fifty-six RBIs.

"When I hit .298 in Hawaii, I knew I could hit in the big leagues. I always wanted to call Gene Mauch and tell him, 'I can hit now.' I've fantasized talking with Gene about that."

Joe reflected on 1956 and his backup role to Tappe.

"Elvin Tappe was the right decision for our team to handle our young pitching staff. He was more experienced and better. I learned a lot from him that helped me in my later playing days. Pitchers loved to pitch to me and I have to give a good deal of credit to Tappe."

Joe began 1963 with Toronto, a Class AAA team, and mid-season, was back in Hawaii where he appeared in ten games, batting .323. He finished the year, and his career, in Class A, hitting .306 for San Jose in the Califor-nia League.

"I didn't hit all that well except the last two years, and nobody re-members it except me," Joe said. "Baseball was a great disappointment, but I loved it. I never felt I got shafted. If I had worked harder and listened to others, I would've learned how to hit and made it to the major leagues. All I ever wanted to do was play in the major leagues."

"You play the game to make the major leagues."

That sums up the feelings of Joe Hannah and all the others who have played pro baseball. For every player who makes it to the majors, there are thousands who can only dream about it.

"Look at the Baseball Encyclopedia," said Russ Kemmerer, a former major league pitcher, referring to a book that lists all of the players who have appeared in the big leagues. "There is about what, 13,000 names listed in there? Heck, you could find that many lawyers in the phone book."

With both the Cubs and the Angels, Joe's primary competitors were Tappe and Fanning.

"Joe had more potential than either one of us because he could hit better and had power," Fanning observed. "Tappe was a very fine defensive catcher but he didn't run or hit very well. We were a lot alike."

In sixty-four games with the Cubs from 1954 to 1957, Fanning totaled only twenty-four hits for a .170 average. Tappe's cumulative 145-game record over six seasons shows a mere sixty-three hits, a .207 average. Neither of them hit a home run in the majors.

What distinguished Fanning and Tappe from others was their almost professorial knowledge of the game, especially catching.

When Tappe joined the Angels in 1956, he was twenty-nine and in his tenth year of pro ball. Fanning was twenty-eight and in his seventh year. Both had already logged time in the majors and would return as players before getting into baseball management.

Fanning wrote his master's degree thesis at the University of Illinois titled *A Cinemagraphic Study of the Catcher's Throw*, which compared three professional catchers, including Fanning and Tappe, with three college catchers. "We took very meticulous movies of everything we did in catching and throwing a ball to second base—the position of our hands and our feet," Fanning said. "I found out a whole bunch of stuff I never knew."

In 1960, Tappe wrote an instructional manual for all positions called, *The Cubs Method of Play*.

"It was a thick book," recalled Anderson, a Cubs pitcher at the time. "There wasn't anything different in the manual than what every player should know anyway."

In presenting the manual to Cubs owner P. K. Wrigley, Tappe proposed rotating coaches in the Cubs' minor league system.

"The mistake was when Mr. Wrigley rotated the managers," Tappe acknowledged later. "I just wanted to rotate the coaches. I wanted to get coaches, hitting and pitching instructors, to coach our players in the minor leagues and major leagues. Everybody is doing that now."[4]

When Wrigley proposed rotating managers, Tappe warned Wrigley, "All you're going to do is present an alibi for the players."[5]

One critic scoffed: "The Cubs have been playing without players for years. Now, they're going to try it without a manager."[6]

During the two years the head coaching system was used, Tappe served four terms, three in 1961 and one in 1962. The Cubs were a combined 46–70 under his leadership. Altogether, there were five head coaches. In 1961 the Cubs placed seventh with a 64–90 record and the next year, after the National League expanded to ten teams, they lost 103 games and finished ninth.

"We all felt we were under a microscope and what people were seeing was not very exciting," Anderson said. "It just added an additional psychological burden to the ball club."

Of the head coaches, Tappe was the most popular and respected among the players. He was still catching in 1962, the last year for the scheme.

"Elvin was more one of the players than anything else," Anderson explained. "We had a lot of respect for him as a catcher. He was trying to do a decent job. There were some of them that you hoped they knew what the hell they were talking about. But there was always that big question mark."

Fanning became a player-manager in the minors at the end of his catching career, and then moved into the front office as a special assignment scout for the Milwaukee Braves.

This led to Jim establishing a centralized scouting bureau for baseball—the forerunner to the system that serves the majors today.

The purpose of the program, he said, was "to provide more information on players we do not know enough about."[7]

Fanning left the scouting bureau to become general manager of the Montreal Expos, an expansion team that joined the National League in 1969. He immediately picked Gene Mauch to be the Expos' first manager.

"I flew out to Los Angeles, met him at the airport and we made our deal."

Jim remembered their playing days together with the Angels and how much Scheffing relied on Mauch. "I had a lot of admiration for Gene. He was a great aid to Bob."

Fanning recalled looking at some of the Angels' players and thinking, "How come they aren't in the major leagues?"

Mauch was one of those players.

"Gene knew everything. He had the greatest retentive memory of anybody I have ever been around—anybody. He never took a note. He never forgot anything. He would say to me in the early years of the Expos, 'You remember so-and-so? He played for San Francisco.' Heck, I couldn't remember the name. That's the way he was. He would remind me what happened last year in a game. I mean his memory was unbelievable."

Mauch managed the Expos for seven years, creating a solid foundation that Fanning continued to build on with a farm system that produced Hall of Famers Gary Carter and Andre Dawson, as well as Tim Raines, a seven-time all-star outfielder.

With three weeks left in the strike-shortened 1981 season, Jim replaced Dick Williams as manager and guided the Expos into the playoffs—the only time in the franchise's thirty-six-year history. The Expos beat the Philadelphia Phillies in a division series before losing the fifth and deciding game of the National League championship series to the Los Angeles Dodgers on a ninth-inning home run.

Fanning managed the Expos to an 86–76 record in 1982, but a disappointing third-place finish in the National League East prompted him to resign and go back to his first love of developing players in the Expos farm system.

"Jim Fanning treated us like men," said the Expos' Al Oliver, the National League's 1982 batting champion. "He had every opportunity in the world to knock us. It's not often that you will find a manager who will totally protect his players."[8]

Meanwhile, Hannah, the only one of the three 1956 Angels catchers who didn't make it to the majors, was shaping the lives of junior high students as a teacher-coach in Visalia.

After leaving baseball, Joe taught music, history, and physical education and coached baseball and football for twenty-one years.

In his choral music class, he focused on helping young boys overcome their fear of singing. On one occasion, a boy told Joe that he was being called a sissy because he sang in the choral group.

"The next time someone makes fun of you for singing, poke 'em in the mouth," Joe advised.

"Do you really mean that, Mr. Hannah?"

"Sure, I mean it."

Of course, Joe didn't want the boy hitting anybody. But his words served their purpose. The boy felt he had the backing and encouragement to continue singing. Nobody was going to call him a sissy and get away with it.

The Hannah brothers had just received a humanitarian award honoring their contributions to society as well as their baseball achievements.

The event was the 2001 Texas Wesleyan University baseball banquet at the Will Rogers Memorial Center in Fort Worth, Texas.

Rich "Goose" Gossage, the Hall of Fame pitcher, was a special guest. "The innocence of the game is gone," Goose said. "A lot of guys are playing for the money and they are playing for the wrong reason."

Rafael Palmeiro, a star for the Texas Rangers at the time, was in the audience. So was Jim Gentile, a slugging first baseman for the Baltimore Orioles in the 1960s, and Bobby Bragan, former manager of the Pittsburgh Pirates (1956–1957), the Cleveland Indians (1958), and the Milwaukee/Atlanta Braves (1963–1966).

The alleged steroid usage scandal had yet to tarnish the image of Palmeiro and the Cubs' Sammy Sosa.

Two of Palmeiro's Rangers jerseys sold for $2,000 apiece at an auction to fund the Texas Wesleyan baseball program. A bat autographed by Sosa sold for $1,000. A jersey worn by Gossage when he pitched for the New York Yankees sold for $1,000. A Brooks Robinson autographed print of a painting that artist Norman Rockwell did of the Hall of Fame third baseman sold for $900.

"Cowboys and baseball are two of America's most colorful and storied traditions," Bragan said in presenting the award to Joe and Jack. "So when we encounter someone who has made significant contributions to both traditions as well as the education of our sons and daughters, they deserve to be recognized."

Bragan told about the game Jack pitched eighteen innings, allowing only three hits—one in the first nine innings and two in the last nine.

"How good was Jack?" Bragan asked.

He described a dinner in Fresno, California, when Joe Gordon, the flashy second baseman for the Yankees and Cleveland Indians, called Jack one of the two hardest throwing pitchers he had ever faced. The other was Bob Feller, the great Indians pitcher often referred to as Rapid Robert.

Bragan ticked off the accomplishments of the Hannah brothers in education and music.

Jack was a high school counselor and coach for thirty years in Fresno. In 1980 he was named Baseball Coach of the Year for the Western region of the United States. He is a member of the Fresno State University Baseball Hall of Fame and the City of Fresno Hall of Fame.

Eight times the Western Music Association has named the Sons of the San Joaquin as the best traditional group. Jack has been honored as the best songwriter in the cowboy music category six times.

"For Joe and Jack," Bragan said, "a cowboy song is more than just a song. It's also an entertaining way of educating people about cowboys and their important role in the history of the American West. Jack is committing the rest of his life to writing books that help children develop character and an academic mindset early in life."

After the banquet in the lobby bar of the Hotel Worthington in downtown Fort Worth, Goose said he liked to sing in the shower. "We dream of being musicians and you all dream of being baseball players."

Everybody laughed.

Jack is as good a storyteller as he is a songwriter.

On seeing Jack pitch in high school, the Baltimore Orioles arranged for him to meet their manager, Paul Richards, and pitching coach, Harry "The Cat" Brecheen. Richards, a catcher in his playing days, was considered a shrewd judge of pitching talent.

"Now, son, what do you weigh?" Richards asked.

"About 212 pounds," Jack replied.

"Are you six-foot-one?"

"Yeah, I'm about six-one."

"Throw hard?"

"Yeah, I do."

"I'm going to watch you throw today. Get ready to go."

Richards left the room, leaving Jack alone with Brecheen, sitting in a nearby chair.

"Do you chew?" Brecheen asked.

"No, sir."

"Hell, you ain't goin' to make the majors."

Joe had a chewing tobacco story of his own.

At Macon in 1955, Joe shared catching duties with Verlon "Rube" Walker.

"Another player was bumming chew off of him," Joe began. "And, of course, ol' Rube was generous. He'd let him have a chaw. The guy would come up and Rube would feel this hand in his pocket. He'd pull it out and get him a wad, fold it up and put it back in Rube's pocket.

"He got tired of it so one time he got a bunch of new tobacco, opened it up, spit in it and kneaded it around. He made sure the guy was watching him. He spit in it again and kneaded it around some more.

"What the hell are you doing?" the guy asked.

"Oh, I do this all the time," Rube said.

"The guy never bummed another chew off Rube again."

"Who was the guy, Joe," Jack asked, "who liked to mimic Hank Williams?"

"Jake Jacobs."

Joe picked up on the story.

> When he joined the Macon team, he didn't have any luggage. Supposedly, it was lost on the bus. He roomed with Rube Walker. Jake said, "Rube, my luggage hasn't come. Can I borrow some of your clothes?" He borrowed shorts, t-shirts, everything.
>
> One day Rube wakes up and sees Jake wearing his suit out the door. Well, they had this swimming hole down where the river was dammed up. Everybody from Macon would go there and swim. So Jake decides to go swimming. Rube walks up and Jake just dives in the water with his suit on.

Joe mentioned Pepper Martin, the Macon manager who always wanted Jake and Joe to sing for fans between games of doubleheaders. Jack and Pepper crossed paths when the younger Hannah pitched for Austin in the Texas League.

"He really thought the world of you," Jack said.

"Is that right?"

"He told me flat out: 'Joe is one of the best catchers I've ever seen.'"

"He thought I was a good catcher?"

Louis "Satchmo" Armstrong, the legendary jazz musician, said, "There ain't but two kinds of music in this world: good music and bad music. And good music, you tap your feet to."

The folks at Smith Family Theatre in Pigeon Forge tapped their feet as the Sons of the San Joaquin sang "There's a Rainbow over the Range" and "Charlie and the Boys."

"The cowboy was a cowboy," Jack likes to remind people. "He wasn't a gunslinger. Hollywood has developed a myth about the cowboy and they put a gun on his hip. The cowboy didn't carry a gun on his hip. He carried it in a saddlebag."

About halfway through one show, Jack reminded folks, "Nobody has ever committed suicide after one of our concerts."

"It's uplifting music," he explained. "It's music about challenge. It's music about the beauty of the West, how it's a magnet that draws the human heart to its challenges."

The Pigeon Forge crowd was enjoying a musical trip back to a simpler time. The Sons were rebounding from the death of Kay Hannah, Joe's wife of fifty-one years, and a serious neck injury that sidelined Lonnie most of the previous year.

Joe began,

> Well, folks, this next song, we changed the words a little bit, You might notice it if you know this song, "Happy Cowboy."
>
> I've got a friend sitting in the audience who realized that when I was singing this song a lot, I said, "I ain't got a wife to bother my life, I'm just a happy roving cowboy."
>
> He called me up one time and said, "Joe, you know, with Kay like she is with cancer and not expected to live much longer, don't you think you ought to quit singing that?"
>
> I said, "Well, Steve, it's just a song. Heck, I ain't even a cowboy. I mean, not a real one anyway."
>
> He said, "Well, you ought to think about that."
>
> Well, I did think about it, I said, Honey, does that bother you when I sing, "I ain't got a wife to bother my life?"
>
> She said, "Well, no, I guess not."
>
> Well, I sang it one more time and I couldn't stand it.
>
> I said, "Jack, I can't sing that song anymore."
>
> And one day he came up with different words: I don't have the strife of big city life.

After the concert, Joe said to a friend, "I like the new words better, don't you?"

NOTES

1. *The Sporting News*, January 12, 1955, 11.
2. *Los Angeles Times*, July 17, 1955, B6.
3. *The Sporting News*, May 11, 1955, 10.
4. *Sports Collectors Digest*, January 8, 1993, 164.
5. John C. Skipper, *Take Me Out to the Cubs Game: 35 Former Ballplayers Speak of Losing at Wrigley* (Jefferson, NC: McFarland & Company, Inc., 2000), 116.

6. Golenbock, *Wrigleyville: A Magical History Tour of the Chicago Cubs* (New York City: St. Martin's Griffin), 366.

7. *The Sporting News*, February 17, 1968, 23.

8. *The Sporting News*, October 18, 1982, 30.

ELEVEN

No Room at the Top

"Most people would give their right arm to play one day in the major leagues." —Russ Kemmerer, pitcher, San Francisco Seals, 1956

Gene Mauch had just played his last game for the Angels, getting three hits to beat the Hollywood Stars. There were five games left on the schedule but a few days earlier the Boston Red Sox purchased his contract from Los Angeles and he was headed for the majors.

Lorenzo "Piper" Davis, the Angels' thirty-nine-year-old super-sub and the only African American on the team, sidled up to Gene in the team's Wrigley Field clubhouse as he was packing his baseball gear. Piper handed Gene his infielder's mitt.

"Take that glove with you," Piper said. "That's the only way it's getting to the big leagues."[1]

Piper never made it to the majors despite an outstanding career in the Negro Leagues and "white folks' ball"—the term he used to describe the segregation in pro baseball that existed until 1946 when Jackie Robinson broke the color barrier with the Montreal Royals of the International League. Robinson made history in the majors with the Brooklyn Dodgers the next year.

Bob Coats, the Angels' reserve outfielder who hit .312 over nine minor league seasons, didn't make it to the big leagues either. And neither did Raymond "Moe" Bauer, the left-handed relief pitcher who teamed with Bob Anderson to give the Angels the best bullpen in the league.

All three players had excellent years in 1956.

Piper appeared in sixty-four games, batting .316. As a pinch-hitter, his thirteen hits in twenty-nine at bats for a .448 average led the league. He played every position in the field except shortstop, centerfield, and pitcher.

Coats also hit .316, getting seventy-five hits in 237 at bats as a backup outfielder and pinch-hitter. Of his twenty-nine runs batted in, ten were by pinch hits.

Bauer appeared in forty-nine games, all in relief, posting a 6-1 won-loss record and 3.16 ERA.

Mauch likened the six-foot-three-inch, 188-pound Piper to George Hendrick, a similarly built outfielder who hit 267 homers in the majors during the 1970s and 1980s. "With a bat, he was just like George Hendrick. The day didn't come that they could throw a fastball that Piper couldn't get around on."

Two of Piper's home runs in 1956 came as a pinch-hitter.

"Oh, man, he could crank up on a fastball," recalled Gene Fodge. "He was strong—even at 38, 39, whatever he was at that time."

Piper's contributions as a player went far beyond what he did with a bat.

"Piper Davis was the most consummate professional player that I ever played with," said Mauch. "I'm not saying that he was the best player. Hell, I played with Ted Williams, Stan Musial—a bunch of great players. I'm talking about consummate professionalism. He said all the right things at the right time. He was very, very astute."

"The biggest catalyst on the ball club was Piper Davis," said Bob Speake. "He spent most of his time in the bullpen, warming up the pitchers. He helped the young pitchers, sharing all of his wisdom gathered when he was in the Negro Leagues."

Piper played seven years in the Negro Leagues (1942–1948), mostly for the Birmingham Black Barons. "In 1944 Artie Wilson at shortstop and Piper Davis at second base made up an all-star combination that was hard to beat anywhere in baseball," said Monte Irvin, a Negro League star who went on to play for the New York Giants and be elected to the Baseball Hall of Fame.

"We made plays and people would say, 'Gee, how in the world did you get over there?'" Artie said. "Well, we knew what was going on."

In 1948 Piper was player-manager of the Black Barons, guiding the team to the Negro American League title.

"Piper had everything," said Rev. Bill Greason, a pitcher who later became a Baptist minister. "Good ball player. Good manager. He could have managed in the major leagues. He had all the savvy. He was smart. He knew the game."

Piper was a second father to another Black Barons player, a sixteen-year-old named Willie Mays. "In so many ways Piper was the most important person in my early baseball years," the legendary centerfielder wrote in his autobiography, *Say Hey.* "I learned one thing about him very quickly. He told you something only once, and he expected you to go on from there."[2]

"He was what we would call fun but serious," added Greason.

"I remember one game I was pitching. It was a close game. Somebody hit the ball to third baseman Johnny Britton and it went through his legs. The next two pitches I didn't throw very hard.

"Piper stormed in from second base and jumped all over me: 'Do you throw strikes every time?'

"I said, 'I try.'

"He said, 'What do you think he was doing?'

"I used to be kind of hot-headed. That turned me completely around. I was able to recognize that we all try. We all fail sometimes."

Just prior to the start of the 1956 season, the twenty-six-year-old Coats was described as "a terrific spring hitter" by Angels manager Bob Scheffing.[3]

The "spring hitter" label was typical of managers failing to give Coats the credit he deserved. The Angels' 1956 yearbook said as much: "On three different clubs he was the first rookie the manager wanted to send away but each time he remained and the telling effects of his bat made the managers glad they changed their minds after those first impressions. Perhaps the glasses he wears fooled 'em."[4]

The six-foot, 180-pound Coats didn't wear glasses his first two years in pro baseball when he hit .352 for Elizabethton, Tennessee, and .317 for Sioux Falls, Iowa. "One night in Sioux Falls two balls in a row dropped within twenty feet of me in the outfield."

He was wearing glasses in 1950 when he played for the Grand Rapids Jets in the Class A Central League. Dubbing him "the Jets' John Doe," the *Grand Rapids Herald* reported, "Coats is a study in white when it comes to color. Quiet, modest, and soft-spoken, he is the Lou Gehrig and George Kell type when it comes to personal mannerisms."[5]

"I was not a colorful ball player," said Coats. "I had been raised to believe that if you're good, you don't have to tell people. They'll know it."

Coats hit .314 for Grand Rapids, but a contract dispute forced him to sit out the 1951 season. He returned to the Cubs' farm system in 1952 to bat a combined .271 for Topeka and Des Moines.

In 1953 he won the Three I League batting title with a .327 average for Cedar Rapids, Iowa. The following year at Macon, Georgia, of the Sally League, he batted .310 and ranked second in the circuit in hits and runs scored. He joined the Angels in 1955, playing in 122 games batting .276 with two home runs.

"I was a singles hitter, had speed and played decent outfield," said Coats.

After a game against the Oakland Oaks early in the 1955 season, Coats was on a bus, waiting to go to the team's hotel. Piper, playing for the Oaks at the time, spotted Coats, sitting next to an open window.

"You're another Artie Wilson," Piper said.

"He grinned and walked away," Coats said. "I didn't know who Artie Wilson was."

Most of Coats' hits were to the opposite field—just like Wilson, another left-handed hitter. Artie won the Pacific Coast League (PCL) batting title in 1949 without hitting a home run.

"I always classified Artie as the greatest singles hitter," Piper said.

L.A. pitcher Dwight "Red" Adams called Coats "The Little Professor."

"He'd wear those glasses and looked like a guy working in the post office or maybe the principal at the high school. He was one of those quiet, easy-going guys that would go out there and hang a rope every chance he got to hit."

"Bob was a very patient utility guy and, on most clubs, he could've been a starter," Speake said.

"Coats slapped that ball around," explained Casey Wise, the Angels' shortstop. "Speake, Bolger and Wade were so much stronger and could hit the ball harder. They were a threat to hit the ball out of the ballpark at any time."

When Speake arrived in L.A. the second week of the season, Coats was out of the starting lineup and on the bench.

The six-foot-three-inch, 165-pound Bauer was a relief specialist long before they were common in baseball.

The most innings he pitched in any one season was 168 at Des Moines in 1954, where he had a 12–10 record. With the Angels in 1955, he appeared in thirty-four games, pitching forty-two innings and posting a 3–3 won-loss record and excellent 3.00 ERA.

Moe turned twenty-eight midway during the 1956 season and was well on his way toward earning master's and doctorate degrees in education from the University of North Carolina in Chapel Hill.

He already had a bachelor's degree from Wake Forest University where he graduated in 1950, compiling a 19–1 record his last two years.

As a junior in 1949, he pitched the Demon Deacons to a second-place finish behind the University of Texas in the College World Series. In 1950, Moe was 11–0, pitching thirty-five consecutive scoreless innings at one point. "I went about sixty innings without walking a batter," Moe said.

For his accomplishments, Bauer was selected the most outstanding athlete at Wake Forest along with golf great, Arnold Palmer.

"Basically, I was a curveball pitcher," Moe said. "Control was the thing I had. If I didn't have it that day, it was Katy bar the door!"

Katy didn't have anything to worry about as Moe walked only twenty-five in eighty innings pitched in 1956.

"We were kind of a one-two punch," Anderson said. "Moe was the left hander, I was the right hander. I got in more ballgames than Moe but he sure got in his share. When he got in there, we did well. And when I got in there, we did well."

Anderson and Bauer were one-two on the Angels in appearances (seventy and forty-nine, respectively) and earned run average (2.63 and 3.16). They combined to win eighteen games while losing only five.

"Ol' Moe," mused Adams, "he pitched in the big leagues some, didn't he?"

Adams was surprised to learn Moe never made it to the majors. "Never at all? That's too bad. That sonofagun could be tough on those left-handers. He was a guy who maybe wouldn't pop your eyes as far as being overpowering but he'd get you out. I thought that he'd get a shot up there."

Angels manager Bob Scheffing was overheard as saying, "With that curveball, he can help somebody up there."

But Moe wasn't among the nine Angels players Scheffing took with him to Chicago in 1957.

"The closest I came was at the end of the 1957 season," Moe said. "The Cubs were going to bring me up to finish the year. The night before we were to play our last game, they sent word that they had filled their roster and wouldn't have me report. But I'd go to spring training the next year. That didn't come to pass either."

Moe paused and then finished the thought.

"I wished I'd had a cup of coffee around the league. I really do."

Piper Davis is a legend in Birmingham, Alabama. He is best remembered as Mr. Birmingham Black Baron in recognition of his contributions to one of the Negro Leagues' perennial powerhouses.

In December 1999 he was selected one of Alabama's Fifty Greatest Sports Performers of the Century along with some of the greatest athletes of our times—Jesse Owens, Joe Louis, Bo Jackson, Joe Namath, Kenny Stabler, Charles Barkley, Henry Aaron, Satchel Paige, Willie McCovey, and Willie Mays.

Displays at the Birmingham Civil Rights Institute and the Alabama Sports Hall of Fame pay tribute to Piper. He was inducted into the Hall of Fame in 1993. Birmingham's Piper Davis Youth Baseball League is named in his honor.

When Piper died in 1997, the *Birmingham News* reported that the seventy-nine-year-old Davis "came along too late for the major leagues, but just in time to become one of Birmingham's most respected names in baseball."[6]

Some of the Angels' veterans, such as Mauch and Adams, knew of his exploits in the Negro Leagues and with Oakland in the PCL prior to joining the Angels late in the 1955 season. A few players heard Piper talk about playing basketball for the Harlem Globetrotters but most of them had no inkling a legend was in their midst.

"To talk to him, you'd never know it," said Fodge. "He never talked much about himself."

That's unfortunate because as Piper's daughter, Faye, puts it: "My daddy had a thousand and one stories."

There's the story about how he was named "Piper Colina" after two coalmines near his home in Piper, Alabama. The nickname was later shortened to Piper.

There's the story about how Piper was about to sign a Black Barons contract when Abe Saperstein, owner of the Harlem Globetrotters, discovered he could also play basketball.

"I've got the pen in my hand to sign for a certain figure, $350 or something like that."

Bob Williams, owner of the Savoy Café in Birmingham, went to the table where Piper was sitting with then Black Barons manager Winfield Welch.

"Welch, that boy can play basketball, too."

"What?"

"Yeah, that's my best player."

"You play basketball?" Welch asked Piper.

"Yeah, I played one year in college."

Welch left the table to call Saperstein. "Abe, this boy can play basketball, too. Bob says he's his best player"

"Give him another sixty-five dollars a month," Abe replied, "and tell him he's got to try out for the Globetrotters."[7]

Piper played for the Globetrotters from 1943 to 1946 and then coached the court wizards, participating in their worldwide tour of 1960–1961.

There's the story of Piper informing the mostly veteran players on the 1948 Black Barons that a sixteen-year-old kid was starting in centerfield.

"Here's the lineup today, men. Willie Mays is playing in centerfield."

"What the hell is wrong with Piper?" one of the players complained. "He's gone crazy puttin' that damn little ol' boy out there in centerfield."

"Anybody that don't like it, you know what you can do," Piper shot back.[8]

And there are the stories about Piper and Artie Wilson, possibly the best double-play combination in the history of baseball.

They played together for nine years—four with the American Cast Iron Pipe Company (ACIPCO) in the Birmingham industrial league and five more with the Black Barons.

As a shortstop, Piper said Artie "was right at the top—him and Jackie Robinson. He was at the top all the way in hitting."

At ACIPCO, Piper and Artie would take the field early to catch short hops between their legs. "We'd get calls from the fans: 'Okay, Piper and Artie, put it on now. Let's have some fun.'"

Everywhere they played, fans were wowed with their double-play artistry.

After playing in a Negro League all-star game in Chicago, Piper and Artie were late for a Black Barons game in Chattanooga. When they arrived, the game was delayed to give them time to put on their uniforms. "The people came to see us play," Piper explained. "We dressed, threw a couple of balls and said, 'We're ready to go.'"

In the second inning a ball was hit to Artie behind second base. "If the ball was hit that way, one of us was to say right away if he could get it. There were never two of us in short right field or short left field."

Artie's nickname for Piper was "High"—short for "Highpocket" because he was so tall.

"I got it, High," he said.

"I went to the bag. I was hanging onto the back of the bag. He caught it, flipped it to me and we got a double play."

The public address announcer exclaimed, "That was worth waiting for, folks."

"Willie Mays, he played for the fans," Piper said. "Artie played for the fans."

Piper elaborated in a *Southern Exposure* magazine interview with Theodore Rosengarten in 1977, "The Negro ball player gave big league baseball the unexpected—daring. Because we loved the game, and we played more for the fans than for ourselves because there wasn't much money involved in Negro ball."

Baseball needed black players to attract new, black fans.

"Do you know what the quota was?" Piper asked. "The quota at first was three. It wasn't a written thing, but just among the owners, they said, 'We'll have about three of 'em.'"[9]

There may not have been a written quota but there's a scouting report in the files at the Hall of Fame in Cooperstown, New York, that helps explain why Piper didn't get a chance to play in the majors.

The author is not identified, but he's clearly with the New York Yankees.

The typed document begins

> Davis is thirty-two, they tell me, and Wilson is about the same age. They are both good ball players. The St. Louis Browns scouted Davis in 1946, took option on him. If he wasn't good enough for the Browns two years ago I don't believe he could make it with the Yankees now.
>
> There isn't an outstanding Negro player that anybody could recommend to step into the big league and hold down a regular job. The better players in Negro baseball are past the age for the big leagues.
>
> I am aware of how these committees apply the pressure on the big leagues to hire one or perhaps two players. If you hire one or two, then, they will want you to hire another one. There will be no compromise with them and they are mostly bluff.[10]

The Browns actually signed Piper in July 1947 along with two other Negro League players, Hank Thompson, a third baseman, and Willard Brown, an outfielder. Recent research has turned up evidence that a fourth player, Chuck Harmon, was signed, although it was not reported widely.

"We hope and trust that the action of the Browns' organization in signing players Willard Brown and Henry Thompson and the option to buy Lorenzo Davis is a sincere effort to bolster the ball club," wrote the *St. Louis Globe-Democrat.*[11]

At the request of the Browns, Piper played first base for the Black Barons during a thirty-day option period so one of their scouts could evaluate him at that position. When the Browns asked Piper to play in the minors and go to spring training with them the following year, he opted to stay with the Black Barons.

Thompson appeared in twenty-seven games and Brown twenty-one before the Browns returned them to the Kansas City Monarchs in the Negro Leagues.

The Red Sox made a deal for Piper in 1950, paying Black Barons owner Tom Hayes $7,500 for the opportunity to look at him, and promised to double that amount if he were signed to a major-league contract.

Piper was sent to Scranton, Pennsylvania, Boston's Class A affiliate in the Eastern League. "If he makes good, I'm going to waste no time in moving him to Boston," declared Red Sox general manager Joe Cronin.[12]

At the end of the 1949 season, Tom Baird, president of the Kansas City Monarchs of the Negro American League, wrote Lee MacPhail, president of the Yankees, "I can't see what some clubs see in players like Pennington [Art Pennington], Parnell Woods, Perry [Alonzo Perry], who went to Oakland, and Piper Davis who went to the Red Sox. He must be in his early thirties. I can't see any of 'em going higher than AAA."[13]

Baird was right about none of the players making it to the majors, but he didn't help matters with his comments.

Piper was leading Scranton in hitting (.333), runs batted in (ten), and home runs (three) when he received a phone call from his wife, Laura, telling him to contact the Red Sox.

"So I called them up and they said, 'We got to give you your release.'

"I said, 'For what, man?'"

"Economical conditions," Piper was told.

"When Boston released me, that took all the joy out of it for me. That was one of the toughest moments of my career."[14]

Piper was shaken but not for long. He returned to white folks' ball in 1951 to play eight years and become a role model for future black major leaguers like Charlie Beamon, a pitcher for the Baltimore Orioles from 1956 to 1958, and Elijah "Pumpsie" Green, the infielder who finally succeeded in breaking the Red Sox' color barrier in 1959.

Beamon and Green were students at Oakland's McClymonds High School and became big fans of Piper when he joined the Oakland Oaks in 1951, replacing Wilson, who got his lone shot in the big leagues that year with the Giants.

"It was a respect thing that I had for them," Beamon said of the two Black Baron stars. "I used to talk to them and I asked, 'Do you think I could've played in the Negro Leagues?' I always thought that if I could play there, I could play in the big leagues."

By 1954, Charlie, then nineteen, was pitching for the Oaks.

"Piper was a father figure to a lot of young players. Not just the black players; all young players. They looked up to Piper. He liked to talk baseball but he liked to talk more about people, about human beings getting along together and what you had to do to be a good player.

"He was just a positive person. You always felt good around him, no matter whether you did good. There wasn't any such thing as doing bad or a bad play."

After baseball, Beamon worked in a jobs-training program where he often counseled young people. "I could hear some of his words that are still appropriate today."

"Piper taught us a lot," said Green. "He knew all of the old ball players, which I'd never heard of nor seen. He had played with most of 'em. He used to talk to us about Josh Gibson, Satchel Paige and he told us about Willie Mays before he became a Giant. He was just an all-around good guy—one of the two or three great guys I've met in baseball."

"He just took Pumpsie and me under his wings," Beamon added.

> If it hadn't been for him, I doubt if the two of us would've got to the big leagues. He had us mentally tough. And we knew how to develop the social skills needed to be able to communicate in racial situations that were strange to young people coming out of an environment that was different.
>
> Pumpsie and I used to sit back and say sometimes, 'Man, I wonder what Piper was like when he was a kid?' You just could see the ability that he had at that age and you could just imagine how good he was when he was younger.

Mel Ott, the all-time National League home run leader until Mays topped his 511 total in 1966, managed the Oaks from 1951 to 1952.

Piper began the 1952 season as the Oaks' starting catcher. If any of his teammates were hurt or needed a rest, Ott simply said, "Piper, you're playing third." Or first, or shortstop, or second, or right, center, or left field.

"Never saw a more versatile player," Ott added. "One reason for his versatility is his desire to play any place any time."[15]

When Ott proposed playing Piper at all nine positions during a single nine-inning game, someone suggested, "Let's make it a ten-inning game—and have Piper sell beer in the tenth."[16]

Piper also showed the way with his bat, posting a team-high .306 batting average. Pitchers learned there was a price to pay if they threw at Piper or one of his teammates.

One pitcher, Bill Boemler of the San Francisco Seals, regularly aimed fastballs at Piper and Ray Noble, the Oaks' other black player.

In a game in late July, Piper singled after being knocked down twice by Boemler. On the next play, Piper tried to score from first with Boemler covering home plate. "I said, 'Here's my chance,' and I bowled him over."[17]

In one newspaper account of the collision, Piper "came into the plate high, with spikes flashing, and Boemler grabbed him by the leg and hung on." Piper was out but he had delivered a message to Boemler and triggered a fight Ott described as "the best I ever saw in baseball."[18]

"More punches were thrown in those few moments than at the last three boxing programs at the Cow Palace," the *Oakland Tribune* reported.[19]

"Noble came from the dugout as though it were a cave," the *San Francisco Call-Bulletin* wrote. "His first swipe just missed the fence. His second almost beheaded a customer in the front row and a radio announcer. Counts on how many Seals he tagged vary from a half-dozen to fifty-two, although only twenty-three men were present."[20]

The free-for-all led to Piper, Noble, and a white teammate, Hank Schenz, receiving letters and postcards from a group threatening violence the following month when they played the Seals in San Francisco.

"Not a shot was fired from the stands, nor a bomb thrown on to the field and every Oakland Acorn showed up," the *San Francisco Chronicle* wrote after the first game of the series.[21]

With plainclothes FBI agents and San Francisco policemen scattered throughout the stands, Piper ripped a double and three singles in four at bats "to prove he was little alarmed over the written threats to his person."[22]

To recognize Piper's outstanding performance and leadership, the Oaks declared the last day of the 1952 season as Piper Davis Day, presenting the "one-man ball club" a five-hundred-dollar U.S. savings bond and other gifts.

After the pregame ceremony, Piper walked to the pitcher's mound, where he retired all three batters he faced. He went on to play a different position each of the next eight innings.

Piper could do it all. And he proved it time and again until the end of his playing days with the Fort Worth Cats in 1958. In a game against the Texas League All-Stars, who were babes in arms when he started his career, the forty-one-year-old Piper smashed a two-run pinch-hit homer over the left-field fence at Fort Worth's LaGrave Field. The hometown crowd of 9,485, black and white folks, roared its approval as Piper circled the bases like his most famous pupil.

"Play when you're out there," Piper taught young Willie Mays. "Give it all you got."

The teacher was true to his own teachings.

Robert Lee Coats lived seventy-seven years in Woodlawn, Illinois—from December 24, 1929, when he was born to his death on September 13, 2007.

A town of 300 people when he was growing up, Woodlawn is located seventy miles southeast of St. Louis.

Coats was a life-long St. Louis Cardinals fan. "Every Sunday, when the Cardinals were home, my friend and I would go to Mount Vernon and catch a Greyhound bus to St. Louis and then take a street car from the bus station to Sportsman's Park, watch the ballgame and then come back."

In his home office, baseball books neatly lined the bookcase shelves: *The Image of their Greatness*, *Wrigleyville*, *The Minors*, *Boys of Summer*, *Late Innings*, and *Angels*, to name a few. "The book I really enjoyed was *Boys of Summer*," Coats said, picking up another book. "This is Louis L'Amour. I've got all of his books."

He handed me *Angels*, a history of the Los Angeles Angels in the Coast League from 1919 to 1957. "Have you seen that?"

I pointed out the first edition was out of print and selling for $300 on eBay.

"You're kidding? Give me that book back.

"Holy cow, Mona," he commented to his wife, standing nearby.

Several baseball photos decorated the walls—a team shot of the 1956 Angels; a photo of Coats, catcher Jim Fanning, and Scheffing taken during the 1955 season; and a photo of the 1931 "Gashouse Gang," the nickname given the Cardinals team that won the World Series that year. "I'm a Cardinal fan, have always been a Cardinal fan, and will die a Cardinal fan."

The Coats family lived in a four-room house attached to the Coats' Service Station and Restaurant. "In those days, all soft drinks were sold in bottles with caps. I saved the caps."

Using the caps for baseballs and broom handles for bats, Bob and a friend pitched to each other. "You can make a bottle cap do all kinds of things: drop, curve, shoot up. The idea was not to hit the bottle cap so hard but to make contact. That's how I learned to hit."

Bob starred in baseball, basketball, and track in high school. He was attending Southern Illinois University on an academic scholarship when Cubs scout Tony Lucadello signed him to a $140 a month contract. "They sent me to a baseball school, all expenses paid, after I graduated from high school. I felt an obligation to the Cubs because of that."

Starting in 1948 at Class D, the bottom of the minors, Coats worked his way up to Class A in 1950 and was headed higher when he got into a contract hassle with the owner of the Grand Rapids Jets. "This is the black mark in my baseball career," Bob said.

Despite leading the team in hitting, the Jets offered a miserly twenty-five dollar increase to $300 a month. "We had our first child. I asked for

$350. They wouldn't budge an inch; I got hard-headed and wouldn't budge an inch. So I didn't play that year."

Bob took a job with Caterpillar Tractor Company in Peoria, Illinois, and played semipro ball on Sundays. "I loved baseball; I decided the next year to give it another shot."

But the year away from baseball was a major setback. "I went from Class A, having a very, very good year, to Class C and starting over again."

"White slavery," C.W. Coats termed baseball's treatment of his son.

"You were blackballed," Lucadello, the scout, acknowledged several years later.

"In those days, you just didn't do what I did," Bob said. "They [management] called the shots."

The opportunity to play for the Angels in 1955 was a redemption of sorts for Coats and the next best thing to playing in the big leagues.

"The Pacific Coast League was high cotton for me. We flew. You could eat a lot more on road trips than the two dollars a day in the low minors. It was a good league with a lot of good ball players. I was playing against guys that I had seen play in St. Louis when I was in high school."

One of those players was Vern Stephens, a third baseman for the Seattle Rainiers. "I saw him when he was a Brownie."

Three of Bob's teammates in L.A. once played for his beloved Cardinals—outfielder Hal "Hoot" Rice, Bilko, and Mauch. "I was kind of in awe playing with these guys. I was just glad to be there."

In Bob's first start twelve games into the season, he rapped three singles, stole a base and scored two runs. As he rounded second base on a teammate's hit, the opposing shortstop, a wily veteran, elbowed Bob in the ribs to throw him off stride and perhaps set up a play at third. "I didn't know the tricks."

The following day, Bob went to L.A. trainer Joe Liscio.

"Joe, my side is killing me."

"You've got cracked ribs," Liscio said after checking them out.

Bob instructed Liscio to tape him up and not say anything to L.A. manager Bill Sweeney.

"I saw a chance to stay in the Coast League, which was unbelievable to me. A kid from a town of 300 people and I'm playing in the Coast League? So I played with cracked ribs."

Through the Angels' first thirty-three games, Bob was the team's top hitter with a .361 batting average. When Scheffing replaced Sweeney on May 23, he was batting .300 with forty-two hits in 140 at bats.

Coats went from playing every day to sharing left-field duties with Rice and Piper, recently acquired from the Oaks. Matters got worse later in the season when Solly Drake joined the team. Billed as "the fastest man in baseball" by the Cubs, Scheffing had orders to play Drake regularly.

"Sweeney gave me a chance. And when I performed, he kept me in there. When they changed managers, I was taken out. That's just the way it was."

The pattern carried over to the next season. Coats would pinch-hit and fill in for the starting outfielders as needed.

"Bob was the nicest guy—maybe a little too nice," said Wise. "I wondered at the time if he had been more aggressive, a little meaner, perhaps he would've played more."

"When Scheffing sat me on the bench," Coats said, "I would've been better off to ask to go somewhere I could play every day."

The 1957 season was Coats' last in baseball and he proved what he could do playing every day in centerfield for the Memphis Chicks in the Class AA Southern League. A unanimous all-star pick, Bob led the league in hits (184), was a coleader in triples (eleven), and ranked third in batting average (.327).

"Some hitters' goal is to hit the ball out and some is to hit the ball hard. My goal was to get on base. If I played regularly, I knew I'd get on base."

Johnny Goryl was a teammate in Memphis.

"He came into spring training and started hitting line drives like all of the great hitters that I've watched over the years—Tony Oliva, Rod Carew, those guys. Bobby just never got the opportunity. There's no question in my mind that, given that opportunity, he would probably have made a pretty good major league player."

For all of his success in Memphis, the Cubs didn't bother to call or place him on their spring training roster for 1958. Instead, he received a contract to play for Portland in the PCL. "I sent it back and said I was retiring."

Thinking it was a ploy for more money, the Cubs sent another contract. Tommy Heath, the Portland manager, also called. "I'm planning on you being my centerfielder this year, Bob. I'll try to get you more money."

Bob was offered the same $900 a month salary he had at Memphis.

"I'm retiring," Bob reiterated to Heath. "I'm through playing baseball."

The week before the Cubs opened the 1958 season against the Cards in St. Louis, Bob got another call, this time from John Holland, a Cubs vice president.

"I want you to join us in St. Louis," Holland said. "You'll play right field and back up Dale Long at first base. We'll pay you $12,000 a year."

That was far more money than Bob had ever made in baseball. But he was wary. Right field was not his best outfield position because of a so-so throwing arm, and he had little experience playing first.

"I need to think about that, Mr. Holland."

Holland called back the next night. "I've been thinking about this and we're going to pay you $13,000."

"Mr. Holland, we've made up our mind. I'm not going to play. I'm in the insurance business now and liking it real well."

He paused to reflect on the decision to quit baseball at age twenty-eight and sell insurance for Equitable Life.

"They weren't going to keep me in Chicago," Bob said. "I would've been there maybe thirty days to get in shape and then I'm on my way to Portland. It seemed like God opened up the opportunity with Equitable for me. The insurance business is competitive just like baseball."

Bob served Equitable clients for thirty-five years, earning permanent membership in the Company's Hall of Fame.

"I am super competitive. Any sales campaign I was in, I was going to win it if I possibly could. I was the same way with baseball. I wanted the team to win and I wanted to do well."

Bob held up a photo of Ray Blades, the former Cardinals player and manager who was also a trusted friend and mentor. The photo is signed by Ray with this personal message: "Baseball's loss but Equitable's Gain. May you always bat 1.000."

One of Moe Bauer's prized possessions from his two seasons in Los Angeles is a black-and-white photo showing Steve Bilko, wearing a chef's cap, serving a meal to Moe, Fanning, and Coats. The trio is toasting their slugging teammate with glasses of milk.

The photo appeared on page one of the *Los Angeles Mirror News* sports section in August 1955. The headline of the story reads, BILKO SWEATS OVER HOT STOVE FOR 3 TEAMMATES.

"What a salad he whips up," Fanning raved. "He cooks anything — steaks, meatloaf, chicken."[23]

The significance of the photo is that it captured Bilko, the biggest sports celebrity in La La Land, serving his teammates. "Steve was a star but he was just a regular guy with us," explained Bob. "He did the cooking. He didn't want you to wait on him."

During the 1955 season Steve, Moe, Bob, and Jim lived together in an efficiency apartment at the Wellington Hotel in downtown L.A.

"Jim and I each had a bed over by one wall," Moe recalled. "Coatsie had one that was on the other side from us. Steve had the pull-down bed in the living room. He was usually the last one to turn the lights out at night. You'd better get to sleep before he did. Because if you didn't the whole building trembled when he was snoring."

The only other concession made to the Angels' star was the refrigerator. "We had the upper part for our milk; the bottom was for Steve's beer."

A bartender from Steve's hometown in Nanticoke, Pennsylvania, kept the refrigerator fully stocked with beer, adding a case almost every day.

Figure 11.1. Steve Bilko often cooked for roommates, left to right, Raymond "Moe" Bauer, Jim Fanning, and Bob Coats during the 1955 season as they lived together at the Wellington Hotel in downtown Los Angeles. *Courtesy Raymond "Moe" Bauer.*

Moe documented some of their activities with an eight-millimeter camera. As we watched the footage in the home of his son, Paul, in Rocky Mount, North Carolina, Moe and his wife, Mary, provided commentary.

"That's you," Mary said.

"That's Don Elston," Moe corrected, referring to another L.A. pitcher.

"That's Bilko!" Mary said. "All I heard about was Bilko's snoring and how they had to go to bed before he did so they could get some sleep."

Ray added, "I asked Steve's wife, Mary, 'What in the world do you do with him?' She said, 'I've got a real sharp elbow.'"

The old movie projector droned on.

"This is when we went fishing," Moe announced. "You're going to see some sick characters here shortly."

During a series in San Francisco several Angels, including Moe, Bob, and Steve, chartered a boat to go salmon fishing near the Farallon Islands, about twenty-seven miles offshore.

"That's the forty-pounder I caught," Moe said. "See the rig that's broken. That's how most of them ended up. We're coming back in.

There's the Golden Gate. That's the roughest spot of water I've ever been on in my life."

All of the players got seasick. They were still feeling the effects that night at Seals Stadium.

"Before the game we're standing in the outfield—still rocking." For emphasis, Moe swayed his slender body from side-to-side.

Behind the grandstand at Seals Stadium, there was a Hamm's brewery building topped with a huge 3D neon chalice. The glass filled with rings of lights to form a rich foam head on top.

"Ol' Steve looked at it and said, 'Wouldn't that be just great to dive in that place and drown?'"

Moe laughed at the thought of Bilko plunging into a vat of beer.

"We developed into a bunch of guys that wanted to get to the ballpark and wanted to play ball because we wanted to win."

Moe quit baseball after the 1958 season with a career 49–32 won-loss record and 3.37 ERA. He returned to North Carolina to complete his graduate studies and begin building a legacy of his own at North Carolina Wesleyan College in Rocky Mount.

Moe transformed a soybean field into a baseball field that in 1988 was named Bauer Field in his honor.

As the school's first baseball coach and athletic director, he built a highly respected sports program, earning election posthumously in 2012 to the USA South Athletic Conference Hall of Fame. Moe died in 2005 at the age of seventy-seven. He is also a member of the Wake Forest and North Carolina Wesleyan Sports Hall of Fames and North Carolina's American Legion Baseball Hall of Fame.

"Mauch, Piper, Bilko . . . the guys were baseball knowledgeable people," Moe said. "As I got involved in coaching that is what I emphasized, not teaching a boy to hit or pitch. My emphasis was always on knowing how to play the game."

On Moe's induction into the USA South Hall of Fame, Paul Bauer explained that the New York Yankees paid for his father's education at Wake Forest with the stipulation that they got first shot at signing him on graduation. "That was his obligation to them," Paul noted.

The Yankees offered Moe $3,000 to sign.

"Three thousand?" Moe asked. "That's all you're going to give me?"

"Yeah, that's all we're going to give you," he was told.

The Cubs offered Moe $5,000, so he signed with them.

"My father could not stand that the New York Yankees had spent $8,000 putting him through school and he never signed with them," Paul said.

Moe repaid the Yankees the entire amount. "It was against the better judgment of my mom," Paul said. "But he did it anyway."

"I miss my daddy," Faye Davis said as we stepped into her office at the Greater Birmingham Convention and Visitors Bureau. "I miss my daddy."

Faye had just attended a Negro League Conference presentation on her daddy, Piper, almost becoming a member of the St. Louis Browns in 1947.

Photos of Piper as well as his Negro League baseball card were on a table in the corner of her office. Nearby was a copy of *Willie's Boys*, the excellent book about Piper and the 1948 Black Barons. The screensaver on Faye's computer showed a distinguished-looking Piper in a suit and tie. And on the wall in a large picture frame above Faye's desk was the *Birmingham News* article, "Born too Soon," published on Piper's death.

Even today Piper is inseparable from baseball in Birmingham. At Hoover Stadium where the current Barons played until moving into a new downtown ballpark in 2013, a life-sized mural of a young Piper graced one of the breezeways leading into the stands. Go to Rickwood Field, the well-preserved ballpark that was home to both black and white folks' ball, and images of him are everywhere.

"I have yet to be able to walk into Rickwood without crying," Faye said.

Piper moved in with relatives in Birmingham so he could stay out of the coalmines and continue his education at Fairfield High.

"Dad gets here and they've got their starting five at basketball. They kind of kept him out."

During one particularly close game, Fairfield students started chanting, "We want Piper Colina! We want Piper Colina! We want Piper Colina!"

Fairfield's coach leaned over to the equipment manager and asked, "Spates, is that Piper Colina boy any good?"

"Yes, sir, he can play."

Piper Colina entered the game, Fairfield won, and the legend of Piper Davis was born.

Before the Angels released Buzz Clarkson in 1956, Scheffing checked with Piper to make sure he was all right with being the lone black on the team.

"It won't bother me at all," Piper said.

"Dad was a pretty solitary type. If you didn't mention baseball, you wouldn't get fifteen words out of him. But if you ever got him started . . . "

One story Piper liked to tell was the time he was catching for the Oaks and called for three straight fastballs to strike out the batter, Mauch. When they became teammates in L.A., Mauch asked Piper why he had the pitcher throw three successive fastballs, defying all baseball logic.

Piper grinned and said proudly, "Element of surprise, my dear brother!"[24]

Piper was a man of few, carefully selected words.

Asked about the segregation that kept baseball white, Piper said, "Wasn't the game's fault." On playing in the Negro Leagues with Satchel Paige and Josh Gibson: "Hit everywhere from .275 up. Be a million-dollar ball player today."[25]

He verbally flagged something important by saying "put it in the computer" long before there were computers. Piper referred to a hard-hit ball as "tattooed" or "buggy whipped."

"Daddy liked to say, 'Hold your point.' And then he'd say, 'Come back to your point.'"

Piper had stories galore.

"I'll tell you one of the most interesting experiences I ever had. When my grandmother died, all of the old guys from [the town of] Piper came to the house one evening. And their visit went on through the night. It was the best history anybody could've had in the life of a coal mine—racial relationships in a coal mine—and how Daddy was deadly with a slingshot."

Faye was reminded of the time a plumber came to their house in Birmingham. On seeing Piper, he exclaimed, "Knocks?"

"Yeah," Piper said, confirming the nickname he picked up as a kid in Piper because of his ability to "knock your eyes out" with a slingshot.

The plumber pointed to a spot on his head and said to Faye, "Look, I got the biggest hickey on my head from your daddy's slingshot."

Faye leaned back in her office chair to demonstrate how her daddy napped while watching television. "All he watched was baseball games until momma got him hooked on a soap opera."

"Does your wife watch *Edge of Night*?" people would ask.

"Yeah," Piper said, "and her husband, too."

"That was typical dad: 'Yeah, and her husband, too.'"

Faye turned to her computer to pull up comments she made at Rickwood Field to commemorate Birmingham's 125th anniversary in October 1997.

"They played the game so well," Faye told the crowd.

"Many of the men whose names have echoed during this event and are synonymous with the glory days of the Negro League are no longer in our midst. But they left us with unmatched memories—memories of baseball brilliance, of unparalleled talent and savvy. Most never played in the major leagues but most major leaguers would have a hard time carrying their gloves to the ballpark. They received much smaller salaries than we hear of today, but they managed to take care of their families and educate their children. They were men.

> They were men who could read the hops, go to the hole, steal signs with the best of them, turn the double play, cut the ball, drive the bus, hit with power, run like gazelles, play through pain, deliver blazing

fastballs and wicked curves. They were quiet and reserved and some flamboyant to the end. Yes, they played the game so well.

They rode the bus all night, laced spikes on swollen feet, entered the field of play and proceeded to tattoo and buggy whip the ball while stopping the opponent with dazzling defense. And when their playing days were over each went on his way, making it hard, at times, to know who was still around. Yes, many have gone on—so in the name of many we call but a few who played the game so well: Winfield Welch; Lloyd "Pepper" Bassett; Mr. Rudd, the bus driver; Nathaniel Pollard; Alonzo Perry; Ed Steele; Wiley Griggs; Harry Barnes; Johnny Cowan; Roosevelt Atkins; "Cap" Brown; and Lorenzo "Piper" Davis.[26]

NOTES

1 John Klima, *Willie's Boys* (Hoboken, NJ: John Wiley & Sons, Inc., 2009), 266

2. Willie Mays, with Lou Sahadi, *Say Hey* (New York: Pocket Books, 1988), 33–34.

3. *Los Angeles Times*, April 9,1956, C1.

4. *1956 Los Angeles Angels Yearbook*, 13.

5. *Grand Rapids Herald*, July 2, 1950, 4 (Sports).

6. *Birmingham News*, May 22, 1997, 8D.

7. Christopher D. Fullerton, *Every Other Sunday* (Birmingham, AL: Boozer Press, 1999), 81–82.

8. Birmingham Black Barons video documentary, Birmingham Civil Rights Institute, Richard Arrington, Jr., Resource Gallery.

9. Southern Exposure, Summer/Fall 1977, *Reading the Hops*, interview by Theodore Rosengarten, 78–79.

10. Document from National Baseball Hall of Fame files, Cooperstown, NY, author and source unknown.

11. *St. Louis Globe-Democrat*, July 18, 1947, C3.

12. Jules Tygiel, *Baseball's Great Experiment: Jackie Robinson and His Legacy* (New York: Vintage Books, 1984), 262.

13. Letter dated October 28, 1949, from Tom Baird of Kansas City Monarchs to Lee MacPhail of the New York Yankees, National Baseball Hall of Fame, Cooperstown, NY.

14. Fullerton, *Every Other Sunday*, 93.

15. *Oakland Tribune*, August 21, 1952, 27.

16. *Oakland Tribune*, March 31, 1952, 22.

17. Tygiel, *Baseball's Great Experiment: Jackie Robinson and His Legacy*, 256.

18. *Oakland Tribune*, July 28, 1952, 20; and *San Francisco Examiner*, July 28, 1952, 28.

19. *Oakland Tribune*, July 28, 1952, 20.

20. *San Francisco Call-Bulletin*, July 28, 1952, 6.

21. *San Francisco Chronicle*, August 27, 1952, 1H.

22. Ibid.

23. *Los Angeles Mirror-News*, August 10, 1955, Part 3, 6.

24. Klima, *Willie's Boys*, 266.

25. *The Sporting News*, June 30, 1997, 6.

26. Davis, Faye J., *They Played the Game So Well!* Copyright 1997. Written on the occasion of the Alabama Negro League Players Salute celebrating the 125th Anniversary of the City of Birmingham.

TWELVE

Mr. Automatic

"Dave Hillman was Mr. Automatic. He went out there time and time again and pitched you that good ball game." —Dwight "Red" Adams, pitcher, 1956 Los Angeles Angels

There's no game clock in baseball, but Darius Dutton "Dave" Hillman could hear the minutes ticking down on his career as he prepared to pitch against the Seattle Rainiers.

The Angels were twenty-seven games into the 1956 season and Hillman had faced only one batter because of a sore right shoulder. A series of cortisone shots and x-ray therapy treatments failed to stop the pain. When Dave started his motion and brought his right arm forward to throw the ball, he felt like his shoulder was being stabbed by an ice pick. Doctors told Dave his body wasn't producing the fluids needed for the shoulder muscles to move freely and without pain.

The Angels had a 17–10 record, but their pitching staff was giving manager Bob Scheffing headaches. His best pitcher, in terms of won-loss record, was Hy Cohen. Hy was a perfect 5–0, tops in the league. But he also had a lofty 5.70 earned run average and struggled to go deep into the games he started.

The cut-down date for team rosters in the majors and Pacific Coast League was five days away. The parent Chicago Cubs would be sending down fresh, young arms, and Scheffing needed to know if Dave could pitch on a regular basis because he had his own roster cuts to make.

"I knew that it was the do-or-die acid test as to whether I would get over the sore arm or I'd be going on down farther in the minor leagues," Dave said.

Arm trouble plagued Dave's rookie season with the Cubs in 1955. After starting the season with the Cubs, he was optioned to L.A. where he pitched twenty-four innings before returning to the Cubs. He pitched fifty-eight innings for the Cubs, mostly in relief. "Once the shoulder loosened up, I was foot loose and fancy free and the arm didn't bother me."

It took the twenty-eight-year-old Hillman six years to work his way up through the minors to the majors.

Hillman started his professional baseball career in 1950, winning fourteen games at Rock Hill, South Carolina, in the Class B Tri-State League. He won twenty for Rock Hill in 1951, one of them a no-hitter. He also led the league in strikeouts with 203.

Dave won only eight games the next two seasons, but he pitched another no-hitter, this time for Springfield, in the Class AAA International League. A 16–11 record in 1954 for a seventh-place team, Beaumont, Texas, in the Texas League, earned him a shot with the Cubs.

"I played with Dave in 1950 and then I was with him off-and-on along the way," said Jim Fanning, a catcher for the Cubs and Angels in 1955 and briefly for L.A. in 1956. "He had a good fastball, a super changeup and excellent control. You sit on the outside or inside of the plate and he hit it."

"He knew where the ball was going," said Dwight "Red" Adams, a veteran pitcher for the Angels. "He had good control in the strike zone. There's a difference between throwing strikes and keeping the ball out of the middle of the plate."

"Whenever you played behind Dave, you never had to worry about bases on balls," explained Gale Wade, the Angels centerfielder. "The ball is going to be hit or he's going to strike somebody out. You can play a lot better defense behind a control pitcher like Dave."

When Scheffing handed the ball to Dave to pitch against Seattle, he said, "Let's go!"

The clock was about to strike midnight for Dave.

"It was a make-or-break game for me. I had to go out and pitch or I was going to be shipped out."

The Rainiers jumped ahead 2–0 in the second inning; the Angels answered with three runs in the third. Each team scored in the seventh. Dave had a 4–3 lead going into the eighth inning when Bill Glynn, formerly a first baseman for the Cleveland Indians, stepped to the plate. "I knew to keep the ball out and away from him—nothing high. But I got it up and in. He hit a home run off a pitch high and tight that got away from me."

Glynn's two-run homer put the Rainiers up 5–4 entering the ninth. The Angels bunched a walk, three singles and a double error by Glynn to score four runs and regain the lead 8–5. Bob Anderson, the Angels hardthrowing closer, pitched a scoreless ninth to preserve Dave's first of twenty-one wins.

Dave went eight innings, allowing seven hits and three walks while striking out five. "I got out there and just kept on going."

In his next start, Dave tossed a five-hitter. Two weeks later against the Rainiers at Little Wrigley, he pitched a four-hit shutout.

He wound up with a 6–0 record against the Rainiers, the defending PCL champion and eventual runner-up. Half of those victories were at Seattle. He was undefeated against three other teams: third-place Portland (2–0), fifth-place Sacramento (5–0), and sixth-place San Francisco (2–0). Overall, he was 10–3 against first division teams, all three losses coming at the hands of the fourth-place Hollywood Stars.

"It never did bother me as to who I was pitching against. We'd have our meetings in the clubhouse and go over the hitters. I let the boys know how I was going to pitch them in different situations. And fortunately that's the way it went."

Dave had an 8–3 won-loss record entering July when he reeled off seven straight victories. He won his twentieth game in Seattle where it all started.

He was an amazing 11–2 at Wrigley Field, a hitter's paradise that most pitchers wanted to avoid. "It made me a better pitcher. You don't take unnecessary chances. In a larger ballpark, you can make a mistake. I was always aware that being in a small ballpark, I had to be real careful."

Despite missing the first month of the season, Dave's 21–7 won-loss record, 3.38 earned run average, three shutouts, and fifteen complete games paced the Angels pitching staff.

Scheffing knew that he was going to get a good game out of him," said Anderson. "I probably saved a few games for Dave but when he was pitching, I had a little more chance to relax. Mr. Automatic is a good description of the kind of pitcher that he was that year."

Dave's performance earned the respect and admiration of Scheffing. The night the Angels clinched the pennant in Seattle—nearly four months after his make-or-break game—Scheffing told Dave: "The things you've done in so short a period of time, let me know if you ever need anybody to go to hell for you."

"I appreciate that, Bob. I loved playing for you."

"You let me know."

Hillman's birth names are Darius Dutton. Dave is a nickname given to him by his boyhood hero, John S. Blackwell, in their hometown of Dungannon, tucked in the Appalachian foothills of southwest Virginia near the Tennessee border.

Darius was born September 14, 1927—the fifth of Carmel and Ollie Hillman's seven children. Carmel was a carpenter for the Clinchfield Railroad, now CSX, which runs through Dungannon to the coal mines in the area.

About 400 people lived in Dungannon while Hillman was growing up. Everybody knew each other because, in many cases, they were related.

John and Dave, for example, were distant cousins. "My grandmother was a Blackwell."

One day Dave Macon, a banjo player in the Grand Ol' Opry, came to town to perform at the local school. While picking and singing, Macon flipped his banjo in the air, caught it and continued playing without a break in the music.

John was a jovial guy with a hee-haw type of laugh that filled the school auditorium. "I was sitting behind him and laughed until I cried. The next day he started calling me Uncle Dave Macon. As the years went by he cut it down to Uncle Dave. And then it became Dave."

John was sixteen years older than Dave. He left Dungannon briefly in the early 1930s to pitch professionally for Richmond, Virginia, before returning to operate his father's grocery store and play baseball on weekends in the semipro Lonesome Pine League. Dave was only five the first time he saw John pitch, but he remembers it well: "He had the darnedest curveball of any human being I had ever seen in my life. And he could throw hard."

Dave was a scrawny nine-year-old when he started playing catch with his hero. "He'd monkey around throwing the ball. He could throw a knuckleball, curveball, and everything else. We played burn-out."

On graduating from high school, Dave weighed only 138 pounds. He wasn't much bigger (160 pounds) when he pitched for the Angels in 1956. "I didn't do like a lot of kids and throw with my arm; I used my legs to leverage my weight. And I figured out what I had to do to get more spin on the ball."

There was no baseball team or coaches at Dave's high school. All he had to go on was what he learned from playing catch with Blackwell. "It stuck with me all my life."

At 8:30 the morning of February 14, 1939, Dave, then eleven, was sitting in class at school when his teacher, Carrie Addington, received news that her brother, John Blackwell, was dead after a shootout with a deputy sheriff at Dungannon's Poplar Cabin Filling Station.

John was a free spirit who liked to drive his truck through the streets after a big rain storm, splashing water everywhere. He carried a pistol and was known to be trigger happy. The day before the gun battle, he shot out Dungannon's new street lights for the fun of it.

Word spread quickly that Ben Sluss, a deputy sheriff, was going to arrest John for vandalism.

John was sitting behind the counter as Sluss crossed the street to enter the service station. John removed a pistol from his pocket and placed it on top of a nearby safe. He thought Sluss was coming to take him to jail.

Sluss actually was on his way to deliver money John had asked him to collect on bad checks he had been given.

"How are you, John?" Sluss inquired.

"All right," replied John.

When Sluss reached in his pocket for the money, John grabbed his pistol and started shooting. Sluss was struck by three bullets but somehow fired back after falling to the floor. John was killed by a bullet to the head. Sluss died the next day from his gunshot wounds.

"They let us out of school," Dave recalled. "I went to the filling station where he was shot. The filling station was next to the barber shop. They put his body on the pool table in the barber shop. They had his shirt off. There was no blood but plenty of bullet holes. There was one through the shoulders, another in the chest. I was in shock because I loved the fellow. I thought a lot of him."

Dave went on to pitch two years (1948–1949) for the Coeburn Blues in the Lonesome Pine League—the same league Blackwell was pitching in when Dave was a kid. He soon was dubbed "Fireball" as scouts came to see if he was as fast as his nickname.

Tim Murchison, a scout for the Cubs, was in the stands for a Saturday night game in St. Paul, Virginia. He sat next to Dave's parents.

"I was firing away. They didn't have big catcher's mitts in those days—just small ones with very little padding. Every time I threw a fast ball, the catcher backed up. And, then, the umpire kept backing up."[1]

After the game, Murchison told Dave's mother, "I'm going to sign that boy if it takes everything I got."

Dave signed with the Cubs in 1950, moved to nearby Kingsport, Tennessee, with his wife Imogene and their one-year-old daughter, Sharon, and began his climb up the pro baseball ladder.

By the end of the 1956 season in Los Angeles, Dave had another nickname—"The Slim Virginian."

A few years later, *The Virginian*, a tough ranch foreman played by actor James Drury, became a popular western television series. Nobody knew the real name of the foreman. He was known only as *The Virginian*.

Ironically, few people know Hillman by his real name—Darius Dutton. And virtually nobody in baseball knew of the impact Dave's boyhood hero, John S. Blackwell, had on his pitching career.

Back in L.A. after winning the pennant in Seattle, Dave lost in a blowout to the Stars before going the distance to beat the Padres for his twenty-first victory—second best in the league.

He had now pitched 210 innings and was looking forward to going home three days later when the PCL season ended.

John Holland, the Angels president, and the Cubs had other plans.

"Dave, they want you to come up," Holland told Dave.

"I don't want to go."

"Why?"

"I've pitched my heart out here for this ball club, and for you and Bob, and I don't want to go. I'm worn out."

"Go on back up, Dave."

"No, if I go up there, they'll want me to sign a contract for next year. I don't want to. I feel like I can negotiate a little bit with the kind of year I've had out here. I don't want to go."

"You go on up. I'll take care of you."

Dave was well aware of the news stories about Holland and Scheffing moving up to the Cubs. So he headed to Chicago for the last two weeks of the season.

"I think Hillman can win up there," Scheffing said. "He's got everything a winning pitcher needs."[2]

Dave lost the two games he started for the Cubs even though he pitched well. In the second game, the Cubs committed four errors leading to four unearned runs. Counting the twelve innings pitched for the Cubs, he toiled 222 innings.

As expected, Holland and Scheffing were selected to lead the Cubs in 1957. Holland was given the title of vice president, but he essentially operated as a general manager, negotiating trades and contracts.

Dave was one of six Angel pitchers Scheffing took with him to spring training. Dave was anxious to meet with Holland and discuss a new contract. "I kept waiting for Holland to call—tell me to come on up and re-do my contract."

Dave got a call just before the May 15 cut-down date when major league teams reduced their rosters to twenty-five players.

"I knew what was going on. I was going to go out."

The Cubs were disappointed in Dave's performance despite a respectable earned run average (3.38). He was used sparingly, pitching seven innings in six games.

At one point, Ernie Banks asked Hillman if he needed help finding the pitcher's mound.

"No thanks, Ernie, I'll find it. But I might get a nose bleed when I get up there."

Dave wasn't in a joking mood when he arrived at Holland's Wrigley Field office.

"Dave, we're going to send you out to Portland."

Portland was the Cubs new affiliate in the Coast League.

"I'm not going to Portland. I proved to you last year that I could pitch. You told me to come back up here at the end of the season, sign a contract with the Cubs for the remainder of the season, and you would take care of me this spring. I want to play somewhere else where I can prove to them, and to myself, that I can pitch up here. If I can't, I know the way home."

"Dave, don't be that way. I'll guarantee you one thing. If you're not back up here within two weeks, I'll have you sold to somebody else where you can play."

"I had faith and confidence in you, Mr. Holland. But I will not believe another thing that you tell me even if you put your hand on a stack of Bibles and swore to it."

Holland worked his way up the Cubs organization from Visalia to Des Moines to L.A. and to Chicago like many of the players. He was widely respected as a fair and decent man. Perhaps he forgot about his conversation with Dave in L.A. Certainly, he was surprised by Dave's diatribe.

"He just hung his head," Dave recalled. "That's the only time I ever talked to a superior the way I did. But I was hurt."

Dave told Holland he was going home.

"Dave, I'll call Bob Lewis [Cubs' traveling secretary] and tell him to write you a check for $1,500 to go to Portland."

As Dave left Holland's office, he thought to himself: "Dave, get that $1,500, and get your ass out of here and go home."

Before leaving, he went to the Cubs clubhouse to pack his gear and talk to Scheffing.

"Bob, you once told me that if I ever needed anybody to go to hell for 'em to let you know."

"What's wrong?"

"Mr. Holland wants me to go to Portland. He told me he would guarantee me that within two weeks time, I'd be playing back in the major leagues, if not with the Cubs, with somebody else. I'm going home."

"Don't do that, Dave."

"I need your help."

"Dave, I can't do a thing. The decisions come from up there." Scheffing pointed to Holland's office.

"Well, I thought that all along."

Dave cashed the check and headed home to Kingsport.

After numerous calls urging him to reconsider, Dave decided to go to Portland. "I missed baseball."

The two-week layoff didn't impact his first start for Portland—a complete game victory over the Angels at Little Wrigley. He allowed two runs and nine hits while striking out five. He lost his next start but he gave up only two earned runs and six hits in seven innings.

Just as Holland promised, the Cubs recalled Dave approximately two weeks after being sent to Portland. He hopped on a late-night flight for New York City, arriving the following afternoon to see a story in a New York City tabloid about a Cub pitcher being lost, strayed, or stolen.

Hillman didn't know it but he was late reporting—the Cubs recalled him two days earlier but the Beavers didn't tell him until after he pitched in relief in another game.

The Cubs were playing the Dodgers in Jersey City. Holland and Scheffing greeted Dave warmly. "I want you to be ready to go in Philadelphia," Scheffing said.

Before the game with the Phillies, Dave discussed how he was going to pitch each hitter in the lineup. "We came down to Chico Fernandez. I'd played against Chico in the minor leagues and I knew how I was going to pitch to him—down and away."

Scheffing spoke up. "No, Dave, I want to change your way of thinking on that. I want him pitched high-and-tight."

Fernandez came to bat in fifth inning with the bases loaded. Dave threw a pitch high-and-tight. Chico hit the ball in the air to left field deep enough to score the runner from third base on a sacrifice fly.

Dave pitched a masterful four-hitter but the Cubs lost, 1–0.

The next morning Holland asked Dave to come to his hotel room. "After the game I pitched, I thought he'd give me a new contract."

"Dave," Holland began, "you can't pitch Chico Fernandez high-and-tight in a situation like that."

Hillman told Holland about the clubhouse meeting and Scheffing's instructions on how to pitch Fernandez.

"I didn't know that, Dave."

"Well, Mr. Holland, there are a lot of things that go on in that clubhouse that a lot of people don't know anything about."

Dave eventually got a $1,000 raise for his performance with the 1956 Angels. And he didn't have to pitch another inning in the minors.

Dave finished the 1957 season with a 6–11 won-loss record and 4.35 ERA. He pitched five more years in the majors, two each with the Cubs (1958–1959) and Boston Red Sox (1960–1961) and one with the Cincinnati Redlegs and New York Mets (1962). The 1962 Mets were the worst team in baseball history, winning only forty games.

Dave went home to Kingsport to work in a men's clothing store owned by an uncle. He figured selling shirts and shoes was better than being with the Mets and getting kicked in the pants every time he pitched.

Soon after his major league debut with the Cubs in 1955, a Chicago sportswriter referred to Hillman as "a Murry Dickson type pitcher" because of their similarities in size, pitching style, and tenacity. "He's a kid with lots of guts and no one up here is going to scare him," Cubs manager Stan Hack said of his rookie pitcher.[3]

Hillman and Dickson also had something else in common—pitching for losing teams.

Dickson won an impressive 172 games in the majors. He would've won a lot more if he hadn't played for the lowly Pittsburgh Pirates in 1952 and 1953 and the Philadelphia Phillies in 1954. He lost sixty games those three seasons. In Dave's three full seasons with the Cubs, they never finished above .500.

Hillman showed only flashes of the brilliance Dickson demonstrated over eighteen years. But from mid-1958 through 1959, Dave's last season with the Cubs, he was arguably their most effective and consistent starting pitcher despite won-loss records of 4–8 and 8–11.

In August 1958, the *Sporting News* reported, "Hillman, in many respects has been the Cubs' most dependable pitcher, even though he had a 3–5 record. Four of his losses came in low-run games and had his teammates given him better batting support it is conceivable he would have a 7–1 or 8–1 mark."[4]

He was at his best in 1959, posting a 3.58 ERA, completing four games and pitching seven or more innings in nine others. He tossed a two-hit shutout against the Pirates; struck out eleven in seven innings of relief to beat the Los Angeles Dodgers; and in the next-to-last game of the season stopped the Dodgers in their bid to wrap up the National League pennant.

The Dodgers were one game ahead of the Milwaukee Braves with two to play. A win over the Cubs and Hillman clinched a tie.

"I went out there, honey, and I'll never forget the control that I had," Dave recalled. "I could thread a damn needle with that ball. I was just sitting back and sh-o-o-o-m-m-m . . . throwing that thing in there."

The normally quiet Cub bats came alive to produce three runs in the second, six in the third, and three in the fourth. Hillman even batted in two runs with two hits.

Dave had a 12–0 cushion going into the sixth when the Dodgers scored twice, bringing Scheffing to the mound.

"What's wrong, Dave?"

"It ain't nothing. For five innings, they took the first pitch. Now they're starting to hit it. I've got to go to work."

Dave blanked the Dodgers the rest of the way, scattering nine hits and striking out seven for a 12—2 Cubs win.

"That's the easiest game I've had all year," Dave said after the game. "All the way through my idea was to make them hit the breaking pitches. I used fastballs and slip pitches mostly in the early part of the game and switched to curveballs later."[5]

Meanwhile in Milwaukee, the Braves beat Philadelphia to tie the Dodgers going into the last game of the season. Both teams won their final game to force a best-of-three playoff. The Dodgers won that and then beat the Chicago White Sox in the World Series.

After the 1959 season, Hillman was traded to the Red Sox and Scheffing was fired. He was managing the Detroit Tigers in 1961 when Dave pitched six and two-third innings of scoreless relief to beat the Tigers and knock them out of first place. Dave allowed only three hits, reminding Scheffing of the 1956 season in L.A. "Dave won twenty-one games and we romped to the pennant," he said after the game. "Dave is not an overpowering pitcher but he knows what he's doing out there."[6]

"I thought the world of Bob Scheffing," Dave said.

Figure 12.1.   Dave Hillman, right, shows Ernie Banks the knuckler he used to blank the Pittsburgh Pirates on two hits in a 1959 game for the Chicago Cubs. Hillman's won-loss record of 21–37 in the majors belies a respectable earned run average of 3.87 over eight seasons with the Cubs, Boston Red Sox, Cincinnati Redlegs, and New York Mets. *Associated Press Wirephoto/National Baseball Hall of Fame Library, Cooperstown, NY.*

To know that Scheffing respected his abilities as a pitcher was the kind of respect Dave strived for his entire baseball career.

NOTES

1. L. M. Sutter, *Ball, Bat and Bitumen* (Jefferson, NC: McFarland & Company, Inc., 2009), 59.

2. *Los Angeles Times*, September 13, 1956, A1.

3. *The Sporting News*, June 15, 1955, 6.

4. *The Sporting News*, August 27, 1958, 15.

5. *Chicago Sun-Times*, September 27, 1959, 93.

6. *Detroit News*, April 28, 1961, D1.

THIRTEEN
Grump's Old Men

"There are a million old broken-down minor league ball players and I don't know what you can say about them. Except they just kept playing." —Dwight "Red" Adams, pitcher, 1956 Los Angeles Angels, as quoted in *Los Angeles Times*, May 17, 1974

Most managers would look at a sore-arm pitcher with a bad foot and walk away as quickly as possible.

But the pitcher hobbling around on crutches was Dwight "Red" Adams, a wily thirty-four-year-old right hander with 145 Coast League wins to his credit, including twenty-one for a weak L.A. team in 1945. With the fifth-place Portland Beavers in 1955, he won twelve games and had a 2.05 earned run average in 220 innings pitched. He started the 1956 season with the Beavers, allowing eleven runs in fourteen innings, before he was placed on the disabled list to recover from foot surgery.

L.A. manager Bob Scheffing was feeling as his nickname, "Grump," might suggest—grumpy. The Angels had lost four of five games, the pitching staff roughed up for an average of eight runs a game. "We can't win the pennant with the pitching we got on the road last week," he grumbled.[1]

So when Scheffing spotted Red at Little Wrigley before a Beavers-Angels game, he saw an answer to the team's pitching woes.

Scheffing wanted to know how Red was doing and if he'd be able to pitch by the end of the year.

"I wouldn't bother with trying to get me," Red said. "I wasn't throwing worth a damn before I had my foot operated on and my shoulder is still sore."

"Hell, you've pitched with a sore arm your whole life," Scheffing replied.

The Beavers wound up releasing Adams and the Angels immediately picked him up.

"Just take your time," Scheffing advised Red, "and when you think you can go a couple of innings, we'll get you in a game."

Red hadn't pitched in two months and the injured foot was preventing him from getting much velocity on his pitches.

"I didn't have enough to spare even when I was at my best," Red said. "I'm feeling sorry for Bob, quite frankly. He's got all these young guys and a helluva team. They don't need me. And yet I've got to do the best I can because he's gone out on the limb for me. I wasn't very optimistic about what I was going to do."

In his first appearance, Red retired all four batters he faced. "The Angels may have found a discarded jewel in Red Adams," one writer reported.[2]

A week later, Red started and beat the Seattle Rainiers, pitching into the seventh inning.

Red's next start against the Hollywood Stars was a defining moment in the season for him and the Angels.

"It was the damnedest game that I was ever in," Red said.

The first two hitters singled, and then, Gene Freese, brother of the Angels' George, belted a three-run homer. The next hitter singled, bringing Scheffing to the mound.

"No question in my mind but what he was going to take me out of the game," Red said.

"How do you feel, Red?"

"Well, other than my feelings being hurt a little bit and slightly embarrassed, I feel all right."

"Stay with them," Scheffing said. "I want you to get a few innings under your belt."

As Scheffing returned to the dugout, Red turned around, picked up the rosin bag and looked at the scoreboard. The Stars had a 3–0 lead, a runner was on first, and there were no outs.

"I'm thinking: Scheffing, I always had a lot of respect for your judgment. But I'm questioning it now. How in the hell do you think I'm going to get a few innings in if I can't get a son-of-a-bitch out?"

Red decided he wouldn't throw any more strikes.

"I started threading that needle outside the plate and all around the joint—everywhere but the strike zone. They were so anxious to get at that stuff, they were jumping at it."

In the bottom of the first inning, the Angels scored four times to go ahead, 4–3. That was the final score. Red finished the game, blanking the Stars on three hits the rest of the way.

"The good Lord was looking after me," Red chuckled.

Red won five straight games and finished with a 6–2 record, completing five of his twelve starts.

"He was pitching from memory," added Portland's Ed Mickelson. "Some of those guys are harder to hit than the kids who throw the ball hard."

"Red was pitching with his heart and head then," said Johnny Briggs, one of the Angels kid pitchers. "He was a smart son-of-a-gun. The rest of us, we all had blazing fastballs and a ten-cent brain."

"If you sit back and analyze it, Scheffing felt like he had to have Red Adams and Marino Pieretti with these kids," said Bob Coats.

"Bob wanted some older guys around for balance," Red said. "And it worked."

"Here's how you break up the pitching staff," said Bob Anderson. "You had the young guys, the old guys and the left-hander—Harry Perkowski. The way he wore his hat. When you looked at him walking out onto the field you said, 'There's a left-hander.'"

In addition to Red, the Angels had Pieretti and Perkowski.

The thirty-three-year-old Perkowski was the only one around at the start of the season.

"Harry Perkowski has been dangling on the brink of becoming a regular, starting major league pitcher for so long that he feels like a professional cliff-hanger with a hole in his parachute," *Los Angeles Times* columnist Ned Cronin wrote.[3]

Perkowski pitched six seasons in the majors, winning twelve games for Cincinnati in both 1952 and 1953. Control problems in 1954 elevated his earned run average to 6.09 as his record slipped to 2–8. He had a disappointing 3–4 record and 5.25 earned run average with the Cubs in 1955.

"There were times when he was unbeatable," Scheffing said, "but he also suffered periods when he had difficulty locating the plate and he'd let in too many runs to establish himself as a fixture in the lineup."[4]

Perkowski was the Angels' opening day pitcher, stifling the San Diego Padres on six hits. He won only three of his next nine decisions and was sent to the lower minors soon after L.A. signed Adams.

The thirty-five-year-old Pieretti joined the Angels in May after failing to stick with the Philadelphia Phillies.

Pieretti pitched six years in the majors with the Washington Senators, Chicago White Sox, and Cleveland Indians.

He had a 115–103 record over seven seasons in the Coast League, winning nineteen games with a 3.01 earned run average for last-place Sacramento in 1955. He led the league in innings pitched (293) and was second in complete games (twenty-five). Most amazing were the 270 innings he averaged pitching the previous five years.

"When you took Marino out of a game, you had to have a gun and point it at him," said Briggs, a teammate in Sacramento as well as L.A.

The story goes that Marino was getting clobbered in a game at Sacramento's Edmonds Field. Solons manager Tony Freitas went to the mound to change pitchers.

"Tony tried to take the ball away from Marino and he got mad and threw it right over the top of the press box," Briggs said. "Tony said nothing."

Marino stomped off the field and into the dugout. Tony calmly brought another pitcher into the game, walked back to the dugout, and sat down. Briggs was nearby.

"Marino," Briggs recalled Tony saying, "If you'd thrown the ball during the game like you did over the press box, you'd still be out there pitching."

"Marino went berserk," Briggs said. "He threw crap all over the place."

Described variously as a "prodigious half-pint" and "vest-pocket pitching gamecock," Marino was listed as a five-foot-seven-inch, 153-pounder.

"Forget about five-seven; he was only five-foot-five," said Charlie Silvera, a catcher who grew up with Marino in San Francisco.

And he weighed closer to 140 pounds.

"From the waist up, he was built like a man that was over six feet tall," said Dino Restelli, a former teammate and life-long friend. "He had a big chest, big sinewy arms."

"He would throw a lot of stuff up there," Silvera said. "He wasn't overly fast. He would curveball you, knuckleball you, screwball you, do anything to get you out. He'd run in front of you when you went to first base, tried to trip you. He'd do anything."

"He wasn't afraid of anybody and he pitched the same way," said Dante Benedetti, a boyhood friend and long-time baseball coach at the University of San Francisco. "When he was on that mound, he was the boss."

Born in Lucca, Italy, Marino was nine months old when his family emigrated to the United States.

Benedetti recalled Marino's mother chastising her son, "You stupid American! Learn how to play with *your* balls instead of all those balls you go out there and play with."

"We'd go out and play from nine o'clock in the morning to six o'clock at night," said Restelli. "We played three or four games. And Marino played every game. He pitched in one, played third base in another and shortstop the next game. He never got tired of playing."

Pieretti pitched better for the Angels than his 7–9 won-loss record indicated. In three of his losses, the Angels failed to score and in two others they tallied only twice. He was a workhorse, pitching 156 innings as a starter and reliever.

Marino and Red gave Scheffing the role models he wanted for his young pitchers. They were battlers and knew pitching was all about out-smarting hitters, not overpowering them.

"They realized that they could pass on some wisdom to us," said Anderson, one of the kid hurlers. "When they saw something that we were doing, or maybe a little change that we were making that took away some of our effectiveness, they were willing to talk to us."

In Marino and Red, the Angels had two pitchers who had fulfilled the dream of every frustrated pitcher—heaving a ball out of the park.

A new balk rule in 1950 required pitchers to pause one full second with runners on base, before throwing to home plate. Red was called for twenty balks. Two of them came on successive pitches in a game at Vaughn Street Park in Portland.

"I threw my glove up in the air out of disgust."

"You're out of the game," the third-base umpire hollered.

"That really pissed me off," Red said. "So I took a hop, skip and jump and fogged the ball over the bleachers in right-center field. After I turned it loose, I thought to myself: 'I hope to hell it makes it.' With this arm I got, it might not get out of here."

Red was relieved to find out the ball wound up across the street in front of a bar.

It's not unusual for a city to name public places after its sports heroes.

San Francisco named a playground after Joe DiMaggio, and near AT& T Park, there's the Lefty O'Doul Bridge, Willie Mays Plaza, and McCovey Cove. All are legends, symbolic of the city's amazing baseball heritage.

So why would San Francisco name a baseball field after Marino Pieret-ti, a journeyman pitcher with a 30–38 won-loss record in the majors?

The answer to that question has nothing to do with statistics and everything to do with the heart of a man committed to helping kids learn how to play the game he loved.

"If I had to pick a Mr. Baseball, it would be Marino Pieretti," said Dante Benedetti. "He's the only one."

Marino went to the same high school as DiMaggio and followed him from the diamonds of North Beach to the diamonds of the American League. The similarities stop there.

Joltin' Joe was a natural. The only thing that came naturally for Mari-no was fighting to survive.

He didn't make his Galileo High School baseball team.

He pitched well for local semipro teams, but the hometown Seals and Oakland Oaks of the Coast League considered him too small.

A scout for the Cincinnati Redlegs said his bosses were interested only in big pitchers, not a little guy called Pee Wee. But the scout recognized that Marino had qualities that cannot be measured, and arranged for him to pitch for El Paso in the Class C Arizona–Texas League, where he won sixteen games in 1941.

A contract dispute in 1942 prompted Marino to remain home in San Francisco where he played virtually every day for sandlot and semipro teams. "I love baseball like nobody's business," he said. "When I go to bed, I lie awake thinking about it. I dream about it. And when I wake up the next morning, I can eat baseball for breakfast."[5]

In 1943, Marino moved to Portland and the then Class AA Coast League. He was 9–1 and the next year 26–13 with a 2.46 earned run average for 322 innings pitched. Of his twenty-six victories, eleven came the hard way—one-run battles that came down to the last out.

At the time, major league teams could draft only one player from minor league rosters for the draft price of $7,500. Portland didn't expect an undersized pitcher like Marino to be selected so he was on the draft list.

The lowly Senators picked Marino, causing Portland to complain it was ripped off. "Pieretti is a $50,000 pitcher," Portland argued.[6]

"Portland made a mistake in not selling Pieretti for all he would bring before his name went on the draft list," said Clark Griffith, owner of the Senators. "They were right about one thing, though, he's a $50,000 pitcher!"[7]

World War II was coming to an end in 1945 but the majors were still depending on wartime players to fill in until many of its stars and established players returned.

Three years earlier at El Paso, Marino suffered a severe concussion from being hit on the head by a pitched ball. This kept him out of the war, but resulted in frequent migraine headaches that nagged him throughout his career.

For one season, however, Marino was a headache for American League teams. He pitched 233 innings, posting a 14–13 record and 3.32 earned run average as the Senators finished in second place.

"His record would read even better with a fair break in the luck," Shirley Povich wrote in his *Washington Post* sports column. "Pieretti, like the other Washington pitchers, suffered for lack of batting support in the early weeks of the season, and suffered some brutal defeats!"[8]

With the war over and big league teams at full strength, Marino saw limited action with the Senators in 1946–1947. He was traded to the White Sox in 1948 and the Indians in 1950. Altogether, he won sixteen games.

As fate would have it, Marino was pitching for Cleveland when DiMaggio got his 2,000th career hit June 20, 1950. After the ball was returned to Marino, he walked off the mound and handed it to his North Beach pal. "He was the greatest I ever played against," Marino said.[9]

"If you could've taken Joe's ability and given it to Marino, or Marino's personality and character and given it to Joe, you'd have the champion of the world," said Benedetti.

Marino pitched eight more years in the minors, ending his pro career in 1958 with the Modesto Reds. He had a 6–3 record at the time, but the Reds were in financial trouble. He asked to be released and his monthly salary of $1,400 be divvied up and given to three young prospects on the team.

"With conditions as they are now in the minor leagues, I've got to face the fact that I've had it in baseball," Marino said. "But my arm is still strong and I feel I could do a good job of relief pitching, even in the majors." [10]

Marino's professional career was over but he continued to play semi-pro ball. He was being paid fifty dollars a week by one team when he approached Benedetti about playing for his New Pisa Restaurant team. "I'll play for you for nothing," Marino said, "because you've got a bunch of guys that like to play ball."

Marino went to work for New Pisa and started pitching and managing Benedetti's teams. "He'd pitch every day if you asked him to. He didn't care if it was five days in a row. He was ready to pitch any time." And he was always ready to play third base, catch, pinch hit, and share his baseball knowledge with youngsters.

"The thing I enjoyed," Marino said, "was taking those kids, putting them in a park and teaching them fundamentals, discipline, seeing them develop."

The park where Marino usually could be found was Crocker Amazon in San Francisco.

"Every day he'd be out there from three o'clock until eight at night working with the kids," said Restelli. "He was always willing to help somebody."

"If you made a mistake," said Frank Strazzullo, another ex-ball player, "he'd get right on you and bury it into your mind: 'don't make it again; practice what I'm telling you.'"

Marino and his friends conducted baseball clinics at Crocker Amazon Park.

"They'd come from all over the state," said Strazzullo. "We showed them the fundamentals of the game. And then we told them to go home and practice. We had some promising kids come out of that."

Two of them were about the same size as Marino—Joe Morgan, five-foot-seven, 160 pounds; and Walt "No Neck" Williams, five-foot-six, 165 pounds. Morgan became a Hall of Fame second baseman, while Williams played ten years in the majors.

But the greatness achieved by a few pupils isn't why a baseball field was named after Marino. He was honored "for his devotion, desire, and deep love of baseball."

Those are the words inscribed on a bronze plaque displayed over a grandstand entrance to the Marino Pieretti Baseball Field in Crocker Amazon Park. Outside, one of the murals on the clubhouse wall shows a determined Marino wearing a 1956 Angels cap and jersey. He has his game face on and looks ready to pitch both ends of a doubleheader.

When ceremonies were held to dedicate the field in February 1980, Marino was battling what he called "The Big Three"—heart disease, diabetes, and cancer. He was fighting them all at once.

Marino listened as his friends showered him with praise.

"If ever I saw anybody who wanted to be a ball player and made himself a ball player, it was Marino Pieretti," said Dario Lodigiani, who played for the White Sox and Philadelphia Athletics. "He's the only person I've known in baseball who gave more back than he took out."[11]

Marino, frail and weakened by The Big Three, took the microphone. He thanked city officials for renaming the field in memory of a living person and "all my ball players, 10,000 of them over the past thirty-four years." He closed with a comment that resembled one of his fastballs aimed at a batter's chin. The target was a local politician who promised to make the Marino Pieretti Baseball Field one of the finest in the city: "If I have to come down here with a flashlight," Marino said, "I'll be sure it's taken care of."[12]

The banquet room of Nick's Seashore bar and restaurant at Rockaway Beach in Pacifica, California, was buzzing with the sound of some 125 old men in green jackets.

"You are wearing Marino Pieretti on your back when you wear the green jacket," said Frank Strazzullo, leader of the pack known as the Friends of Marino Pieretti.

Marino was sixty when he died January 30, 1981—eleven months after the dedication of the Marino Pieretti Baseball Field. Frank died in 2012. The group keeps going, meeting for lunch in the San Francisco area the third Wednesday of every month.

"This is old San Francisco, guys who played baseball and other sports," explained Charlie Silvera, the ex-Yankees catcher. "They show up in tribute to a man who gained so much respect for what he did for baseball and San Francisco."

"San Francisco was very close," Frank said. "No matter what part of the city you came from, you hit the baseball fields. That's how we all grew up. It was a beautiful city. It was a beautiful way of living."

"We had good guys in those days," said Rinaldo "Rugger" Ardizoia, who pitched briefly for the Yankees in 1947. "No fancy Dans, no earrings, no necklaces, no batting gloves, no shin guards and arm guards."

Everybody had a nickname on the playgrounds. There was Charley the Weasel and Potatohead. Frank was Babe. Marino was Chick.

The first gathering of Marino's friends took place at Nick's in 1977.

Marino had cancer of the liver and was told he didn't have long to live. Marino stopped eating and went into seclusion. "He gave up," Frank said. "He wanted to die."

Marino's wife, Flora, didn't know what to do. Neither did the doctors.

So Frank and Dante Benedetti went to the Pieretti home, unlocked the door of his room, got Marino dressed, and took him to Nick's. "We said, 'Chick, if you're going to die, let's die happy.'"

The friends drank and swapped stories and bawdy jokes. Marino started eating again. "It was like a miracle. Everybody was amazed."

"If you want to do this again next week," Frank told Marino, "you'd better straighten out and live a little."

The friends returned to Nick's and when others joined them, they moved to Benedetti's New Pisa Restaurant. "We started with three," Frank said. "It kept growing and growing and growing."

Marino called the luncheons "my medicine" and told the guys he felt lousy, but not as lousy as they look. He asked for the luncheons to continue after he died and that the group raise money to buy baseball equipment for kids.

"If you don't do all of that, I'm going to haunt you bastards," he said. "You're gonna be sitting around and feel a little flick behind your ears. When you do, you'll know it's me, serving you up one of my little knockdown pitches . . . my little warning." [13]

Every month the group makes a donation to the baseball program of a local boys club. The luncheons are loud and loose like a men's locker room.

"Listen up!" Frank hollered to begin one luncheon. "Quiet down. Let's go, I got a hot date at 1:30. Our motto is: the will to live. While I'm on this earth, I'm going to give you hell with all I can. Because you guys need it."

And the guys love it.

"We've got two priests that turn their collar around when they come to the luncheons," Frank said. "We converted them."

"Tough exteriors; gentle hearts," said Father John O'Brien, one of the priests. "Some people brag about camaraderie; these guys live it."

Frank once handed out batteries for guys with hearing aids. "If you don't know what I'm talking about, how do you know what you're going to be doing next?"

There are no membership fees or monthly dues.

"You don't have to be a ball player," said Frank. "Just be a human being."

Joe DiMaggio's nephew, also named Joe DiMaggio, attended one of the luncheons.

"What was it like to have Joe DiMaggio as an uncle?" he was asked.

"It was better having Marilyn Monroe for an aunt," young Joe quipped.

Joe DiMaggio himself showed up at a luncheon in 1985.

"Hey, Frank, don't make a big issue of me being here," Joe said. "I don't want to go through all this shit, signing autographs."

So Frank announced, "We all know that Big D is in the house. He's one of the boys. Leave him alone."

And the boys did just that.

After the luncheon, Joe visited with Vincent "Niggy" Marino, a boyhood buddy who grew up to be a professional boxer.

"Give me the twenty bucks you owe me," Niggy said, referring to money he loaned Joe when he played for the Seals in the 1930s.

"I thought you forgot about that," Joe said.

"I don't forget about nothin', you cheap Dago bastard!"

Joe was grinning as he signed a baseball and gave it to Niggy.

"What the hell am I supposed to do with this?" Niggy asked. "Shove it up my ass? I want my twenty bucks."

Niggy never got his twenty dollars. He didn't care. He was telling the story fifteen years later and still laughing about it.

Laughter was the medicine that kept Marino Pieretti going. And it's why the group was still going thirty-five years later after the death of his pals, Dante Benedetti and Frank Strazzullo, who rousted him out of bed for the first luncheon.

"This group represents Marino Pieretti's spirit," Benedetti said.

"The green jacket is a symbol of Marino's spirit," Frank said. "It's not one you hang on the wall or you keep in a closet. You wear it."

Sally John had heard about Red Adams from her husband, Tommy, a pitcher for the Los Angeles Dodgers but she had never met the team's pitching coach.

"Is this the guy that's going to coach you, Tommy?" Sally asked. "The guy that pitched the twenty-two-hitter?"

Red Adams was the pitching coach for the Dodgers from 1969 to 1980 and helped develop John, Don Sutton, Bill Singer, Andy Messersmith, Rick Sutcliffe, Bob Welch, and many other outstanding pitchers. Most of them can tell you about the time Adams went the distance in a game, scattering twenty-one or twenty-two hits. The number sometimes changes in the retelling of the story.

"I think it was a twenty-two-hitter," he said of the game that took place in 1939 when he pitched for Bisbee, Arizona, in the Class D Arizona-Texas League. "It was a mile-high there . . . a small park. We only had five or six pitchers. One guy had a bad arm.

"Carl Dittmar was the manager. And when he gave you the ball, he'd say, 'Red, I don't know if you're going to get a win or a loss but you're going to have a complete game.' You went nine regardless of the type of game you pitched. You learned to throw from all angles. Because if one angle wasn't working too well, you could throw submarine, over the top, mix it up.

"Anyway, I pitched this game. I always tell people that we made ten errors. I don't know how many unearned runs there were but I lost 16–15 in twelve innings and I gave up twenty-two hits. And I always threw this in—I don't know if it was true or not—but I told the guys: I came back with three days' rest and jerked up a nineteen-hitter."

In a *Los Angeles Times* story in 1974, Don Sutton said, "Red pitched in the minors half a century. He knows what it is to work hard and never really get any time in the majors. Chances are anything we run into he's been through it."[14]

Sutton was right about that.

In nineteen years in the minors, Red had a 193–182 won-loss record and 3.78 ERA for 3,318 innings pitched. Compare that with his 0–1 record and 8.25 ERA for twelve innings in the majors with the Cubs in 1945.

"I was a sore-armed pitcher," Red said.

He also was one of the smartest pitchers to step on the pitcher's mound.

After baffling the Hollywood Stars in a game, Stars' manager Bobby Bragan asked Red, "Have you ever had any less stuff than you beat us with last night?"

"I'm sure I have," Red said. "But I didn't have to use it."

Richie Myers was an all-star shortstop for Sacramento before he joined the Angels in 1956.

"I never saw a straight ball," said Myers. "It was always a slider or breaking ball because he knew I liked to pull the ball."

One of Myers' teammates at Sacramento was Bob Dillinger, a .306 hitter during his six years in the majors and the 1953 PCL batting champion with a .366 average.

"Red will pitch you that way until you start hitting 'em," Dillinger told Myers. "And, then, he'll change on you."

Dillinger taught Myers "to wait a little bit longer and learn to hit guys like Red."

"When you go to the big leagues, you're going to have more of these guys that are going to work on you," Dillinger said. "They'll get a book on you. The more things you can do to keep out of their book the things you can't do, it's going to benefit you."

"Bob used Red as an example because he's the one who would pitch to your weakness all the time," Myers said.

In 1956, when Red and Gene Mauch were teammates in L.A., it was a foregone conclusion that Mauch would manage in the big leagues.

"If I do," Gene told Red, "you're my pitching coach."

When Mauch became manager of the Phillies in 1960, he offered Red a job as pitching coach.

Red was a scout for the Dodgers at the time and declined the offer. But that didn't keep Mauch from using Red to challenge his Phillies pitchers.

"The nagging memory of Red Adams may help explain why three times within two weeks last year, Mauch demanded that his pitcher pitch to a talented hitter with runners on second and third," Stan Hochman wrote in the February 1963 issue of *Baseball Digest*.

"You never walked anybody with Red pitching," Mauch said. "He would find some way to make a hitter swing at a pitch over his head or down around his ankles."[15]

Tommy John joined the Dodgers in 1972 after nine solid but unspectacular years in the American League. He was 11–5 his first year in L.A. and 16–7 in 1973. He was 13–3 in 1974 when he hurt his right throwing arm and had what is now widely known as Tommy John surgery.

After eighteen months of rehabilitation, Tommy returned in 1976 to go 10–10, followed by 20–7 and 17–10 records the next two seasons before he signed as a free agent with the Yankees in 1978.

In his autobiography, *TJ*, Tommy wrote, "Red told me that in the National League, I would do better relying on my fastball more than my curve. Red was exactly right, and under his coaching, I prospered in Los Angeles."[16]

Red hung out with his pitchers on the road. "If he isn't talking to a pitcher," Sutton said, "he is probably talking to a catcher about a pitcher."[17]

"The first thing you need to do is to get know the person before you even attempt to do any coaching," Red said. "Get to know the guy—how he thinks; how he goes about his work; how he handles a rough spot; how consistent he is with his focus or his mechanics. If you know about him, you're hopefully making a friend out of him.

"I always looked at pitchers like my little brother. You're just trying to help them when you can, if you can. And you hope to hell that the ones you don't help, you don't hurt. Sometimes you can try to do too much."

For Red, pitching is an art that takes years to develop.

"When a guy has it all figured out, then, I think he's in trouble. There are certain things you can be pretty set about—conditioning, things of that nature. But as far as any one way to throw a baseball, there are many effective deliveries. The fun part of coaching was the analyzing. Why is this guy effective? What does he do well?"

Tommy John won eighty-seven games in six seasons with the Dodgers. He won 164 games after his surgery, retiring in 1989 at age forty-six with 288 career victories.

Don Sutton was inducted into the Hall of Fame in 1998 with 324 wins over twenty-three seasons. When Red became the Dodgers' pitching coach in 1969, Sutton had lost more games than he won (34–42). Under Red's tutelage, his won-loss record was 196–133.

After the 1980 season, Red retired and Sutton signed as a free agent with the Houston Astros. Before leaving L.A., Sutton gave Red a new four-wheel drive Datsun pickup truck, saying, "I can't say enough about what he has meant to my career."[18]

Sutton and John obviously remembered Red's twenty-two-hitter.

NOTES

1. *Los Angeles Times,* June 13, 1956, C3.
2. *Los Angeles Herald-Express,* June 25, 1956, B4.
3. *Los Angeles Times,* April 4, 1956, C3.
4. Ibid.
5. *The Sporting News,* August 9, 1945, 5.
6. *The Sporting News,* March 15, 1945, 8.
7. *Washington Post,* July 17, 1945, 8.
8. Ibid.
9. *San Francisco Examiner & Chronicle,* November 27, 1977, B1.
10. *Modesto Bee,* August 5, 1958, A10.
11. *San Francisco Examiner,* February 26, 1980, 27.
12. Ibid.
13. *San Francisco Sunday Examiner & Chronicle,* California Living Magazine, May 6, 1979, 23.
14. *Los Angeles Times,* March 17, 1974, Part III, 1.
15. *Baseball Digest,* February 1963, 67.
16. Tommy John with Dan Valenti, *T.J.: My 26 Years in Baseball* (New York: Bantam Books, 1991), 153.
17. *Los Angeles Times,* March 17, 1974, Part III, 10.
18. *The Sporting News,* September 27, 1980, 8.

FOURTEEN

The Kid Phenoms

"'Pour it on 'em, Tony,' we roared, and he tipped his cap to us as he walked off the field after pitching out of a jam. He won the game, and for years I looked for his name on some big-league rosters, but he disappeared into the heart of America. One of the multitude who was not chosen." —Ray Kinsella in the book *Shoeless Joe*, by W. P. Kinsella

A month into the 1956 season, Frank Finch of the *Los Angeles Times* wrote, "If there is any such animal in baseball as a lead-pipe cinch, Dick Drott, Bob Anderson and Bob Thorpe of the Angels' pitching staff belong in that category. They're can't-missers, destined for stardom in the majors." [1]

This was not just hyperbole from a hometown sportswriter.

"He [Drott] reminds me of Allie Reynolds," said Charlie Silvera, a former New York Yankees and Chicago Cubs catcher who caught both pitchers. Silvera likened Drott to the six-time all-star Reynolds because "he murders those hitters with a fastball, curve and guts." [2]

Anderson inspired comparisons with two of the best relief pitchers of all time. "He was not quite like Mariano Rivera but at least as good as Troy Percival," Gene Mauch said.

Thorpe won twenty-eight games in 1954 at Stockton, California. His manager, Gene Handley, was involved in the Cubs' signing of Greg Maddux in 1984.

"He was the same type of pitcher as Maddux—not an overpowering fastball but effective because he set up the hitters with off-speed pitches," Handley said. "He had an outstanding changeup. And that's something for a young man coming out of high school."

Drott, Anderson, and Thorpe were can't-missers. And there were times during the 1956 season when the can't-miss label applied to two other right-handers, Gene Fodge and Johnny Briggs.

211

"I would've loved coaching those guys," Dwight "Red" Adams said. "If I'd been managing, we either would've won it by more or maybe I would've screwed it up because I would've gotten rid of all the old pitchers and used the young guys."

Drott was nineteen years old to begin the season, Anderson twenty, Thorpe twenty-one, Briggs twenty-two, and Fodge twenty-four.

Anderson, used only in relief, was the most consistent with a 12–4 won-loss record, team-best 2.65 earned run average (ERA), and twenty-eight saves, although the save was not recognized as an official statistic at the time.

"He was like a machine," Adams said. "He could throw strikes. He could overpower you. He just went in there and nailed them to the wall."

"He had a fairly good curveball but he would just come in and blow smoke at 'em for an inning or two," said Angel shortstop Casey Wise.

Anderson had all of the qualities of the starting pitcher he later became in the majors with the Cubs.

"He had the body, the arm, decent delivery, a well-coordinated guy," Adams said. "He should've been starting over some of us old dudes."

Drott had a 13–10 record and was the most dominant of the whiz kids, striking out a league-leading 184 in 197 innings pitched. He also was erratic as reflected in his 108 walks and 4.39 ERA.

The six-foot, 185-pounder won six of his first seven decisions and, then, lost four of his next five. He was still the talk of the league with his lively fastball and devastating curveball.

"His curveball snarls up and bows like a head waiter," reported the *Los Angeles Herald & Express*, "and his lively fastball exposes every batter to a siege of pneumonia."[3]

"It was the sharpest curveball that you ever want to see," said Wise. "When his curveball was good, just forget about it."

"Dick had as good of stuff as anybody I ever caught," Silvera said. "The only problem he had at that time was his command and knowledge of pitching."

Fodge wasn't as flashy as the others and didn't attract attention until he reeled off nine straight victories in July and August. He finished with a 19–7 mark and 4.31 ERA, tossing two shutouts and completing eleven of the twenty-five games he started. He appeared in relief in nineteen other games.

"Gene was a worker that didn't have outstanding stuff but was capable of getting the job done," said Raymond "Moe" Bauer. "He had the kind of thing that you can't measure."

"He had a good arm and he did it easy," said Adams.

Despite a 7–7 record and 4.86 ERA, Adams was especially high on Thorpe. "Bob didn't throw as hard as Drott, Fodge, or Anderson. But he threw good enough. He was a serious-minded guy on the mound and about his work."

Adams thought Thorpe had a chance to become a major league star like "a Johnny Sain, Lew Burdette or Sal Maglie."

The Cubs outbid fifteen other major league teams for the hard-throwing Briggs after he won fifteen games for last-place Sacramento in 1955.

Briggs was 5–5 with a 5.63 ERA, injuries limiting him to only thirteen starts in eighteen games.

"He had a good curveball but he could put some mustard on his fastball," said Richie Myers, who played with Briggs in Sacramento and L.A. "He didn't try to dazzle you with changeups or a lot of off-speed stuff."

"I didn't like him when he was with Sacramento," George Freese said. "He tried to nail me every time I came to the plate."

"He was a bulldog-type guy," said Adams. "He had that look about him. The way he carried himself, you could tell that he was a battler."

Briggs lost a battle with his temper after Hollywood shelled him for five runs in two innings of a game in early August. He slammed his pitching hand against a dugout post, fracturing a finger.

"That's a pretty strong temper," Myers said. "You can take yourself right out of baseball swinging at the wrong part of the dugout."

In the 1950s, few teams had specialty coaches for pitching or hitting so players helped each other.

"I needed all kinds of coaching," Adams said. "I had a terrible curveball. I improved my curveball when I was in my thirties from some kid that came to our club from Class B. You either could do it or you couldn't."

Scheffing and Marino Pieretti worked with Drott to develop a changeup. Adams mentored Thorpe. Piper Davis encouraged the kid pitchers. Mauch and Elvin Tappe made sure they remained focused.

"Most young pitchers have a tendency to stray sometime during the ballgame," Adams said. "I can remember Don Sutton, as great as he was, doing that. It's part of growing as a pitcher. I call it, 'Staying on your stick every pitch.' All you've got to do is wander just a little bit and trouble crops up."

Adams used hypothetical situations to teach young pitchers when he was coaching for the Dodgers.

> First guy up, you make a perfect pitch and he hits it on the fist and just dunks over the infield . . . one of those dying seagulls.
>
> Next guy, you got three-and-two on him and you throw a perfect strike on the outside corner and the umpire calls it a ball. You've got two guys on and nobody out. You're throwing great.
>
> Next guy hits a perfect double play ball to shortstop and he's just getting ready to field it and it hits a rock and bounces over his head. Now, you've got a run in, two on and nobody out. What are you going to do then?

Are you going to take stock of things and take another hitch in your belt like they say ol' Walter Johnson used to do? He just took another hitch in his belt and he let out a little more shaft. But the rest of us don't have that kind of talent.

Are you going to lose your composure? Are you going to start looking to see if somebody is warming up in the bullpen? You're going to figure out how to get out of the situation with the least amount of damage. And you can only do it one pitch at a time. That's how good pitchers do it.

The Angels' kids learned a lot about pitching in 1956 just from watching Adams. In one complete game victory, he didn't walk nor strike out a batter. In another, he scattered sixteen hits, twice working out of bases-loaded jams by getting hitters to ground into inning-ending double plays.

The kid phenoms soon found out that talent alone doesn't bring success and that can't-missers often miss out on the stardom others predict for them.

The size of the towheaded kid throwing at Chicago's Wrigley Field was impressive enough. But the popping sound of his fastball hitting the catcher's glove was all the Cubs coaches needed to hear.

"Don't let that kid out of the ballpark unsigned," said Scheffing, a coach for the Cubs at the time.[4]

The kid causing the commotion was Bob Anderson of Hammond, Indiana, a Cubs fan for all of his eighteen-year life.

One look at the six-foot-four-inch, 210-pound right-hander and his blazing fastball and Scheffing was seeing stars in his future.

You can teach a kid how to throw a curveball but not a fastball. He either has one or not. Anderson had a fastball that, if radar guns had existed then, would've been clocked around ninety-five miles per hour. He also had the kind of fastball that hitters feared.

"Oh, God, he could bring it," said Ed Mickelson of the Portland Beavers and one of the Coast League's top hitters in 1956.

"Oh, God!" was the reaction to an Anderson fastball that hit Pueblo's Don Musto in the head during the second inning of a game May 25, 1955, between Des Moines and Pueblo in the Class A Western League. Anderson was pitching for Des Moines.

The ball smashed into Musto's left temple just above the eye. "He dropped straight to the ground," Anderson said. "Home plate was crimson. I thought he was dead."

So did everybody else in the ballpark.

"It scared me. I've never had control over somebody's life like that. The shock going through me was just incredible. Watching him being carried off on the stretcher really unnerved me."

Musto was taken to the hospital where he was treated for a concussion and damage to his left eye that caused him to temporarily lose sight in the eye. Anderson went on to strike out fourteen and finish the game, but he wasn't the same pitcher for a while. "I was afraid to come in tight so I was wild and outside most of the time. My record, of course, suffered."

Musto recovered from the injuries and returned to action a month later. "Of all people, the first person he faced when he came back was me. After that, both of us were all right."

Prior to the incident, Anderson was 5–1 with two straight shutouts. He was 6–4 the rest of the season to wind up 11–5.

When Anderson reported to L.A. in 1956, he expected to be reassigned to a team in the lower minors, especially after a shaky spring performance.

In an exhibition game against the University of Southern California (USC), he was roughed up for nine earned runs. He gave up a whopping twenty-seven runs in four other games he started.

"I didn't deserve to be a starting pitcher at the beginning of the season," Anderson said. "I was lucky to be there because of the roster requirements."

Scheffing obviously saw something in Anderson that made him think he could be the team's ace relief pitcher, replacing Omar "Turk" Lown who had moved up to the Cubs.

In the 1950s, relief pitching was just beginning to emerge as a specialty. Most relievers started some games and virtually all of them were veterans. Lown was thirty-one when he pitched for the Angels in 1955. The prototype reliever of the era, Ellis "Old Folks" Kinder, was in his late thirties when he starred for the Boston Red Sox.

Scheffing had time to experiment with Anderson as Coast League teams could carry thirty players the first month of the season before trimming their rosters to twenty-one.

Initially, Anderson was used in games where there was little pressure because the Angels either had a big lead or were far behind. Gradually, he got into closer games.

After eight relief appearances, Anderson had pitched fifteen innings without giving up an earned run. By mid-May, he had appeared in fifteen of the Angels' thirty-two games, allowing only four earned runs in twenty-seven innings for an amazing 1.33 ERA.

"Scheffing never came to me and said, 'Bob, we want to make a relief pitcher out of you.' It just happened. I didn't question it. I wanted to play and if that's the role I was going to be used in and be effective, that's what I wanted to do."

Anderson adapted quickly to his new role.

"I could get ready in about ten or twelve pitches. And, then, I would just throw loose until I was needed."

He had good control, walking fifty-two batters in 105 innings. "My strengths were that I was young, I could throw hard and I was wild

Figure 14.1. Steve Bilko (left) was the Pacific Coast League's most valuable player in 1956 and pitcher Bob Anderson the league's top rookie. Angel manager Bob Scheffing looks on proudly in the background. *UCLA Charles E. Young Research Library Department of Special Collections, Los Angeles Times Photographic Archives.*

enough to keep them on their toes. They were expecting a fastball from me. They just weren't sure exactly where it was going to be."

Scheffing put Anderson and the other young pitchers at ease with his firm yet laid-back style of managing.

Anderson and Drott showed up for a night game with bad sunburns from spending the afternoon at the beach. "Our backs and fronts were really red. We were really uncomfortable."

"Look, guys," Scheffing told them, "I'm not going to say anything at this point as long as you can pitch. But if you can't pitch, I'm going to fine you."

Not only did Anderson and Drott pitch, they spent very little time at the beach the rest of the season.

Anderson developed a special kinship with Scheffing, who was managing the Cubs when he became a starting pitcher.

In 1958, Scheffing sent Anderson to Fort Worth in the Class AA Texas League to work on becoming a starter. Anderson came up with a decent curveball to go with his fastball.

"I can pinpoint exactly when I became a pitcher. I remember one specific hitter."

The hitter was Keith Little, batting cleanup for Dallas.

"I had two fastballs that were outside so I had a two-and-oh count on him. I thought, 'Well, he'll probably chase the next one.' So I'll come up high and inside.' I did and he chased it. Then I threw him a curveball exactly where I wanted, right on the outside corner, which he took for a strike. The next one I wanted to throw him up tight again. And I did. Everything just worked perfect. And I thought: 'you know, this is what pitching is all about. This is fun.'"

Scheffing had the starting pitcher he wanted.

In 1959, Anderson won twelve games and was the workhorse of the Cubs pitching staff, starting thirty-six games and pitching 235 innings. The Cubs finished fifth with a 74–80 won-loss record, their best in seven years. But Scheffing was fired at the end of the season. "Was I surprised when the Cubs bounced me?" Scheffing said. "Have you ever had someone set off a firecracker behind you?"[5]

"I thought the world of Scheffing," Anderson said. "It was a sad day for Chicago when he left. It was a very, very difficult time not only for the players but also the fans."

Over the next three years, Anderson played for seven different managers and head coaches. In 1960, he won nine games as a starter. In 1961–1962 under the so-called College of Coaches, he pitched primarily in relief.

"There was no rhyme or reason as to the way we were used," Anderson said. "I remember warming up and pitching six games in a row. There was no concern for what could happen to the pitchers."

In late August 1961, Anderson appeared in three straight games against Pittsburgh, recording two saves and a win. He pitched one inning in the first game, two and one-third innings in the second, and three innings in the third. On the last pitch of the third game Anderson hurt his arm.

"I remember vividly when I hurt my arm. It was against Roberto Clemente and it was a pitch that didn't need to be thrown because I had struck him out on the previous pitch but the umpire called it ball two. Even Clemente dropped the bat and started to walk away from the plate. I threw him a fastball that moved in on him, but when I threw it, I felt something in my shoulder. The day after that I warmed up to go into a ballgame and I couldn't throw."

Anderson appeared in nine more games in 1961, finishing with a 7–10 record, eight saves, and a 4.26 ERA.

"The year after that, 1962, why, it was dog crap," Bob said, referring to his 2–7 record and 5.02 ERA.

Anderson hung on for two more years. In 1963, he was 3–1 for the Detroit Tigers and in 1964 he was back in the minors where he was a combined 7–15 for two Kansas City Athletics farm teams.

During a medical examination some twenty-five years later, Bob asked a doctor to check the shoulder of his right throwing arm. With his fingers, the doctor pressed on the area that hurt when Bob pitched. Pain shot through the shoulder much like it did the night he struck out Clemente.

"That's it!" said Bob. "That's it!"

"That's your rotator cuff," the doctor said.

Anderson had a torn rotator cuff the last four years he pitched. Today, the injury can be repaired surgically. In the 1960s, doctors didn't know what to do about a torn rotator cuff except tell a pitcher to get on with the rest of his life.

Bob's promising baseball career was over ten years after it began. He was twenty-eight.

Dick Drott was cruising along and, then, suddenly, the hitters were smashing fastballs they couldn't touch earlier in the game.

Angel catcher Joe Hannah called timeout and walked to the mound to tell his young pitcher he needed to start mixing up his pitches.

"Just go back there, Joe, sit down, relax and enjoy the game," Dick said. "I got this express going tonight."

Drott was proud of his fastball.

"In the first inning he's fast, the next time you're up he's real fast and the third time around he throws bullets at you," marveled Jim Westlake, first baseman for the Vancouver Mounties.[6]

"He had a live fastball and major league plus curveball," said Red Adams. "I've never seen a guy grip a curveball like he did. Usually you use the seams to grip the ball. He gripped the ball right in the middle—no seam at all. If you were teaching someone to throw a curveball, it's the last place you'd ever show them where to grip it."

"I was always amazed by his curveball," said Jim Brosnan, a pitcher for the Cubs. "It was a beautiful pitch. It reminded me of Sandy Koufax's curveball and Koufax, in my opinion, was the best pitcher of all time."[7]

Drott was good and he knew it.

He was pitching for the Cubs against the St. Louis Cardinals. There were two outs in the ninth inning and the Cards had the tying run on third base and the winning run on first. The next batter was Stan Musial.

Scheffing went to the mound to talk with Dick.

"Listen," Scheffing said, "don't give this guy a fastball and keep your stuff away from the plate. Make him chase it if you can."

Drott looked his manager in the eye.

"Skipper," he said, "Mr. Musial is overmatched."[8]

Scheffing returned to the dugout and watched his kid pitcher whiff the great Cardinals slugger to end the game.

"Dick was a typical cocky young guy," Adams said. "That's one of the things that made him good."

Drott was sixteen years old in 1952 when he helped pitch his American Legion Junior team in Cincinnati to the national championship. He won fifty-four of sixty-one decisions in high school, attracting offers from all but two major league teams.

"I signed with the Cubs," Dick explained, "because they didn't have a very good pitching staff at the time and I felt that I had a better chance to move up quickly."[9]

And he was right.

In 1954, he went directly from high school to Cedar Rapids, Iowa, in the Class B Three I League where he was 5–7 and fanned ninety-three batters in 108 innings. He pitched for Burlington in the same league in 1955, improving both his record (10–8) and strikeout ratio (151 in 158 innings).

That earned Drott a spot on the Angels roster in 1956 and an invitation to the Cubs' spring training camp in Mesa, Arizona. Scheffing also was there.

Dick had the camp buzzing after hurling three scoreless innings in the Cubs' first exhibition game against the Baltimore Orioles.

Concerned he might lose Drott to the pitching-starved Cubs, Scheffing ordered him to take the first train to L.A.

Dick got his "express" going early for the Angels, fanning seventy-four batters in his first fifty-nine innings. After striking out fourteen and fifteen in successive games, one of the Angels said wistfully, "Gee, but I'd like to own twenty-five percent of that guy."[10]

"Dick had some of the finest natural stuff I've ever seen in a pitcher," said Anderson, who shared an efficiency apartment with Drott near Hollywood. "He was nonchalant about it."

Anderson said off the field Drott was laid back "like a lamb," but "he was a tiger" on it.

> He really challenged them. He knew he had good stuff and he was extremely confident in his ability to strike people out. He had a live fastball and one of the best curveballs that I've seen in my life. He could throw it at various speeds. He had great control over it. And he loved to throw it. Had he not hurt his arm with the Cubs, he probably would've been one of the outstanding pitchers of that era.

Drott's rookie season in 1957 was amazingly like another first-year Cub pitcher—Kerry Wood in 1998.

Dick, who turned twenty-one during the 1957 season, had a 15–11 won-loss record, 3.58 ERA, and his 170 strikeouts ranked second in the

Figure 14.2.   Dick Drott was being compared with the great pitchers of his time after striking out a league-leading 184 batters for the 1956 Angels and winning fifteen games as a rookie for the Chicago Cubs in 1957. "Dick Drott had the best curveball I ever saw in a nineteen-year-old kid," said Gene Mauch, the Angels' veteran second baseman. *Author's collection.*

National League. Kerry, also twenty-one, was 13–6 with a 3.40 ERA and 233 strikeouts, third in the league.

When Wood fanned twenty Houston Astros in a one-hit shutout at Wrigley Field May 6, 1998, it brought back memories of Drott whiffing fifteen Milwaukee Braves on the same field May 27, 1957.

"Tiger Woods, Kerry Wood," Cubs first baseman Mark Grace said after Kerry's gem. "Hello, world." [11]

"That boy," future Hall of Famer Robin Roberts said of Drott, "is as good a pitcher at his age as anyone I've ever seen." [12]

Frank Lane, the Cardinals' general manager, predicted Drott "can't miss" before lamenting, "If only we had him." [13]

Dick's fifteen strikeouts were just three shy of the major league record at the time. He had Henry "Hank" Aaron, the Braves' legendary slugger, so confused that he was called out on strikes three times—twice on fastballs and once on a curve.

"Dick Drott has a chance to be one of the great ones," Scheffing said after the 1957 season. [14]

The similarity in the careers of the two Cubs pitchers doesn't stop there. Wood hurt his arm and spent the following season on the disabled list recovering from Tommy John surgery. Over his fourteen-year career, he was on the disabled list sixteen times, never fulfilling the potential he showed as a rookie.

After a 7–11 record and 5.43 ERA his second year, Drott served six months active duty with the Army Reserve. In the spring of 1959, he returned to the Cubs out of condition and some twenty pounds under his playing weight, complaining the Army food wasn't fit to eat. Dick hurt his arm when he tried to throw too hard too soon. He was 1–2 and spent most of the season on the disabled list or in the minors trying to regain the form that made him a "can't-misser."

It never happened. He was 2–10, and on and off the disabled list the next three years before a 2–12 record in 1963 with Houston ended his major league career.

Drott had one shining moment his last season when he was as good as he ever was and almost as good as one of the all-time greats—Juan Marichal of the San Francisco Giants.

Dick had a one-hit shutout going into the bottom of the eighth inning of a classic pitching duel with Marichal. He gave up a bloop double, struck out the next batter, and got Marichal to fly out before another double gave the Giants their only run of the game. Drott struck out seven and allowed three hits. Marichal fanned five and pitched a no-hitter.

Marichal wound up winning 243 games in a Hall of Fame career while Drott finished with a 27–46 record in the majors.

Drott went to work in 1965 for the Chicago Park District, running community baseball programs until he died of stomach cancer in 1985. He was forty-nine.

Scheffing succeeded in whisking Drott out of the Cubs' spring training camp in Arizona to L.A. before anybody knew what was going on. But the Angels manager knew he couldn't get away with putting Johnny Briggs on the same train.

Scheffing had big plans for Briggs after the Cubs acquired him from the Sacramento Solons. But the five-foot-ten-inch, 165 pounder showed so much stuff in the spring that the Cubs kept him through the first month of the 1956 season.

When Briggs arrived in L.A. in mid-May, he had a bone chip floating in the elbow of his throwing arm.

"One big bone chip," said Briggs. "It was like a front tooth when they took it out."

"When he was pitching well, the chip was in one location and when he didn't, the chip was in a place where it created pain," said Anderson.

"In those days, if a guy had chips or something, he was a little bit suspect if he wouldn't play hurt," Casey Wise said.

Briggs pitched well for the Cubs—one earned run in five innings for a 1.69 ERA. In his lone start for the Angels before he was placed on the disabled list, he allowed one earned run in six innings. Johnny returned to action ten days later to win his first game of the season but the elbow bothered him so much that surgery was required, sidelining him for almost a month.

During a ten-day stretch in late July, Briggs won three straight games prior to winding up on the disabled list again with a fractured finger in his pitching hand.

"Johnny Briggs' sore arm really hurt us," Scheffing said. "I figured he would be our number one or number two pitcher with Dave Hillman."[15]

"I remember him showing me the scar from the operation on his pitching arm," said Adams. "During that era, it was pretty unusual for a young pitcher like that."

"I wasn't quite right," Briggs said. "Later my arm got better and the next year a lot better."

In Sacramento, Briggs pitched for the worst team in the league so the opportunity to pitch for a run-scoring machine like the 1956 Angels was too much to resist. "They didn't want me to, but I came back and pitched as soon as I could. I wanted to pitch for that ball club because it was pretty hard to lose a game. We were the top minor league team in the top minor league."

In 1955, Briggs was the top pitching prospect in the top minor league. Briggs won his first three starts for the lowly Solons, two by shutouts, and he went thirteen and two-thirds innings in his fourth game without a decision.

A caravan of big league scouts began following the twenty-one-year-old dubbed the "Folsom Phenom" by the local media because he graduated from Folsom High School about twenty-five miles from Sacramento.

One of the scouts was the Detroit Tigers' Joe Gordon. He was manager of Solons in 1951–1952 when Briggs showed up at a tryout camp.

In American Legion Junior competition, Briggs averaged eighteen strikeouts a game. He hurled two no-hitters, allowing only sixteen hits in fifty-four innings. "But that was in Folsom, not Sacramento," Johnny said. "When I graduated from high school, nobody even asked me to try out let alone sign a contract."

He got a job at McClellan Air Force base near Sacramento where a coworker urged him to try out with the Solons.

Briggs pitched the first inning of a practice game.

"Joe Gordon stood behind me as I pitched," Briggs recalled. "I struck out a couple of guys and as we were walking off the field, he said, 'Kid, I want you to go upstairs. We're going to sign you up.'"

In 1952–1953, Johnny pitched for Idaho Falls in the Class C Pioneer League. He was 13–11 the first year and 10–8 the second, walking more batters (281) than he struck out (277).

Johnny's control and record improved dramatically in 1954 at Salem, Oregon, in the Class A Western International League. He was 20–8, walking 161, and striking out 233 batters in 255 innings.

After watching Johnny yield only five runs in his first four Coast League games, Gordon declared he had a "major league arm." [16]

The financially strapped Solons slapped a $125,000 price tag on him. "Briggs may be the answer to our problems," Solons president Fred David said. [17]

"The price isn't excessive if Briggs is as good as our scouts report," the general manager of one National League team told the *Sacramento Union*. "Briggs could be the best pitcher in the minors—another Herb Score." [18]

Johnny wowed major-league scouts with three more shutouts, including a one-hitter, but by the close of the season his record was 15–15 despite a solid 3.44.

That was good enough for the Cubs, who acquired Briggs and Myers in exchange for cash and two players and then sent them to L.A.

Johnny would never match his success in Sacramento.

He was a combined 5–6 for the Cubs in 1957–1958 before being traded to the Cleveland Indians, where he had another arm operation. In 1959–1960, he was 4–5 with the Indians and Kansas City Athletics to finish with a 9–11 career record in the majors.

"I could never understand why Johnny didn't get more of a shot with the Cubbies," Anderson said.

"At that time, he was just one of many strong arms in the Cubs organization," explained Gene Fodge.

Johnny spent two more years in the minors before returning home to Folsom in 1960 and getting into the real estate business. He was twenty-eight.

Gene Fodge was proud of each of his nineteen wins for the 1956 Angels, especially the one that gave L.A. its first pennant in nine years.

But the victory that brought him the greatest pleasure took place two years later when he was pitching for the Cubs at the Los Angeles Coliseum, about two miles from Little Wrigley.

Fodge beat the Dodgers 15–2 for his first and only major league win.

What made it even more special was that he got the best of two of the greatest pitchers in baseball history—Don Drysdale and Sandy Koufax.

Drysdale, twenty-two, and Koufax, twenty-three, were just starting their careers at the time but so was Fodge, a six-foot, 175 pounder from South Bend, Indiana.

"I couldn't believe all of the telegrams I got from South Bend when I won that game," Fodge said, laughing. "My parents, my teachers in school, coaches around town, even the mayor sent me a telegram. I'm glad they did it then because they didn't get another chance."

Drysdale started the game for the Dodgers, followed by two other pitchers before Koufax appeared. Meanwhile, Fodge pitched a complete game, scattering ten hits and striking out three.

The game was reminiscent of 1956 when Fodge methodically mowed down opponents while his teammates piled up runs.

"When I can win nineteen games and still have a 4.31 earned run average, you know what kind of scoring they're doing," Fodge said. "It doesn't say a whole lot for my pitching, but it does say a lot for their hitting."

Gene was the oldest of the kid pitchers and the most underrated.

"Gene was a real competitor," Anderson said. "He did not have overpowering stuff but he had a good fastball, a good slider and he could spot his pitches pretty well. I thought the Cubs gave him very, very little opportunity. For some reason, they didn't smile on Gene."

Adams echoed this view. "I had the feeling that they underestimated him. No one said it. But just the way they handled him. I wondered why they weren't higher on Gene because I thought he was a very good prospect."

The Cubs thought enough of Gene to put him on their 1956 roster along with Briggs and Thorpe.

He was 16–10 with a 2.28 ERA for Des Moines the previous year but those numbers don't reflect his true impact.

Over a three-week period, Gene pitched forty-two consecutive innings without allowing an earned run and thirty-two consecutive innings of scoreless ball, tying a league record. He gave up only three runs in a seventy-three-inning stretch.

"I could throw as hard as anybody coming up," Gene said. "I knew that and so did everybody else. But I found out, too, that it goes just as far when they hit it. The biggest thing that was ever put into my mind was that you've got to change speeds."

Fodge was inconsistent as a starter the first two months of the season so he was relegated to the bullpen with a 6–4 record and 5.62 ERA, the highest on the team. He responded with four innings of scoreless relief to win a game and then reeled off eight more victories, six as a starter, for nine in a row.

"After that season, I figured I was on my way up," Fodge said. "I was on my way to Chicago and they dropped me off in Fort Worth."

Gene spent the 1957 season shuttling from one Cubs farm team to another—Fort Worth to Portland to Memphis. He hurt his arm in Fort Worth and ended up with an 8–14 record. "Instead of keeping me in the warm weather in Fort Worth, they shipped me to Portland where it's damp and cold. My arm never did come around that year."

In 1958, Fodge made it all the way to Chicago. "I said, 'Well, maybe this is it.' But it didn't work out that way."

After beating the Dodgers in L.A., Gene started three more games. He was 1–1 with a 4.82 ERA when the Cubs sent him to Fort Worth in July where he finished the year and his career with an 8–3 record.

Fodge was twenty-seven when he went back to South Bend to stay.

In 2000, at the age of sixty-nine, Gene was sitting in a South Bend restaurant, reflecting on his career. He arrived in a Ford Ranger with a front license plate reading, CUBS FAN—I BELIEVE IN MIRACLES.

Fodge signed with the Cubs because his father was a diehard Cubs fan, and Gene believed the opportunity was greater in Chicago because "the club was down and in the process of rebuilding."[19]

"I'm still a live-and-die Cub fan," Gene said. "Most of the time you're dying."

He was wearing a Sammy Sosa watch and his PCL championship ring. "Every day was 'Happy Days,'" he said of the 1956 season.

Fodge was the winning pitcher when the Angels clinched the pennant. "I can still feel the champagne in my eyes. That will go to the grave with me.

"There are so many good parts of the game that I had a pleasure of being a part of. And, then, there's a lot of the downfall stuff. If I had to do it again, I'd do it with a different lifestyle."

Fodge's nickname was "Suds."

"Johnny Briggs gave me that because we liked to sip our beer."

Sometimes the sipping got out of control.

"My lifestyle changed a lot after I got into the game and I let it get to me. I didn't take care of myself. And when I finally got to Chicago, that's when it took its toll. They gave me the opportunity and I blew it."

"But I was in sixteen games," he said proudly. "It's sixteen games I'll never forget."

Fodge relished the memories.

"It has been what, forty-two years since I was in the majors? I'm still getting stuff in the mail from fans. I can't wait to open it. I get some of the most interesting letters from people saying, 'We're fans from your era and baseball has never been the same.' I always answer them. My wife says, 'You've never been out of baseball.' I haven't really because people have kept me in it."

Gene died in 2010 at the age of seventy-nine.

At his funeral, family and friends sang along with a recording of Harry Caray warbling "Take Me Out to the Ballgame." It was a fitting tribute to the only Cubs pitcher to beat Drysdale and Koufax in the same game.

Bob Thorpe was different from the Angels' other kid phenoms.

He relied on finesse, not speed. "He was the ultimate pitcher even as young as he was," Bob Anderson said.

He didn't say much, prompting teammates to call him "The Quiet Man." "Bob particularly didn't talk a whole lot about Bob," said Bob Borovicka, a high school teammate and his closest friend.

And he tended to hang out with veteran pitchers like Red Adams. "He always got along with older ball players," Borovicka said, "because there was never that 'me-me-me' or 'I-I-I' stuff with him."

"Bob Thorpe had maturity built into him when he was born," Anderson said.

Listen to those who saw Thorpe play in high school and you'd think he was born with a baseball in his right hand and the ability to pitch like an old pro.

Gene Leek faced Thorpe in high school before playing in the majors for the Indians and Los Angeles Angels.

"I knew he was going to play pro ball," said Leek. "Everybody was talking about how he was going to make it big. Even in high school, he was working the corners on you. He wasn't trying to throw it down the middle. He was pitching."

The pitch that had everybody talking was Thorpe's curveball.

"He had a downer—off the table type like Sandy Koufax," said Leek. "He came over the top with it. When you see a curveball like that, you go 'Whoa!' And he could get it over. He pinpointed that thing."

"I don't know where he got it but, boy, he had it," said Les Cassie, who coached Thorpe for two years at San Diego High School. "Maybe it was God given, I don't know. As he got stronger, it got better."

One of his teammates at San Diego High and in American Legion baseball was Bill Adams.

"Thorpe was a craftsman," said Bill. "He'd throw the breaking ball on a three-and-two or two balls and no strike count. He wasn't looking to get even in the count. He was looking to find a way to make you hit his pitch."

In 1952, Thorpe paced San Diego High to the Southern California baseball title and San Diego's Fighting Bob American Legion Junior team to the national championship finals where they lost to Drott's Cincinnati team.

A six-foot-one-inch, 170 pounder, Thorpe was signed by Cubs' scout Jack Fournier and sent to Stockton in the Class C California League.

"The kid won't impress you right away," Fournier said. "He isn't unusually fast and they'll get hits off him. But he'll be rough with men on base. He's got the poise of a big leaguer now."[20]

When Thorpe joined Stockton in 1953, the player-manager was Tony Freitas, considered by many the best minor league pitcher of all time with 342 victories, tops among lefties.

Freitas was forty-five; Thorpe was eighteen. The pairing of teacher and pupil was perfect as Freitas was a so-called dinker, throwing lazy curves and changeups with impeccable control.

"Bob was like a sponge," said Bill Adams. "He had an unsatisfied curiosity about pieces of the game that most of us didn't even think about."

Freitas helped Thorpe develop a changeup and how to move a hitter around in the batter's box to set up pitches.

"Once he acquired the changeup, he was a pretty awesome pitcher," said Borovicka. "From that point on, he probably wasn't as quick as a Dick Drott or some others, but he was fast enough that if they were looking for his curveball and he threw the fastball, it was by them."

Thorpe was clearly a good student as two years later John Hoffman wrote in the *Chicago Sun-Times*, "In polite company Bobby is a baby-faced kid who is seemingly out of place in the presence of hairy-chested ball players. But on the mound he is a cold-blooded performer with the poise and know-how of a 30-year veteran."[21]

Freitas showed the way on the mound with a 22–7 record and 2.38 ERA. Thorpe had a 16–8 mark and 3.52 ERA.

Handley replaced Freitas as Stockton's manager in 1954—the spectacular season that propelled Thorpe into the national limelight.

Thorpe's numbers speak for themselves: a 28–4 won-loss record, a 2.28 ERA, 197 strikeouts, and only 94 walks in 300 innings. Even more amazing, he completed thirty-three of the thirty-four games he started.

"It was almost like he could throw his glove on the mound and win," said Borovicka.

"He had no real weakness whatsoever," Handley said. "He could do it all. He was a crafty pitcher. I didn't have a pinch-hitter who was any better than him so I'd let him stay in the game. He was a good fielder, ran the bases well, just an all-round good athlete."

In two seasons at Stockton, Thorpe had a 44–13 record.

The Cubs placed Thorpe on their roster for the 1955 season, envisioning him as the first player in team history to jump from Class C to the majors.

The Cubs' high hopes were reflected in a full-page story in the *Sporting News.*

"Watching him on the mound, you would think he was a thirty-year-old veteran major league pitcher instead of just a twenty-year-old kid with only two years' experience in a Class C League," Cubs manager Stan Hack said, adding, "But it's a long haul from Class C to the majors."[22]

"He's certain to be a big league pitcher," Handley said, "and this very well could be the year. The kid's smart as a whip. He's got poise and enough stuff to make it. He's a wonder."[23]

Hack decided Thorpe was up to the task. "He has looked very good and right now I'd say he could win in our league. At least I'll start him in selected spots and we'll find out."[24]

Thorpe had never been to Chicago. "I've never seen a major league park," he admitted.[25]

A crowd of 19,504 watched as Bob took the mound for the Cubs at Wrigley Field to face the Chicago White Sox in the final game of the exhibition season.

"I may be making a mistake sending him against the Sox at this stage," Hack said. "But I think he's the kind of a kid who can take the assignment in stride."[26]

Thorpe struck out the side in the first inning, but not before the Sox loaded the bases with a hit and two walks. He wasn't as fortunate in the second, with the Sox scoring four runs on two walks and three hits, including a bases-loaded triple. In two innings, Bob struck out four, walked five, and gave up four runs on four hits.

"The ordeal of making his first pitching effort in a big league park before the biggest baseball crowd he had ever seen was too much for the twenty-year-old Thorpe," Hoffman reported in the *Sun-Times.*[27]

The Sox ordeal made Hack reluctant to use Thorpe during the regular season. Bob pitched a total of three innings in two games, both in relief and the Cubs far behind. He allowed four hits and one earned run.

Thorpe never pitched in the majors again. The Cubs shipped him to Des Moines where he finished the 1955 season with a 10–10 record and 3.65 ERA. But there was a reason for Thorpe's so-so performance.

"Bob's wife almost died in childbirth and they did lose the baby," explained Wid Matthews, the Cubs' personnel director. "And what made it even tougher for Thorpe was the fact that his wife was in San Diego while he was 2,000 miles away in Des Moines. It isn't difficult to understand the nervous tension he suffered and the misgivings he must have had about being away from home at such a time."[28]

The year before Thorpe was rated among the top rookie prospects in the majors along with Roberto Clemente, Elston Howard, Ken Boyer, Herb Score, and Bill Virdon. The Cubs believed he still belonged in this elite group.

"Thorpe may lack sheer speed, but he knows how to pitch," said Cubs pitching coach Dutch Leonard. "And that will win for him in the end."[29]

He started the season with the Cubs but didn't get into a game. With the Angels, he appeared in twenty-nine games, completing six of the twenty games he started. In 156 innings, he struck out seventy-seven, and walked sixty.

Thorpe was better than his 7–7 record might suggest. In three of his losses, the Angels scored a total of three runs. "Thorpe had a lot of bad luck," said Dave Hillman.

That bad luck continued for the rest of Thorpe's career.

In 1957, he was 7–15 with a 4.05 ERA for the last-place Portland Beavers. This was good enough for the Pittsburgh Pirates to draft him for 1958, but he missed the entire season because of an operation to remove bone chips in his throwing arm. In 1959, he attempted a comeback with Columbus, Georgia, in the South Atlantic League.

"The Pirates had high hopes for him," Borovicka said.

Thorpe visited Borovicka before leaving for spring training. "He told me his arm felt good. It was strong again. He thought everything was going to be okay."

Bob pitched in three games before retiring and heading home to San Diego to work as an apprentice electrician for his father-in-law, Bill Frank.

"If you don't make it in baseball, you can take over my company when I retire," Bill told Bob.

By 1960, Bob had worked off-and-on as an electrician for six years. He was close to qualifying for journeyman status.

Cassie, Bob's San Diego High baseball coach, got a call from a newspaper reporter the morning of March 17, 1960. "I'll never forget that day," Cassie said.

"Les, you'd better sit down," the reporter said. And, then, the reporter described what happened.

Bob was electrocuted while splicing a high-powered electric cable. He instinctively jumped back as the power hit his palm and his elbow grounded against a metal transformer box. The force of the current burned his fingerprints into the metal base of the awl he was using to apply insulating fluid.

"In those days, they did it hot," Borovicka said. "Now, they don't. They turn off the power."

"One of the nicest young men I ever had a chance to coach," Cassie said. "He gave me 110 percent every day."

"Bob was very tightly focused and seemed to know exactly what his plan was for his life," Bill Adams said. "He was baseball, baseball, baseball."

Thorpe and Borovicka, often called "The Two Bobbies," were a combined 29–2 the year San Diego High won the championship.

"The Two Bobbies were great pitchers," Adams said.

"They were together all the time," said Cassie.

Thorpe was twenty-four when he died, leaving his widow, Barise, with two sons, Robert, seven, and Billy, three. A third son, Barry, was born two weeks after Bob died.

Borovicka eventually married Barise and raised his friend's three boys. They refer to Thorpe as "Father" and Borovicka as "Dad."

"I tried my best to raise them the way he would've raised them," Borovicka said. "I think he would be pleased with the job I did, although it's probably not as good as he would've done if he had lived."

NOTES

1. *Los Angeles Times*, May 16, 1956, C2.
2. *Baseball Digest*, December 1956/January 1957, 67.
3. *Los Angeles Herald-Express*, May 18, 1956, D4.
4. *The Sporting News*, July 25, 1956, 31.
5. *The Sporting News*, February 14, 1970, 33.
6. *Los Angeles Times*, May 31, 1956, C2.
7. *Chicago Tribune*, May 7, 1998, Section 4, 11.
8. *Baseball Digest*, May 1962, 9.
9. *Los Angeles Times*, May 16, 1956, C2.
10. *Los Angeles Times*, May 30, 1956, D2.
11. *Chicago Tribune*, May 7, 1998, Section 4, 11.
12. *The Sporting News*, July 17, 1957, 21.
13. Ibid.
14. *Baseball Digest*, December 1957/January 1958, 68.
15. *Los Angeles Times*, June 13, 1956, C3.
16. *The Sporting News*, May 4, 1955, 25.
17. *Sacramento Bee*, August 2, 1955, 22.
18. *Los Angeles Times*, June 6, 1955, D2.
19. *Chicago Daily News*, March 28, 1957, 50.
20. *Chicago Sun-Times*, March 7, 1955, 53.
21. *Chicago Sun-Times,*, April 9, 1955, 32.
22. *The Sporting News*, April 6, 1955, 7.
23. *The Sporting News* January 19, 1955, 7.
24. *Chicago Sun-Times*, April 6, 1955, 53.
25. *The Sporting News*, April 6, 1955, 7.
26. *Chicago Sun-Times*, April 9, 1955, 32.
27. *Chicago Sun-Times*, April 11, 1955, 60.
28. *The Sporting News*, April 11, 1956, 16.
29. Ibid.

FIFTEEN

Perfect Wasn't Good Enough

"I guess I'm one of the bastardized stories of that team, huh?" —Hy Cohen, pitcher, 1956 Los Angeles Angels

On page fourteen of the 1956 Los Angeles Angels yearbook, a glowing profile of Hyman "Hy" Cohen begins, "Regarded as one of the top pitching prospects in baseball, this year could be the big season for Hy Cohen."[1]

The twenty-five-year-old Cohen already had six full seasons under his belt, including a brief fling in the majors with the Chicago Cubs.

In 1954, at Des Moines in the Class A Western League, the six-foot-five-inch, 215-pound right-hander won sixteen games during the regular season plus two in the playoffs. His earned run average of 1.88 set a league record. He won ten games in a row at one point, pitched six shutouts, including a one-hitter, and surrendered only one home run in 196 innings.

Hy's performance at Des Moines followed two years in the military where he won thirty-two games while losing six for the Brooke Army Medical Center baseball team.

One of Hy's teammates at Brooke was Don Newcombe, a three-time twenty-game winner for the Brooklyn Dodgers in the 1950s.

"He's got more stuff than most big league pitchers right now," Newcombe told the *Sporting News*. "His fastball is wicked, his curve breaks very sharp and he has a more effective slider than most major leaguers. I'll be surprised if he isn't a consistent winner for the Cubs in 1955."[2]

Another teammate at Brooke was Bob Turley, a twenty-one-game winner and Cy Young Award winner in 1958 for the New York Yankees. "When you looked at him, he was such a big guy that everybody thought he would be overpowering fast. He wasn't that fast. But he had a good curveball and pretty good control. He always kept you in the game. He was a good pitcher."

Hy was born January 29, 1931, in Brooklyn, the youngest of four children. His father, Joseph, emigrated to the United States from Poland. He was a garment worker and knew nothing about sports except that Hy was a star high school quarterback and spent most of his time during the summer playing sandlot baseball.

In 1947, the Hearst newspaper group sponsored an all-star sandlot game pitting New York City's finest against the best players from throughout the United States—Dick Groat, Bill Skowron, and Gino Cimoli, to name a few future major leaguers. Hy, then sixteen, struck out four in the two innings he pitched for the New Yorkers.

The game was played at New York City's Polo Grounds and attended by 31,232 people, including the legendary Babe Ruth and Babe Didrikson Zaharias, the greatest woman athlete of her time.

Zaharias used Hy's glove to play catch before the game. Joseph Cohen sat next to Babe Ruth, but he didn't know it. "You know who you were sitting next to?" Hy asked his father.

"Okay," Joseph replied.

Joseph had his sights set on other things.

When Hy was fifteen, his father told him, "One day comes a man with a big black cigar and he will ask you to sign a baseball contract."[3] That man was Paul Krichell, a New York Yankees scout. He saw Hy pitch in the Hearst all-star game and came with a big, black cigar.

Krichell signed the great Lou Gehrig and tried to sign Hank Greenberg in 1929. Gehrig still was playing first base for the Yankees so Greenberg, also a first baseman, signed with the Detroit Tigers. He became one of baseball's premier sluggers and the first Jewish superstar in American professional sports. "You're going to be the next Hank Greenberg," Krichell said to Hy.

Never mind that Hy was a pitcher. He was Jewish and, like Greenberg, tall and handsome—destined to be a hero and huge gate attraction in the Big Apple with its large Jewish population.

Hy was seventeen in 1948 when he signed with the Yankees for a $750 bonus plus $175 a month to pitch for LaGrange, Georgia, in the Class D Georgia-Alabama League. But Hy's father died of a heart attack two months before, so he wasn't around to see his prophecy fulfilled.

In two years at LaGrange, Hy was a combined 18–20, lowering his earned run average from 5.50 in 1948 to a respectable 3.33 in 1949.

In a game against Griffin, Georgia, a team led by player-manager Rudy York, Greenberg's home-run hitting sidekick at Detroit, Hy had what he termed an epiphany.

York was thirty-five years old in 1949 and still a menacing figure with a bat in his hands. The bases were loaded when the slugger came to the plate.

Hy's first three pitches were balls. York took a called strike and, then, swung and missed to make the count three-and-two. Another ball would walk in a run. A pitch in the wrong spot would surely end up out of the park for a grand slam homer. Hy reared back and fired the ball. York hit 277 home runs in the majors, but this time he swung and missed.

"Holy cow!" Hy thought to himself. "I think I can make it."

Hy reflected on that moment.

"That was my epiphany. After all, this was Rudy York. He could hit the ball a mile if he ever got a hold of it. And I struck him out."

The Cubs liked what they saw and snatched him from the Yankees via the minor league draft. Krichell was fuming; the Cubs were ecstatic. "You make it in Chicago and you'll own half of Chicago," Hy was told by an advisor to Cubs owner P. K. Wrigley.

Jewish baseball players were somewhat of an oddity at the time—especially one the size of Cohen. "I guess I'm what you call a mutant," Hy said on arriving in Grand Rapids, Michigan, to pitch in the Class A Central League.[4]

"Most people didn't think of a Jewish guy being tall," Hy explained. "Hank Greenberg was tall. He said to me, 'Geez, you're even taller than I am.' He thought he was the tallest Jew in baseball."

Hy pitched well at Grand Rapids in 1950, posting a 12–9 won-loss record and 3.41 ERA. At Des Moines in 1951, he was 16–10 with a 2.86 ERA. And then the U.S. Army called his number.

Fortunately Hy was able to pitch regularly his two years in the military. He returned to Des Moines in 1954 to wow the Cubs and earn a spot on their pitching staff to begin the 1955 season.

With the Cubs, he was roughed up for twenty-eight hits and fifteen earned runs in seventeen innings for a 7.94 ERA. He was sent to L.A. in exchange for Hillman.

Despite a 5–10 won-loss record, Hy displayed flashes of the brilliance that Newcombe had spoken about.

In his second start for the Angels, he tossed a five-hitter only to lose 1–0. Three weeks later, he pitched a four-hit shutout. In a season-ending playoff series against the Hollywood Stars to determine bragging rights in L.A., Hy blanked the Stars on one hit in six innings of relief pitching. His ERA of 3.59 was solid. And he completed four of the sixteen games he started.

Days after Hy arrived in Los Angeles, a local columnist pegged him as a look-alike for Robert Mitchum, the movie actor.

Bob Kelley, the Angels' play-by-play radio announcer, interviewed Hy on a pregame show.

"You're young and a good-looking kid, Hy. What do you think about women?"

"Hey, Bob, I'm not going to get married until I'm at least thirty. That's far from my mind."

Figure 15.1.   The future was bright for pitcher Hy Cohen, third from right, when he joined the Angels in 1955 along with Raymond "Moe" Bauer, far left, and Casey Wise, far right. They are shown here with manager Bob Scheffing, second from left. *Courtesy Raymond "Moe" Bauer.*

Two months and ten dates later, Hy married Terry Davis, a local girl he met through Stu Nahan, an assistant to Kelley who would go on to become a well-known sportscaster in L.A. Chuck Connors, aka *The Rifleman*, attended the wedding ceremony. So did his Angels teammates, including Steve Bilko, Gene Mauch, and Gale Wade.

Hy Cohen, the kid from Brooklyn, was feeling right at home in L.A.

Life was good for Hy the first month of the 1956 season. He was newly married, and the Angels were winning and scoring runs in bunches every time he pitched. They scored eight runs as Hy won his first start, giving up five earned runs in five innings. His teammates produced eleven runs in his next victory—another five-inning stint in which Hy allowed six earned runs.

Hy pitched into the eighth inning in notching his third win—a 5–3 decision. All three runs were earned. The Angels scored nine times as Hy gave up one earned run to post his fourth win and first complete game— a seven-inning contest that was the second game of a doubleheader. He improved to 5–0 with the Angels' 8–4 win over Vancouver on May 5. All four runs were earned and charged to Hy, who was relieved by Bauer in the sixth inning with two outs and the bases loaded.

A headline in the *Pasadena Star-News* set the stage for Hy's next start: ANGELS, SEALS OPEN AS COHEN SEEKS 6TH.[5]

Hy didn't get a shot at that sixth win.

Angels manager Bob Scheffing surprised everybody by announcing he was getting rid of Cohen. "That perfect record belied Cohen's true ability. He had a tough time getting past the fifth inning and his ERA was the highest on the club. I thought I had better pitchers, so I let him go."[6]

Hy's ERA of 5.70 actually was the second highest on the team to Marino Pieretti's 6.09.

"To this day, no one understands it," said George Freese. "His earned run average was high. But nobody could believe it."

"I felt sorry for him," said Eddie Haas. "I thought, 'My Lord, he's five-and-oh, and he's being sent down.'"

"I remember everybody remarking, 'My God, they're sending Hy out,'" said Casey Wise. "The scuttlebutt was that in spite of the fact that he won all the time, we were averaging eight runs a game."

"When it happened, it was one of those hush-hush, it can't be true type of things," recalled Bob Speake. "And, then, Hyman comes into the locker room and starts packing his stuff. So we knew it was true."

"We had more reliable guys," explained Mauch. "He won games but it wasn't because of his pitching. It was because of the offense."

"He might've won twenty-five," Dwight "Red" Adams said, laughing. "It's hard for me to imagine that they would ship a young guy out like that who is five-and-oh when they had a couple of old dudes like me and Pieretti hanging around. No one promised us that it would always be fair."

At a Pacific Coast League Historical Society reunion forty-five years later, Roger Osenbaugh, a pitcher for the Sacramento Solons, said, "When I heard that, I thought, 'what the hell, five-and-oh. What more could a man do?" Turning to Cohen standing nearby, Osenbaugh added, "You scared every pitcher in the league that year when you were sent out five-and-oh."

Osenbaugh elaborated.

"The bottom-line with most people is your won-loss record. The earned run average is certainly important but not a biggie.

"From year to year, what is a good ERA and what isn't changes with the passage of time, the league and the circumstances."

Osenbaugh knows all about circumstances.

In a game against the Angels in 1957, he was hammered for eighteen hits, including nine homers, and twenty-two earned runs, eleven of them in the seventh inning when he was mercifully removed from the game.

You might think that Roger's manager, Tommy Heath, had it in for him but that wasn't the case. "Osenbaugh was ill recently and hasn't been getting enough work to regain his early-season form," Heath explained. "I figured a stiff workout would sharpen him up."[7]

"You throw that game out and my ERA was three-something," Roger explained.

Osenbaugh, considered one of the best right-handed pitchers in the league, was purchased by the Pittsburgh Pirates later in the season. "But if you look at my ERA (4.36) and that one game, you certainly wouldn't have done that. A pitcher has to be analyzed by everything."

The passage of time has eased the pain of the 1956 season. Hy once joked at a Coast League reunion: "With that five-and-oh record and ERA that I had, I'd be making $3 million now."

Hy wasn't laughing when informed he was being shipped out.

"You can imagine how I felt. To win twenty games, you've got to be lucky. You're not going to pitch shutouts or win one-run and two-run games every time. You've also got to win games when you give up five and six runs. I figured I was real lucky and I'm going to get better as I go along. I'll win twenty games."

Tears in his eyes, Hy told Scheffing: "I can't believe you're doing this." And, then, he cried.

"I was so embarrassed that I cleaned out my locker while nobody else was around and just got the hell out of there."

He headed to Tulsa in the Texas League, appearing in five games and losing his only decision. From Tulsa, Hy went to New Orleans in the Southern Association (SA) where he pitched for Andy Cohen, the first Jewish player to star in the majors. "He sat me down and talked to me: 'Look, whatever happened there, I know you still got it.'"

Hy was 11–7 at New Orleans with a 3.52 ERA. His record for 1956 overall was 16–8 with a 3.90 ERA.

Cohen spent the 1957 season with the Memphis Chicks in the SA, winning fifteen games and leading the league with the lowest ERA—2.72. "I had such a great year at Memphis; I thought the Cubs would bring me back up. But nothing happened."

Hy started 1958 at Toronto in the International League. He was 0–1 when he returned to the SA to play for the Nashville Vols. It was worthy of a banner headline in the *Nashville Banner*: VOLS PURCHASE HURLER HY COHEN FROM TORONTO. Ironically, the subheadline referred to the statistic that doomed Hy with the 1956 Angels: EX-CHICK PITCHER HAD LOWEST EARNED RUN AVERAGE IN SA.[8]

Hy's ERA was still the story five weeks later when the *Banner* reported, "Hy Cohen (2–6) failed again Monday night as his earned run average, lowest in the Southern Association last year (2.72) soared to an unmentionable 8.75."[9]

A sore pitching arm bothered him in Nashville but that wasn't his biggest problem. "Mentally I was just blown out because I felt I should've been in the big leagues."

Hy was twenty-seven. In nine minor league seasons, he won 100 games. Three times he won sixteen games, fifteen once. He led two different leagues with the lowest ERA. Overall, his ERA was a highly respectable 3.34. It was time to quit.

"Who knows, maybe 1956 was the turning point of my whole life? That could've been a twenty-win year for me. And that's what every pitcher strives for. But 1956 also was the year I decided to go to college and start looking out for myself. I wanted to be a teacher-coach."

Cohen was a history teacher and coach for thirty years, twenty-eight of them at Birmingham High School in Van Nuys, California, about twenty miles from downtown Los Angeles.

He coached baseball and football for thirteen years and, then, tennis for twelve. Altogether, his teams won eighteen league championships. Birmingham's 1966 and 1969 baseball teams won the Los Angeles city championship.

Hy was inducted into the Southern California Jewish Sports Hall of Fame for his coaching accomplishments. In September 1995, the Los Angeles Dodgers honored him as an outstanding educator in ceremonies at Dodger Stadium.

There are photos from that special night on the wall of Hy's home office. In one, he's pictured with Newcombe, his Brooke Army teammate who once predicted a bright future for him with the Cubs. Another photo shows Hy and Tommy Lasorda, then manager of the Dodgers, talking near the Dodger dugout.

"I had great years teaching and coaching so maybe that was always meant to be for me."

Hy leaned back in his office chair, reflecting on his career as an educator.

Hy's son, Jeff, tried out for the baseball team at another school—Taft High. The coach was a friend. "He said, 'Your kid isn't going to make the team but I could use him to pitch batting practice.' I told him to cut him."

Hy knew from experience that if you're not succeeding at one thing, try something else. Jeff became an accountant and started a highly successful silk flower business that he operates with his sister, Jill.

"When I was coaching at Birmingham, Taft had a kid playing shortstop—Robin Yount. The scouts asked me, 'What do you think of this kid?' I had a kid at the time who I thought was the best ball player in the league. So I said to the scout, 'Yount is not going to make it.' He was tall and lanky and he didn't look strong enough. He's a Hall of Famer now. What does that tell you? What do I know?"

Hy mentioned George "Sparky" Anderson, manager of three World Series champions at Cincinnati and Detroit and a long-time friend. "Remember the speech he gave when he was inducted into the Hall of Fame?"

Anderson said, "I got good players, stayed out of the way, let 'em win a lot, and then just hung around for twenty-six years."

"You win because you have good ball players," Hy said. "I had great ball players in high school. I had kids who were mature and who could hit the ball and did well. We won twenty-six games in a row over a span of two years. But my success naturally depended on the kids."

Hy treated students "a little bit older" than their actual age. "I wanted them to have high expectations. To be successful, you've got to work hard. No one is going to give it to you.

"What you do is motivate the kids to do as well as they can—not only on the ball field but in the classroom."

Hy motioned to the baseball memorabilia in his office.

"I wouldn't give up my years of playing ball for anything. That was a great experience—a great educational experience."

During his brief stint with Toronto in 1958, the Maple Leafs played against the Havana Sugar Kings in Cuba. Fidel Castro and his guerilla rebels were still in the mountains but poised to take over the capital of Havana.

"It was kind of dangerous. When we got there, we were met with guys with machine guns. We stayed at the Hotel Nacional. They wouldn't let us out of the hotel. People in the hotel would take us aside and say, 'Tell everybody that Castro is a good man and all that stuff.'

"We were at the ballpark one night. I happened to be pitching. About the fourth inning I heard a big pop in the stands. All the guys are running from the field into the dugout and I'm on the mound. I said, 'What the hell do I do?' It wasn't a gun. But it shows how nervous everybody was."

Cohen often shared that story with students so they could better understand the Cuban revolution. "When you talk about personal things to kids in the classroom, they pay more attention than stuff out of the textbook."

One of Cohen's star students was David Gregory, the television journalist and *Meet the Press* moderator known for asking tough questions.

"He was asking provocative questions even in high school," Cohen said. "We always had discussions after the bell rang—always. I had to write excuses for him because he was late to the next class."

David also tried out for the tennis team Cohen coached to a second-place finish in L.A. "It was a great team; I had to cut him."

Hy taught American history and economics wearing a sweat suit. Students called him "Coach."

After one history class, a young girl approached Hy.

"Coach," she said, "I never really liked history but now I want to teach history because you motivated me."

Tears came to Hy's eyes much as they did that day in 1956 when he was told he was being sent down with a perfect won-loss record. But these were tears of joy.

"When you are a teacher and a kid comes up and tells you, 'Hey, I like the way you taught the class and I want to do that.' That's one of my greatest thrills. That's the satisfaction of teaching."

When Hy Cohen went to see the movie *Field of Dreams* soon after its release in 1989, he considered himself a failure.

For all of his success as a coach and teacher, he had yet to reconcile his lack of success in major league baseball.

Hy's dream growing up was to play in the majors. He fulfilled that dream in 1955 with the Cubs but the results didn't meet either his own or the Cubs expectations.

"When I was in Chicago with the Cubs, I could throw physically with all of them. I could do whatever they could do. But mentally? I didn't have the maturity, that mental toughness to stay in the big leagues. I recognized that after I was sent down."

Hy made his major league debut against the St. Louis Cardinals. The Cubs were trailing 5–0 when he came in with a runner on second and nobody out.

The first batter he faced, Del Rice, doubled to center, scoring a run. Alex Grammas grounded out. Larry Jackson, the pitcher, walked. Wally Moon lined a single to center, scoring Rice. Red Schoendienst fouled out to the catcher. Up came Stan "The Man" Musial with two runners on base.

The Cardinal great was in a slump—hitless in his last thirteen at bats.

Looking at Musial, Hy was reminded of his old neighborhood in Brooklyn when he and his buddies had a lottery to pick three guys to get six hits for the games that night. "Put up a nickel and get a quarter. I always picked Musial. Now, here I am facing him."

Musial tripled off the left-center field wall to score two runs and scored on a Cubs error before Hy got the third out to end the Cards' ten-run inning.

Hy wound up pitching seven innings, allowing twelve hits and eight runs, six of them earned.

At one point, a Cubs coach, Dutch Leonard, walked up to Hy in the dugout and said, "I'll buy you a tie if you hit Musial in the back."

Players almost fell off the bench laughing because Dutch was well-known for being a tightwad.

"Me? A kid who used to bet on Musial—I'm going to hit him in the back? It never happened. I threw him three different pitches and he got three hits off of me. I sure got him out of that slump quick."

Hy was impressive in his next outing against Pittsburgh and, then, the Philadelphia Phillies knocked him out in his first start with a four-run fourth inning.

He appeared in four more games, pitching a total of four innings. In his last game against the Phillies, he walked two and allowed four hits and three earned runs.

"I deemed myself a failure because I didn't stay in the big leagues. I pitched what, seventeen innings? My ERA was high. The only one good game I had was against Pittsburgh; I threw three shutout innings in relief. I started in Philadelphia, which was okay until all hell broke loose. And then they sent me down and I never got back."

Hy's friends told him he had nothing to be ashamed about.

"My expectations have always been high. I even had it with my kids playing ball. You've got to be the best. When I was pitching, I didn't want to give up a run. And I wanted to go nine innings. I didn't want anybody to relieve me."

He paused and, then, quipped, "Of course, with the Angels it was different."

Not until Hy saw *Field of Dreams* did he come to terms with his base-ball career. He connected with the story of "Moonlight" Graham, a man who played one inning in the majors for the New York Giants during the 1905 season before quitting and becoming a doctor.

"I saw that movie and I said, 'One inning and they are looking for this kid.' You know, when I was playing, we had sixteen teams and only 400 guys could make it in the big leagues.

"In watching that film, I said, 'God, I was there for a couple of months. I played at a time when it was difficult to get to the big leagues.

"I have gradually reconciled myself to the fact that, hey, I did some-thing that not too many people did in their lifetime—play in the big leagues. But also my life after that has been very rewarding with my teaching and coaching. I don't have that feeling anymore that I was a failure."

On Hy's sixtieth birthday in 1991, Diane and Buck Weber presented him with a poem titled, *Cohen on the Mound*:

> The outlook wasn't brilliant for the Chicago nine that day
> The score stood 4 to 2 with but one inning left to play
> The Giants' Mueller hit a single, Antonelli did the same
> And a sickly silence fell upon the Cubs fans at the game.
> From 5,000 throats and more there came a mighty groan
> Which echoed through the stands and came back in a moan
> Willie Mays stepped up to bat, on his way to 51
> And with young Hy Cohen on the mound, the game as good as won.
> An ERA of nearly eight—a third of Cohen's age
> Would end the game for sure this time said Harry Caray, sage
> But Cohen was determined; he'd done this thing before

He'd strike out Mays once again to become part of Chicago folklore.
Two strikes were quickly on the board
Willie was in a shock
He'd hit that ball a mile next time
Hit a tremendous knock.
Then Cohen held the ball and then he let it go
And then the air was shattered by the force of Willie's blow
Oh, somewhere in Chicago the sun is shining bright
The band is playing somewhere and somewhere hearts are light.
And somewhere men are laughing
And somewhere children shout
The Giants went on to win the game
But Cohen struck Mays out.

NOTES

1. *1956 Los Angeles Angels Yearbook*, 14 (1st ed.).
2. *The Sporting News*, October 20, 1954, 16.
3. *Chicago Sun-Times*, March 17, 1955, 66.
4. *Grand Rapids Herald*, June 25, 1950, 4 (Sports).
5. *Pasadena Star-News*, May 11, 1956, 11.
6. *The Sporting News*, June 13, 1956, 33.
7. *Los Angeles Times*, June 23, 1957, C2.
8. *Nashville Banner*, June 10, 1958, 20.
9. *Nashville Banner*, July 15, 1958, 18.

SIXTEEN

From Bombshells to Bomb Threats to Dodger Stadium

"There is one sad feature about a great minor league ball club. It's always broken up, and the better the team the sooner the dissolution."
— Hy Goldberg of the *Newark Evening News* on the 1937 Newark Bears

The first bombshell fell February 21, 1957, when the Brooklyn Dodgers acquired Wrigley Field in Los Angeles and the Angels' franchise in the Pacific Coast League from the Chicago Cubs.

The second bombshell dropped two weeks later when the Dodgers and Cubs divvied up the 1956 Angels between L.A. and Portland, the Cubs new Coast League affiliate.

By the time the 1957 season ended, it was a foregone conclusion that the Dodgers were moving from Brooklyn to Los Angeles the next year and the Angels, Little Wrigley and plans for the PCL to be a third major league would be history.

Paul Andreson, a big Steve Bilko fan, was eleven years old in 1957. "I was probably one of the few people in L.A. who was mad when it was announced that the Dodgers were coming to town, once it dawned on me that my beloved Angels would be leaving."

"When we heard that the Dodgers could possibly come out here, nobody wanted them," said Bob Case, who was thirteen years old at the time. "Are you kidding? We've got the Hollywood Stars and the Los Angeles Angels. Why would we want the Dodgers?"

The Dodgers avoided a local uprising by keeping Bilko in L.A. Five other 1956 Angels—Red Adams, Elvin Tappe, Piper Davis, Bob Coats, and Marino Pieretti—were on the spring roster but only Tappe stayed.

Coats remained in the Cubs organization and ended up at Memphis in the Southern Association with Joe Hannah and Hy Cohen. Davis and

Eddie Haas were assigned to Fort Worth in the Texas League. Adams finished the season at Miami in the International League and Pieretti at Des Moines in the Western League.

Moe Bauer was transferred to the Portland Beavers, where he was joined eventually by George Freese and Casey Wise as well as the nucleus of the 1956 Angels pitching staff: Bob Anderson, Dave Hillman, Bob Thorpe, Johnny Briggs, and Gene Fodge.

For the third straight year, Gale "Windy" Wade failed to stick with the Cubs. He was sold to the Dodgers and sent to L.A.

Gene Mauch had his best season in the majors with the Boston Red Sox while Dick Drott, Bob Speake, and Jim Bolger were the only Angels to last the entire season with the Cubs.

Bilko walloped fifty-six home runs to continue as the "The Sultan of Swat of Grocery League" but his batting average plunged sixty points to .300 as Mauch wasn't around to steal signs and tip him off on pitches to expect. And the Dodgers did not keep their promise to make the Angels their number one farm club. Instead, they sent top prospects to St. Paul in the American Association and Montreal in the International League. The Angels plummeted to sixth, finishing twenty-one games behind the first-place San Francisco Seals.

In early August, a *Los Angeles Mirror-News* headline declared, NO LONGER SAFE TO BE AN ANGEL.[1]

After striking out to end a game, Wade was taunted by fans seated near the Angels' dugout at Little Wrigley. One of them grabbed at his cap and another punched him. "Wade, you're a bum," they taunted.[2]

Wade scaled the rail separating the stands from the field and ripped the shirt of one of his tormentors.

"I don't like to go into the stands, but I also don't like to get punched," Wade said. "As a ball player I expect to get needled, but when the fans get personal—well, I'm the kind of guy who won't take that stuff, whether it be on the street or in the ballpark."[3]

The week before, a heckler took a swing at Bilko, who, the *Mirror-News* reported, "grabbed his wrist and held him until the gendarmes hustled him off."[4]

The season, and the last Coast League games to be played at Little Wrigley, ended with telephone calls to the ballpark's switchboard operator warning of a bomb planted in the home team's dugout.

Most of the players fled to the bullpens as a bomb squad searched both dugouts and the stands. They found nothing and the doubleheader was completed with the Angels losing both games to the Padres.

"There have been numerous threats against the lives of professional ball players but this was believed to be the first such bomb scare," Phil Collier wrote in the *San Diego Union*.[5]

"You didn't think much of a bomb scare back in those days," recalled Jim "Mudcat" Grant, the Padres' starting and winning pitcher in the first game. "It wasn't a huge thing. So I went up in the clubhouse and waited until they told me to come back out."

The entire 1957 season was a bomb for the Angels players relegated to Portland. After winning 107 games the previous year, they lost 108 games with the last-place Beavers, who finished 41 games out of first place.

"If I had to say anything about 1957, I'd say it was the year you'd like to forget," said Anderson, who was 4–9 with a lofty earned run average of 5.04. "I looked forward to going into the military at the end of the year just so the season would be over."

Moe Bauer said the 1956 Angels "developed into a bunch of guys that wanted to get to the ballpark, and wanted to play ball because we wanted to win."

It was a lot different in Portland.

"Many an evening, starting about the first of August, I said to myself: Oh, my gosh, we've got to go out to the ballpark again tonight."

The way the Cubs and Dodgers broke up the Bilko Athletic Club, keeping Bilko and Tappe in L.A. while sending Freese and most of the pitching staff to Portland, upset many of the players.

"When you go up to the majors or down to the lower minors, that's part of the game," Anderson said. "But here we were in the same league and all of a sudden everything was ripped asunder. I don't know if it was a letdown or if we just all felt that going into the season it was not going to be as good. We were very, very disappointed to leave some of the players behind."

Russ Kemmerer, a pitcher for the Seals in 1956 and later the Red Sox, wrote a book on his experiences in baseball titled, *Ted Williams: Hey Kid, Just Get It Over the Plate!*

"The thing that makes a team a team is compatibility," Kemmerer said, "and being able to work together, to pick up the slack for one another. Great teams, whether they are minor-league or major-league teams, have that ability to pull themselves together.

"These players then went to a major-league team and their role was entirely different. You either weren't called on or you were called on sparingly and your skills . . . it doesn't take long to lose them if you don't use them. As a result, they were not particularly great players on the major-league level. But certainly, that has nothing to do with the team itself."

Kemmerer mentioned Williams being yelled at by a Boston teammate, Vern Stephens: "That's right, I'll drive in all the runs and you make the money."

Williams refused to swing at pitches outside his zone. More than one teammate grumbled, "If Williams would've just swung at that damn three-two pitch one inch off the plate, he would've driven in another hundred runs." But Williams never did. He wasn't going to break the discipline that made him a great hitter.

For Kemmerer, Boston's failure to win the World Series for eighty-six years had nothing to do with trading Babe Ruth, known as "The Bambino," to the Yankees.

"It wasn't the 'Curse of the Bambino,'" he said. "It was indecision. They didn't know who to keep or who not to keep."

Cub fans have their own curse to blame for their team not winning a World Series since 1908—the "Curse of the Billy Goat."

The story goes that the owner of the Billy Goat Tavern in Chicago put a hex on the Cubs when he was asked to leave Wrigley Field with his smelly goat during a World Series game in 1945. That's the last time the Cubs appeared in one.

The Cubs' failures can be traced to other decisions such as trading Lou Brock, a future Hall of Famer, to the St. Louis Cardinals in 1964. The Brock trade is generally considered the worst in a long list of bad deals.

A story by Hal Lebovitz in the May 1, 1957, issue of *Sporting News* described a meeting at Wrigley Field in August 1952 between a Cub executive and a seventeen-year-old boy and his father.

"Son, my advice to you is to give up the idea of playing ball," the executive said. "You'll never make it. You're too small."

The father put his arm around his son's shoulder as they headed for the door. Rudolph Maris stopped, turned to the executive, and said, "One of these days you'll see this boy play in Comiskey Park."[6]

Nine years after the Cubs told Roger Maris he was too small to play pro ball, he slammed sixty-one home runs to break Babe Ruth's single-season record of sixty.

"The Cubs' success and reputation is built on their failure," said Bill Adams, former executive director of the San Diego Hall of Champions.

Going into the 1957 season, the Cubs had finished last or next-to-last in the National League seven times since the 1945 World Series. Their best record in the 1950s was 77–77 in 1952. The Cubs hit bottom in 1956 with a decade-worst 60–94 record.

In L.A., Bob Scheffing and John Holland teamed to build the Angels first championship team in nine years. The Cubs were hoping they could do the same in Chicago, naming Scheffing manager and Holland a vice president.

At the press conference announcing his appointment, Scheffing said, "The only reason I'm here is because twenty-one players did a helluva job for me at Los Angeles."[7]

Holland joined a Cubs front office that already had two vice presidents—Charlie Grimm and Clarence "Pants" Rowland.

Like many of the players, John worked his way up the Cubs organization.

"The farm club is the lifeblood of any ball club, but I don't believe that any ball club can be built successfully entirely from the farm system," he said on becoming a Cubs VP. "We're going to make changes because baseball is built on changes."[8]

Thirteen regulars who were on the Cubs roster to end the 1956 season were gone a month into the following season. A league-high forty-three players came and went in 1957.

"It's getting so that you can't tell a Cub player even with yesterday's scorecard," quipped Ed Prell, a sportswriter for the *Chicago Tribune*.[9]

Complicating matters was a power struggle in the front office among the three vice presidents. The *Sporting News* quoted one player as saying, "Can anybody please tell me who is the boss of the show? I signed my contract with Holland and I'm taking orders from Scheffing. That's the way it should be, but every time I look up there's both Grimm and Rowland hanging around."[10]

Grimm, a long-time Cub manager, friend and confidant of team owner, P. K. Wrigley, was really running the show, and banjo-playing "Jolly Cholly" preferred veterans over homegrown talent such as Wise and Eddie Winceniak.

"He [Grimm] was behind the scenes, calling the shots," said Winceniak, an infielder who was sent to Portland after batting .240 in 17 games. "Holland knew more about us and yet he didn't have that much power. If John would've had the final say, I would've been able to stay up there. And Casey probably would've stayed, too, because we were teammates in Des Moines under Holland."

Winceniak also played for Holland in L.A. in 1955.

The day before being demoted, Eddie rapped three hits in a doubleheader, including his first major league homer. "I'm going to cuss you up-and-down," a fuming Winceniak told Holland on hearing the news.

"Go right ahead," Holland said in a show of empathy.

"That goddamn Charlie Grimm, if he had any balls, he would be over here so he could take the brunt of it. But he's got you to take it."

Winceniak never made it back to the majors, playing two more years in the minors before quitting baseball at age thirty.

"I felt I could play up there. And just like when you have a balloon and you bust it . . . that was me after they told me. That [1957] was the most disappointing year of my life."

One of the six Angels gone before the season started was Freese. He was sent to Portland to compensate the Beavers for Ed Mickelson, a thirty-year-old right-handed hitting first baseman overshadowed by Bilko when they were both in the Cardinals organization.

In his memoir, *Out of the Park*, Mickelson wrote, "I tried not to let it get to me, but I felt that no matter what I did, Bilko was their man."[11]

Mickelson was now the Cubs' man but he didn't want to go to Chicago and sit on the bench.

"Bob, I don't want to come," he told Scheffing.

"You're going to play."

"You've got Dee Fondy, what are you talking about? He hits .300 every year."

"No, you'll play against left-handed pitchers. He'll play against right-handed pitching."

Mickelson found himself in the same situation as Bilko three years earlier, wasting away in Wrigleyville.

"The season opens and Warren Spahn is pitching," Mickelson said. "He's left-handed and I'm sitting on the bench."

In six games, Mickelson went hitless in twelve at bats.

Prior to his second and last start, he said to his wife, "Hey, it's cut-down time. If I hit three home runs, they probably won't send me back to Portland."

Mickelson went oh-for-four and headed to Portland.

"We drove about 1,800 miles," he recalled. "I didn't say a word to my wife. I didn't know it but depression really hit me."

Mickelson picked up where he left off with the Beavers, hitting .338 and making only one error in sixty-one games. He even hit a home run in the league's all-star game.

"I was really disillusioned. I lost all my enthusiasm and passion for baseball. I was playing well but it just wasn't the same. I went home before the season was over. I'd had enough."

The Cubs lost twelve of their first fifteen games and they didn't win one at home until the sixth week of the season. They were 26–46 at the all-star break in July and finished 62–92 — two wins more than 1956.

Fans stayed away from Wrigley Field. If they went out on the rooftops of the houses overlooking the playing field, it was to contemplate jumping off, not to watch a game. Attendance dropped to 670,629, the fifth straight year the Cubs failed to reach the one million mark.

Dick Littlefield, a widely traveled pitcher, checked the crowd before one game and said, "Guess nobody put it in the newspapers that I was pitching today. I know I've got more friends than the size of this crowd — and they'd all be here if they knew I was pitching." [12]

Holland and Scheffing acknowledged the chaos they created.

"We can't do that again," Holland said the following spring. "A club can't afford to keep making changes after the season opens. Last year it was the only thing we could do because we had ripped the roster apart." [13]

"We were making so many changes last year that we virtually went through three spring training periods," Scheffing said. "The ball club which started the season was entirely different from that one with which we opened spring training. And then the team was shuffled around quite a bit more later on when we made several trades that brought us new material.

"The general instability, of course, had its effects on the players, too. Nobody knew from day to day whether he'd still be with the club or he'd have somebody different playing alongside him." [14]

Even Banks, an all-star shortstop, was on a merry-go-round.

He switched to third base, a position he disliked, when Winceniak replaced him at shortstop. Six games later they swapped back. Winceniak changed places six days later with Jack Littrell, a shortstop called up from Portland, putting Banks back at third.

"Banks couldn't play shortstop anymore," Winceniak said. "He had good hands but as far as arm and range, forget it."

Ten players shuttled back and forth at third base; six at second base; five at shortstop; and four at first base. Seven players took turns in center-field.

Bobby Adams, a thirty-five-year-old journeyman, wound up playing third. Bobby Morgan and Dale Long, both thirty-one, took over at second and first.

"They've made so many changes that the guys are all afraid they'll be gone if they have a bad day," Winceniak said after being sent to Portland. [15]

When Wise, a switch-hitter, got bogged down in a slump, Scheffing told him to give it up and swing only from the right side.

"I always played better when I had a manager that believed in me," Wise said. "When I knew they were waiting for me to screw up, I screwed up."

That aptly describes the Cubs in 1957—screwed up.

Bill Sweeney, also known as "Tomato Face," was feeling rotten. The manager of the Portland Beavers had watched his team lose again and his stomach was killing him.

After the game, Sweeney returned to the San Diego hotel where he was staying. "I have never had such an awful pain in my stomach," he confided to friends. [16]

Sweeney had lost some twenty pounds during spring training.

"He was a wreck," said Tip Berg, the team's trainer. "But he wouldn't go to the doctor."

Sweeney was the Angels manager in 1955 when a beleaguered Bilko arrived in L.A.

"Do I have to worry about my weight?" Steve asked.

"I don't care what you weigh," Sweeney said. "Just play between the lines."

That's all he asked of his players. At spring training, he told them: "I have no curfews, but don't try to fool me. I'll know by the way you perform. You can't fool an old fooler."

"Managing is overrated," Sweeney often said, "there's nothing to it." [17]

Poor health forced Sweeney out in L.A., but he was back the middle of the 1956 season to guide an underperforming Portland team to a third-place finish, its best in a decade.

In eighteen seasons as a Coast League manager, Sweeney won three championships—one in Portland and two in L.A. His 1957 Beavers were title favorites as he had several 1956 Angels joining Portland stars such as Luis Marquez, a .344 hitter with twenty-five homers and 110 RBIs in 1956.

"We figured we'd win it all or at least be in the first division," Berg said.

The fifty-two-year-old Sweeney was rushed to a hospital the morning after he complained of stomach pains. He died after an emergency operation for a perforated ulcer.

"He was a great minor league manager but what killed him was that he drank too much," Berg said.

Sweeney's death cast a shadow on the rest of the season. The Beavers lost sixteen of nineteen games in April and thirteen straight in July, winding up with a dismal 60–108 record.

"Oh, God, it was an awful team," said Wise. "When they sent me out from Chicago, I really had a bad attitude. I thought, 'I finally made it and now I'm with this bad team.'"

"It was terrible," Winceniak agreed. "This guy was going somewhere, the next guy somewhere else. And we were getting guys that were just, you could say, out of the sandlot. That's how bad it got."

The laid-back Sweeney was replaced by hard-nosed Bill Posedel, a former pitcher for the Boston Braves and chief warrant officer in the U.S. Navy. Bauer appeared in forty-eight games for the Beavers, posting a 4–4 record and 4.15 ERA.

"His concept was that everybody was in the ballgame regardless of whether they played or not," said Bauer. "And after a loss, you need to examine yourself to find out how you contributed to that loss. We lost over 100 games. That's a lot of time after a ballgame to sit in front of your locker with your head in your hands, trying to figure out in the next ten-to-fifteen minutes how you contributed to the loss when you didn't even get in the game. I spent a whole lot of time doing self-examination on games I didn't even play in."

For Mickelson, the season was a roller-coaster ride.

"I was ready for a big year in Portland in 1957," he said.

He hit .309 with twenty-one homers and 101 RBI's for the Beavers in 1956.

"I'm on top of the world. I loved Portland. I loved the Coast League."

Mickelson was talked into going to Chicago. In mid-May, he returned to Portland. "We were just losing one after the other one way or the other," he said.

And Mickelson was feeling lousy. "I couldn't figure out what the hell was happening to me. I'd wake up three in the morning and couldn't go back to sleep. I'd get out to the ballpark like four o'clock and lay down in a little room all by myself and try to get up enough energy to play ball. It was big-time depression."

Richie Myers, one of the 1956 Angels, probably had the right idea. Assigned to Portland for the 1957 season, he decided instead to retire in his hometown of Sacramento.

"Last time I saw Myers," one Sacramento sportswriter mused, "he was sweeping up leaves for the Sacramento parks department. I suppose he's now planting spring roses or fuchsias perhaps."[18]

Red Adams tossed a four-hit shutout and Steve Bilko belted a 410-foot home run in the first game and Angel bats produced eleven runs in the second as L.A. won both games of a doubleheader to take sole possession of first place in the PCL. It was 1956 all over again. Everybody knew better, especially Red.

Except for Bilko at first base, Wade in centerfield, and Tappe behind the plate, there were new faces everywhere Red looked. They were Dodger prospects—mostly those Montreal and St. Paul didn't want.

At one point, the Dodgers considered sending the Angels a twenty-one-year-old Jewish pitcher named Sandy Koufax but instead they sent a twenty-nine-year-old Italian southpaw, Tommy Lasorda.

Rene Valdez, a twenty-two-game winner at Portland in 1956, and future Dodger stars, catcher John Roseboro and pitcher Larry Sherry, initially were ticketed for L.A. but wound up elsewhere.

Mauch was replaced at second base by George "Sparky" Anderson, who would go on to be a Hall of Fame manager for the Cincinnati Reds and Detroit Tigers.

The best of the young Dodgers went to St. Paul—Don Demeter, an outfielder; Norm Larker, a first baseman; Bob Lillis, a shortstop; and Stan Williams, a hard-throwing pitcher.

It was vintage Red the day he blanked the Hollywood Stars. He threw one junk pitch after another and the hitters kept pounding them into the ground for easy outs.

Going into the 1957 season, Red was thinking about something Portland manager Clay Hopper said to him when he was pitching for the Beavers.

The Mississippi-born Hopper managed fifteen teams in fourteen leagues in twenty-five minor-league seasons. He led the Beavers from 1952 to 1955.

The Coast League had been around a half-century but Hopper believed the end was near.

With a syrupy smooth Southern accent, his name came out as "Clayhoppeh."

It was 1953 and the Beavers were in L.A. for a series with the Angels.

"This league is going to fold up, Red."

Hopper paused before delivering the one-liner that Red would always remember: "It's a dead peckerwood."

"This league has been going fifty years, Clay."

"It's a dead peckerwood," Hopper reiterated.

Red realized that Hopper, a manager in the Brooklyn organization from 1945 to 1951, knew a little more about the Dodgers plans than most people.

"He was the first guy that really brought to my attention that the league was going to fold," Adams said. "As a player, you're not thinking along those lines. The league was in about the same position I was in—at the end of the road."

Red started looking at the league and his career differently.

"It was gradual from then until the Dodgers came out. It was obvious the Coast League was going to have some big changes made in it. I thought, 'I'm going to play it out as long as I can in this league and see if I can get a job managing. See what happens.' So that's where I was—sort of marking time. The L.A. club that year was doing just that."

Most of the players, including Wade, belonged to the Dodgers.

Tappe belonged to the Cubs.

Bilko belonged to the Angels and if the Dodgers wanted him for the majors, they had to purchase his contract like any other team. The Cubs had used all their options on Steve so they couldn't acquire him unless every other team in the National League took a pass.

"I didn't belong to anybody," said Adams. "I was an old guy in a new organization. None of the pieces fit."

Wade didn't fit in either.

"Going back to Los Angeles was just a terrible letdown. We had the great desire in 1955. And, then, the great team in 1956. And, then, 1957—that was the year I hated. I worked my ass off to get out of the Dodger chain only to wind up right back in it. Worst year I ever had in baseball."

By August the Angels were in sixth place and all that mattered was how high the "Bilko Meter" and "Bilko Homerometer" would go in the L.A. newspapers.

"If I just shoot at last year's marks I figure that'll be good enough," Stout Steve said at the beginning of the season.[19]

He hit numbers fifty-three and fifty-four in game at Portland. The second was a line-drive shot into the left-field bleachers that hit a woman in the face. "That ball sizzled for the entire distance, nor did it ever rise much than thirty feet above the field," *The Oregonian* reported.[20]

Three days later he slammed his fifty-fifth and the following game he belted number fifty-six to top his previous best. He had eleven games, all at Little Wrigley, to hit four more and tie the Coast League single-season record of sixty. But Steve failed to homer in his last forty-eight at bats.

"He could've hit ten more," said Cece Carlucci, a Coast League umpire. "One game I called him out on strikes four times. He'd just stand there with the bat on his shoulder. He wasn't swinging. I can't figure out why."

"Everything was up here," Bilko explained, motioning to his eyes. "And if I didn't swing, it was outside or over my head. It was getting monotonous. I just didn't want to walk. So I swung at high pitches."

The bomb scare on the final day of the season was a hoax and there were no blasts from Bilko either as the Angels added two more losses to their dismal record.

"What I remember the most about that season was the bomb scare," said John Jancse, an Angel pitcher. "They said it was in the dugout. We all went out to the bullpen. We didn't want to be involved with that bomb going off."

The "bomb" actually went off earlier in the year when the Dodgers took over the Angels as the first step in their move to L.A.

The Coast League was a dead peckerwood, just as Hopper predicted.

In the clubhouse after the last game, a frustrated Jancse confronted Frank Finch, a sportswriter for the *Los Angeles Times*: "Frank, you guys have been asking us questions about what we're going to do next year because the big leagues are coming here. I have a question for you: What are you doing next season?"

"Well, I'll be working for the *Times*," Finch said.

"No you won't," Jancse snapped. "They're going to want big league writers."

"What it really boiled down to was that we all recognized that it was going to screw up the best league in baseball," said Ralph Mauriello, a pitcher who went on to play for the Dodgers. "Playing in the Coast League was actually better and more profitable than playing in the big leagues."

Bill George, a left-handed pitcher for the Angels, put it more succinctly: "They f**ked up the best league in baseball."

As the 1957 season was coming to a close, Bilko was disillusioned.

He hadn't waived his right to be drafted at the end of the year and yet, nobody was calling. "I had been told that some big league clubs wanted me but here I still am."[21]

The Angels were no longer asking $200,000 for their slugger.

"There is no price tag on Bilko," said Bill Heymans, who replaced Holland as general manager in 1957. "We'll dope that out when an offer comes." He added: "But I must admit that no offers have been forthcoming thus far."[22]

The Cincinnati Reds finally made an offer that resulted in Bilko sharing first-base duties in 1958 with Ted Kluszewski and George Crowe. "We bought him because he expressed a desire for another chance in the majors," Reds manager Birdie Tebbetts explained."[23]

Figure 16.1. Despite being named Minor League Player of the Year in 1956, Steve Bilko was still with the Angels the next year while former Angels teammate, Gene Mauch, center, was playing alongside Ted Williams, far left, with the Boston Red Sox. *UCLA Charles E. Young Research Library Department of Special Collections, Los Angeles Times Photographic Archives.*

In mid-June, Bilko was traded to the Dodgers for Don Newcombe, a pitcher whose best days were in the rear-view mirror. A banner headline on the front page of the *Los Angeles Times* sports section heralded the news, DODGERS GET BILKO; NEWCOMBE TRADED.[24]

The Dodgers got off to a miserable start their first year in L.A. and were languishing in last place. Fans were losing interest and Dodgers owner Walter O'Malley was running out of patience.

"The players are hereby put on notice that changes will be made until we get the right combination," he declared at a press conference. "Replacements will come from any place we can obtain them—other major league clubs, our farm system, other minor clubs—whatever is available to help. The club is good enough to win the pennant and I'm getting tired of saying it."[25]

L.A. manager Walt Alston already had two first basemen (veteran Gil Hodges and rookie Norm Larker) and was wondering why he needed another one in Bilko, hitting .264 with four homers at the time of the trade. "The deal's been made," Alston said. "That's all there is to it. We're satisfied. I think it will help both clubs."[26]

What the Dodgers really needed was help off the field where they faced strong and growing opposition to plans for a new ballpark in an area of L.A. known as Chavez Ravine.

City officials already had pledged the land to the Dodgers. But the deal had to be approved by voters in an upcoming public referendum. The Dodgers were losing on the field and they were about to lose at the ballot box. They needed Bilko to rally his legion of L.A. fans with dramatic home runs over the Coliseum's "Chinese Wall"—a forty-foot-high screen in left field and a chip-shot 251 away from home plate.

In his first start at the Coliseum, Bilko lifted a ball over the "Chinese Wall" into the left-center field seats. The ball was hit so high that one of the two runners on base, John Roseboro, fell flat on his face looking for the ball as he rounded second. "I'm glad in a way that he fell," Bilko said. "It gave me more time to go around the bases and listen to the cheers."

After the game, fans gathered around the press box to hear Bilko talk about his three-run clout on the Dodgers' postgame radio show.

"That's our Stevearino," one fan shouted. "That's showing 'em, Bilko." One man broke past a security guard with his boy and said excitedly, "Here he is, son. Shake hands with big Steve."[27]

With one swing of his bat, Bilko had fans and voters excited about baseball again.

The election was still close. It was 351,683 votes for the Dodgers getting the Chavez Ravine location, and 325,878 against—a difference of 25,785 votes that Bilko is credited for making.

"I honestly think Bilko was the difference in winning us the election," said Buzzie Bavasi, general manager of the Dodgers at the time. "No Bilko, no Dodger Stadium."[28]

It may be a stretch to call Dodger Stadium "The House that Bilko Built," but its location in Chavez Ravine can be traced directly to Stout Steve.

NOTES

1. *Los Angeles Mirror-News*, August 5, 1957, Part III, 2.
2. *Los Angeles Times*, August 5, 1957, C1.
3. Ibid.
4. *Los Angeles Mirror-News*, July 27, 1957, Part III, 1.
5. *San Diego Union*, September 16, 1957, B1.
6. *The Sporting News*, May 1, 1957, 7.
7. *Los Angeles Times*, October 13, 1956, A5.
8. *Los Angeles Times*, October 12, 1956, C3.
9. *The Sporting News*, May 15, 1957, 16.
10. *The Sporting News*, April 10, 1957, 14.
11. Ed Mickelson, *Out of the Park: Memoir of a Minor League Baseball All-Star* (Jefferson, NC: McFarland & Company, Inc., 2007), 58.
12. *The Sporting News*, September 11, 1957, 20.
13. *The Sporting News*, February 19, 1958, 28.

14. *The Sporting News,*, March 12, 1958, 5.
15. *Los Angeles Mirror-News*, May 27, 1957, Part III, 1.
16. *The Oregonian*, April 18, 1957, Section Two, 1.
17. *San Diego Union*, April 18, 1957, A15.
18. *The Oregonian*, April 2, 1957, Section Two, 1.
19. *Los Angeles Times*, March 13, 1957, C1.
20. *The Oregonian*, September 4, 1957, Section Two, 3.
21. *The Sporting News*, September 4, 1957, 31.
22. Ibid.
23. *Seattle Times*, March 18, 1958, 28.
24. *Los Angeles Times*, June 16, 1958, C1.
25. *The Sporting News*, July 16, 1958, 10.
26. *Los Angeles Times*, June 16, 1958, C1.
27. *Los Angeles Herald-Express*, July 10, 1958, C6.
28. *Los Angeles Times*, March 14, 1978, Section C3.

SEVENTEEN

Reminiscing in Newland

"As the old saying goes, we've just got to sit back now and smell the roses. See the grass that's on the other side and talk about what we've done." —Dave Hillman, Newland, North Carolina, October 28, 2002

Newland, North Carolina, is located near the Tennessee border in Avery County, the self-proclaimed Christmas tree capital of the world.

The mountains of western North Carolina may seem an unlikely place for a reunion of three players from the 1956 Los Angeles Angels team, but the logistics made perfect sense.

Bob Speake and his wife, Joan, were on a month-long car trip through the eastern United States and visiting Gale "Windy" Wade in Dysartsville, North Carolina. Darius Dutton "Dave" Hillman lives nearby in Kingsport, Tennessee, so Gale arranged for the three to meet half way between Dysartsville and Kingsport in Newland. "Let's meet at Hardee's," Windy suggested.

The night before the then Anaheim Angels beat the San Francisco Giants 4–1 in the seventh, and deciding game, of the 2002 World Series. Darin Erstad, hustling centerfielder for the Angels, told a reporter, "I hope there were kids watching with their fathers, and their fathers told them, 'Watch the way that team plays.' It's refreshing to see that. One reason we were such a great rally team was that we were all on the same page. That's very rare in professional sports."[1]

The three 1956 Angels didn't watch Erstad and his teammates provide the Angels with their first World Series title in forty-two years as a major league franchise. But each of them could relate to what Erstad was saying. As key members of the Bilko Athletic Club—the last Angels team to win a championship—they knew what it was like for a group of talented athletes to be on the same page.

"That particular year all seems like a dream to me," said Hillman, the 1956 Angels pitching ace with twenty-one wins. "Everybody was focused. They knew what they were going to do, what they had to do and they went out and did it. And they did it as a team. It's a dream to me. It was a dream team."

"In those days, we had one-a-comin', one-a-playin' and one-a-goin'," added Speake, the Angels left-fielder who belted twenty-five home runs. "But on that team, you didn't feel the pressure of one-a-comin'."

"Remember how relaxed we were?" asked Wade, the 1956 Angels centerfielder. "We might go down three to nothing or something like that. Not one time did we ever dream that we'd even lose the game. We just sat in the dugout laughing. We knew somebody was going to get on and somebody was going to pop one out of there."

"I still believe this and I will 'til the day I die," Hillman began. "If they had left us alone as a ball club in 1957, and added a little spice here and there—a pinch hitter and a few extra pitchers—I'm confident that we could've won in the National League."

"We could've beaten the Cubs," Wade said.

"We could've beaten Pittsburgh," Hillman added. "We could've beaten Cincinnati. We could've beaten a few others."

"Dave," said Speake, "off that ballclub in 1956, there were you, Drott [Dick Drott], Anderson [Bob Anderson], me and Bolger [Jim Bolger]. We went up to the Cubs in 1957 with great expectations. And then it started to be a parade of players. They just seemed to come in and go around. There wasn't any continuity to the ball club."

For nearly seven hours, the teammates reminisced. They didn't want to let go of the dream season they shared in 1956.

Ray Birch was a catcher in 1948 for Bartlesville in the Kansas-Oklahoma-Missouri (KOM) League—the same league where Wade and Speake started their professional baseball careers. On turning sixty-nine and reflecting on baseball's impact on his life, Burch realized he'd spent "fifteen years dreaming about it, two years playing it and, then, fifty-two years remembering it."

The career of a professional baseball player is brief compared to other professions. Fame is fleeting, if it is achieved at all. Players are relatively young when they retire. Speake was twenty-eight, Wade thirty-two, and Hillman thirty-four.

In the 1950s players moved from team to team so often that they seldom became close. "I hadn't built lasting relationships," Speake explained. "Gale and I stayed in communication with each other. Jim Fanning and I are close. Moe Bauer. But when it really comes down to it, the Christmas card list was kind of thin."

Gale and Dave did not reconnect until 1999. Bob and Dave hadn't seen each other since 1959 when Bob was pinch hitting for the Giants and Dave pitching for the Cubs.

When Bob and Gale arrived at Hardee's, Dave was browsing through a notebook filled with captioned photos of highlights from the 1956 season.

Dave and Bob immediately compared their championship rings and chided Gale for not wearing his ring.

Dave called attention to a photo of Gale on the ground at Lane Field in San Diego. He made a spectacular catch crashing through a gate in the centerfield fence, landing inches from a large grass cutter. Bob was the left fielder.

The bantering began.

"Where was Bob when you went into the lawnmower?" Dave asked Gale.

"He was out there laughing." Gale replied

"That was a wooden fence," Bob said.

"And it had hinges on it," Dave explained. "Before the game we were hitting fly balls to the outfield and Gale slipped over there and unfastened the gate. He wanted to put on a show that day."

"Grandstanding," Bob said, grinning at Gale.

"You probably told me, 'Plenty of room!'"

"'Go get it, Windy, go get it,'" Dave said, imitating Speake. "He didn't want it."

Bob smiled at Gale, saying, "I kept telling you, 'Plenty of room! Plenty of room!' You caught the ball and kept running. At that point, you're on your own."

In another photo Gale is on his feet with Dave standing nearby. "Who's that?" Gale asked.

"See, I played with them and they didn't even recognize me," Dave said.

"You were concerned anyway," Gale laughed.

"Now a pitcher would be out there worrying about you because you'd run down so many mistakes he made," Bob explained. "If you're looking for me and Bolger [right-fielder Jim Bolger], we're over there laughing."

"That's what I'm wondering about," Gale said. "I don't see anybody but San Diego people."

"We all thought you were gone, Honey," Dave said.

"I was for awhile."

"I mean, long gone," Dave said. "We thought you were cut to pieces."

"When those gates open up, everybody is going," Bob said. "Oh dear, I hate funerals."

The conversation shifted to the 1955 season when Bob crashed into the wall at Sportsman's Park in St. Louis, severely dislocating his left wrist. Bob was playing left field and Gale was in center.

"You remember Gale running me into the concrete wall in St. Louis?"

"I told him he had a good chance," Gale said. "He thought I should be worried about his arm."

Wade yelled, "Nice catch, nice catch," and then, suddenly, "My God, you broke your arm!"

"I looked at that thing and it was instant pain," Bob said.

"I'll tell you a story," Bob continued. "This is 1955. We were playing the Dodgers at home and then we went to St. Louis for the last series. I'm playing first base. Carl Furillo gets on first. He said, 'How you'd like to be a Dodger next year?' I said, 'Man, don't kid about things like that.' He said, 'They're upstairs talking about you.' We packed up and went to St. Louis and Gale runs me into a concrete wall. If it hadn't been for Gale, I'd probably wound up a Dodger."

Dave spotted a photo of Gale putting a cross-body block on a second baseman, trying to break up a double play. "Every time I see him he's on the ground or on the lawnmower."

"I never played with a ball player that had a sense for where the camera was as much as he does," Bob needled.

Gale read the photo caption with a quote from Gene Mauch: "He didn't give a damn how many outs there were. If he wanted to run and dive for the ball, he ran and dove for it. It didn't matter. He was just daring."

"Oh, God, that's cruel," Gale said. "That's not complimentary."

Dave read another quote, this one from Gale himself: "Winning one ballgame to me was a whole season. If it meant taking a catcher out at home plate or knocking out the second baseman with a rolling block, I did it. I sacrificed my body to win ballgames."

"There you go," Dave said. "You'd sacrifice your teammates, too."

"We won the ballgame, didn't we?" Bob asked.

"We won the ballgame," Gale replied, changing the subject.

"I was playing golf one day and this guy, a baseball nut, says, 'Gale, I see where you hit only one home run in the major leagues. Who did you hit that off of?' We were walking down the fairway. I say, 'Lord, Frank, I don't remember.' We took four or five more steps and he says, 'Well, I think if I only hit one, I'd remember who it was.'"

Laughter—the kind once heard in the Angels' Little Wrigley clubhouse—filled a corner of the restaurant.

Gale turned to a series of photos showing Steve Bilko putting his heft into a pitch for another of his prodigious home runs.

"Ol' Hump, I tell you what, he was something!"

Gale called Bilko "Hump" because of his batting stance. "He kind of hovered over the plate, hunching his shoulders into a hump."

"I called him, "Mr. Bilko," Bob said.

"I said, 'Yes, sir,' to him," Dave explained.

Figure 17.1. Teammate Gale Wade called Steve Bilko "Hump" because he hunched his shoulders prior to a pitch. *UCLA Charles E. Young Research Library Department of Special Collections, Los Angeles Times Photographic Archives.*

"He was such a laid-back guy," Gale said. "God, he could drink that beer. He'd sit in the clubhouse whirlpool with George Freese after a ballgame and go through a six pack."

"Six pack?" Bob exclaimed.

"That was for starters."

Bob used the series of time-lapse photos to make a point about hitting. "He's got the bat up. The wrists are cocked. That's the reason he hit home runs. He strides, locks the front knee and makes contact at impact—bat on the ball. And it releases all the energy."

"Hey, Speaker, he hit everybody except Ryne Duren," Dave said, referring to a photo showing Bilko throwing his bat in disgust after being called out on strikes—the third time Duren struck him out in the game.

Figure 17.2.   Steve Bilko launches another of his long-range missiles into space. *UCLA Charles E. Young Research Library Department of Special Collections, Los Angeles Times Photographic Archives.*

Mention of the hard-throwing Duren prompted Bob to recount a brawl in Vancouver. "Duren was pitching. And Mauch went up to hit—first inning. Duren winds up and hits him in the ribs. He gets up and goes to first. Third inning, we're coming up. Mauch says to me: 'If Duren throws at me again, you keep Honey Romano off of me.'"

John "Honey" Romano was the catcher. At five-foot-ten-inches and 205 pounds, Romano resembled a football linebacker.

"I looked at Romano and thought, 'Oh man, how am I going to take this guy out?' Gene gets up there and Duren hits him again—same spot. Gene bounces up like a little rooster and runs out there. They meet head on and flop to the ground. Now, Duren's glasses flew off. He couldn't even find Gene. He's crawling around on all fours, looking for his glasses and Gene is beating him to death.

"I'm headed out there between them and Romano. John looks at me and I look at him. We both started laughing.

"Ol' Lefty O'Doul had told Ryne, 'Knock that Mauch down. You can only win this ballgame by knocking Mauch down.' And he landed two of 'em. It was the funniest sight. Here is Duren, crawling around on all fours, looking for his glasses."

"Gene had a lot of guts, tackling ol' Duren," Dave said. "He was big and strong."

"But he was almost blind without his glasses," Bob said.

"Remember Danny Ozark?" Gale asked. "Danny was a first baseman at Fort Worth in 1953. Ryne was going to pitch that night. When Danny came to the ballpark, oh boy, he had a bad stomach problem. He didn't play. And Ryne didn't pitch. Well, the next night, Ryne did pitch. Danny couldn't play sick two nights in a row. We never did let Danny live that one down. Oh, he was scared of Ryne Duren."

Bob pulled out a spreadsheet with detailed team statistics from the 1956 season. "Have you seen this?"

"This will blow your mind," Gale said to Dave. "These don't lie."

"I'm going to show you pitchers' batting averages," Bob said. "Oh, we find that Hillman hit .158."

"That's what I weighed."

"Why you was telling me how you used to pinch hit and everything," Gale said in mock surprise. "You can't pinch hit with an average like that."

One of Dave's favorite stories is the time he pinch hit for another pitcher, Harry Perkowski. "Harry went two weeks, Honey, and never spoke to me. He was mad at me. Harry now says that he don't remember it."

"Harry hit .206," Bob said. "How can you pinch hit for him?"

"It was a left hander pitching," Dave said. "And he walked me. He walked me to get to the lead-off man."

"It's a good thing we had a good-hitting ballclub," Bob said, "because the pitchers only hit .188."

Speake pointed out that the poor hitting by the pitchers caused the team batting average to drop ten points—from .306 to .296.

"Now, there's an explanation for this," Dave said. "They didn't pay me to hit. They paid me to pitch."

"This is the pitching side," Bob said, citing Dave's numbers, "twenty-one and seven with a 3.38 earned run average [ERA]."

"3.38? That's not bad," Dave said.

"Not bad," Bob agreed. "The team ERA was 4.45. That's not overly outstanding."

"With that ball club, Honey, as long as you held a team to under five runs, you were doing good because you were going to win more than you were going to lose."

Dave read his won-loss record against various teams in the league—Portland, 2–0; Sacramento, 5–0; San Diego, 3–1.

"He likes those big parks," Bob teased.

"Is this home games, too? I won most of these in Los Angeles in that little park."

Dave was 10–3 against first division teams, including a 6–0 record against second-place Seattle. Hillman completed fifteen of the twenty-nine games he started—five more than the entire pitching staff of the 2002 world champion Angels.

"You were feeling bad for a while, wasn't you?" Gale said to Dave.

"We had him on the ropes," Bob chuckled.

"I was good against the good hitters but I was poor against the bad hitters," Dave said. "Those .300 hitters? I thrived on them."

The fourth-place Hollywood Stars and cellar-dwelling Vancouver Mounties accounted for six of Dave's seven losses.

"I was pitching at Hollywood on a Sunday afternoon. I knew not to pitch Bill Mazeroski up here," motioning to his chest. "Mazeroski comes up and one gets away from me. I get it up and inside to him and he hits it over the left-field fence. Gene Mauch came in and jumped down my throat. I mean, he got hot. I said, 'Dammit, Gene, go back out there and play second base. Do I get on your ass every time you make an error? You play second base. Let me handle this in here.'"

"Gene couldn't cover a lot of ground," Gale explained. "But he could turn a double play. His greatest asset was his thinking during the game. He really understood what somebody was going to do."

"He was the leader—the field general," Bob added.

Dave spent the last two weeks of the 1956 season with the Cubs; he appeared in twenty-five games the previous year. Gale was the Cubs' opening day centerfielder in both 1955 and 1956. Bob was an early season sensation for the Cubs in 1955, his ten homers in the month of May making headlines across the country.

A notebook with selected Chicago newspaper stories on each player's experiences with the Cubs was on the table to refresh their memories and settle any debates.

Gale noticed the headline of a *Chicago Sun-Times* article by Edgar Munzel: ERROR BY WADE OPENS WAY FOR 2-RUN 7th."[2]

"That was the guy I threatened to throw off the catwalk near the press box at Wrigley Field—Mousey Munzel."

"Edgar is his name," Bob corrected. "You called him Mousey?"

"Mousey. He was a mouse."

"What did he say in the article?" Dave asked. "That you were sunbathing?"

The score was tied 1–1 in the seventh inning when a pop fly was hit to right-center. Munzel wrote, "Walt Moryn was camped under it and the ball had just barely touched his mitt when Gale Wade rammed into him."

Gale wanted to set the record straight.

"I said, 'I got it! I got it! I got it!' The ball wasn't about six feet from my glove when Walt Moryn hit me full bore and knocked me twenty feet. I got up off the ground and said, 'Walt, didn't you hear me?' And he said, 'No, I didn't hear you.' Well, the next day in the darn paper . . . ."

"We've got a problem here," Bob said, producing a *Chicago Tribune* story describing the same play: "Gale Wade banged into Walt Moryn today as the latter was about to close his glove on an easy fly ball."[3]

"I retrieved the ball," Gale said, laughing.

"Well," Bob noted, "Moryn was probably lost. How can two writers see it one way and you explain it to us another?"

"That was totally wrong," Gale objected. "If Walt Moryn was still alive, he'd tell you the truth."

"I'm glad I didn't make those papers," Dave said.

"Hold on!" Bob and Gale said, almost in unison.

They found a story with the following sentence highlighted: "Robinson knocked a two-run homer in the seventh off Dave Hillman, making his Cub and big league debut."[4]

"That must've been Mousey," Gale quipped.

"Jackie Robinson. He hit a line drive and you could hear it ricochet in the left-field seats, just like a jackhammer." Dave imitated the sound of a jackhammer.

"Was you in there in the ninth?" Gale inquired.

"They took me out."

"Wait a minute," Bob interrupted. "Let's talk about the ninth inning."

"Who entered the picture in the ninth?" Dave asked.

Bob pointed to the following account of the ninth inning: "Speake's pinch double past Hodges scored Banks. Speake proceeded to steal third and when Campanella [Roy] heaved the ball into left field, Bob came home."[5]

Gale noticed another story about Hillman titled, COHEN OPTIONED, RECALL HILLMAN.[6]

Hy Cohen had a 5–0 won-loss record with the 1956 Angels when Hillman made his first start five weeks into the season. Dave always believed he was responsible for Hy being demoted until Cohen informed him otherwise in a telephone conversation forty-four years later.

"Poor ol Hy Cohen," Bob said. "Dave ruined Hy Cohen's career completely. We were in Chicago and I was rooming with Hy when this happened. I said, 'Hy, dry your eyes, Dave's a nice guy.'"

"So Dave chased Hy out of Chicago?" Gale added.

"I chased him out of baseball," Dave chuckled.

The teammates enjoyed another hearty laugh.

"It's time to get Speake now," Gale announced.

Everybody waited as Bob read a *Sporting News* story headlined: BOB SPEAKE LETS BAT REPLY TO QUINN'S LABEL OF BUSHER.[7]

"He wasn't quiet, Dave, when it was you and me."

"He's not grinning now."

"The question is whether I'm a busher or a big leaguer," Bob said, "and this guy, of course, doesn't know what he's saying."

Bob continued: "We're in Milwaukee facing Warren Spahn. It's the ninth inning and I hit a home run off of him down the right-field line. We win the ballgame. So the next morning in the Milwaukee newspaper, John Quinn, the Braves general manager, called me a busher because I get a home run off of Spahn."

"Now that's your take," Gale said.

"I'm just an innocent bystander in all this. All I'm doing is hitting home runs. John Hoffman is writing about it. I'm just a pawn."

"Hoffman didn't like me either. But Mousey was the guy that I got after. I told him that if he wasn't so damn little, I'd thrown him off the catwalk."

Speake is asked to explain another *Sporting News* article quoting him as saying it's "easier to hit in the majors than it is in the minors."[8]

"You said that?" Gale said in disbelief.

"You talk about a writer . . . this Hoffman," Bob said. "What ball player in his right mind would make a statement like that?"

"Well, I've known several that haven't been so smart," Dave said.

"You didn't say that, did you?" Gale asked Bob.

"I don't know whether I said it or did not but if I did, it was taken totally out of context. That's my response to it. Always has been. I'd have to be a self-centered egotist to make a statement like that in the face of big league pitching."

"Why is it you think that's taken out of context," Gale said, "but what ol' Munzel said about me is all right?"

"Because it was play-by-play. You ran into Walt Moryn. 'You rammed him' was the expression. This guy, John Hoffman, is the Cubs reporter for the *Sporting News* and so he's got to have something to write about."

"I don't appreciate those guys," Dave said. "They don't write about me."

"You've got to do something!" Bob said.

The conversation returned to the 1956 Angels and the team's manager, Bob Scheffing.

"Scheffing was probably the best that I've ever seen at letting people play," Gale said

"If you were a hitter," Bob said, "he would never take you out when you were in a slump. He would always let you work through it. Then if you would need a few days rest, he would give it to you. He let us do what was necessary."

"That was the smartest playing ball club I was ever on," Gale said.

"The infield shifted as a unit," Bob explained. "We shifted as a unit in the outfield."

"From a pitcher's standpoint," Dave said, "you don't know how great it is to see three damn antelopes in the outfield running."

"When you're winning," Gale said, "you have a good time."

"We had fun with Gene Mauch as much as anybody," Bob said, "because he had the killer instinct."

"A manager has to be a good psychologist," Dave said.

That reminded Bob of the time Whitey Herzog was asked, "What's the hardest thing about being a manager?"

"He said, 'Managing millionaires. And if you have an answer to that, I want to talk to you later.' What you're talking about is using psychology enough to get them to pull together to a common goal."

The 1956 Angels are rated seventh best in the fifty-five-year history of the old Pacific Coast League by Dick Beverage, editor of *Potpourri*, the PCL Historical Society newsletter.

"It was probably our pitching staff that cost us a higher ranking," Bob chided Dave.

The teammates laughed, Dave the loudest. They were reliving a dream season—one that is real and enduring.

Just as the 2002 Angels were on the same page in winning the World Series title the night before, the three 1956 Angels were on the same page—then and now.

NOTES

1. *Sports Illustrated*, November 4, 2002, 37.
2. *Chicago Sun-Times*, April 20, 1956, 73.
3. *Chicago Tribune*, April 20, 1956, 1 (Sports).
4. *Chicago Tribune*, May 1, 1955, 4 (Sports).
5. Ibid.
6. *Chicago Sun-Times*, June 3, 1955, 61.
7. *The Sporting News*, June 8, 1955, 14.
8. *The Sporting News*, June 15, 1955, 5.

EIGHTEEN

Where Have You Gone, Steve Bilko?

Where have you gone, Steve Bilko?
Wrigley Field turns its lonely eyes to you
What's that you say, Angel Annie?
Wrigley Field has left and gone away.

The Cardinals and the Indians at Wrigley Field in Los Angeles weren't that unusual in the 1950s.

At that time major league teams, ranging from the Cleveland Indians to the New York Giants to the Chicago Cubs, visited the friendly confines of Wrigley Field in L.A. for spring exhibition games.

Almost a half century has passed since 1969 when the wrecking ball demolished the old ballpark. Most people are not aware that there ever was a Wrigley Field in L.A.

But on a windy Saturday in September 2007, baseball again was king as the Cardinals and Indians of the Wrigley Little League played.

Mike Garcia introduced himself as president of the Wrigley Little League. "It's opening day of our winter league," he said.

A sign atop the backstop read:

Wrigley Little League Field
At Gilbert Lindsay Recreation Center
Dodger Dream Field

Garcia had big dreams for the Wrigley Little League.

Earlier in the year, a team of youngsters representing the Dodgers traveled with Garcia and two other league officials to Washington D.C. to play a Brooklyn team on the South Lawn of the White House. President George W. Bush was there. So was Frank Robinson, the Hall of Famer. Tommy Lasorda, a pitcher for the 1957 Angels and long-time manager of the Los Angeles Dodgers, attended. Garcia proudly showed pictures of

the occasion that marked the sixtieth anniversary of Jackie Robinson becoming the first African American to play in the majors.

Garcia wasn't even born when the last game was played at Wrigley
Field by the Indians and Los Angeles Angels October 1, 1961.

James Lee III was born two years later—1963. He grew up on Forty-
first Place directly across from the ballpark. When he learned that Steve
Bilko hit the last home run at Wrigley, over the left-field wall in the ninth
inning, he said, "It probably hit my house."

Lee worked for the Gilbert Lindsay Recreation Center that was built
after Wrigley Field was torn down. "Home plate is where our office is
located," Lee said. That's where Avalon and Forty-second Place intersect.

He was wearing a Dodgers cap that he removed briefly to show autographs from Don Newcombe and Lou Johnson, both former Dodgers.
"Sweet Lou Johnson was here earlier today. He was standing right where
you are now. I didn't know who he was until we started talking."

Lee served as a safety officer for the Wrigley Little Leaguers. Between
games, he groomed the field.

He pointed out the houses that were easy targets for home runs hit
over the left-field wall at Wrigley. "Centerfield is at Forty-first Place and
Avalon."

The baseball field was created in 1996. Only recently was it adopted
by the Dodgers and named the Wrigley Little League Field.

Garcia led the way to a storage shed where there was a copy of a *Los
Angeles Times* story on Wrigley Field with a photo that he thought was a
shot of the ballpark. It was actually an artist's rendering of what Wrigley
Field would've looked like if the Dodgers or some other major league
team played there.

Garcia pointed to the nearby soccer fields that were all dirt and fenced
off. "Nike is putting in two synthetic fields. There is a lot more soccer
played here than baseball."

"Where have you gone, Steve Bilko?" *Los Angeles Times* columnist Don
Page wrote as the ballpark was being torn down. "Wrigley Field turns its
lonely eyes to you."[1]

I've gone back to the site of old Wrigley Field three times.

My first visit on May 6, 2001, happened to coincide with the fortieth
anniversary of the New York Yankees' first appearance at Wrigley Field
after the Angels joined the American League in 1961. It was a dream
come true to see major league baseball in my dream ballpark.

The opener on a Friday night was sold out. Somehow my father managed to get tickets. We watched from our grandstand seats as the Yankees came from behind to beat the Angels, 5–4. Mickey Mantle went 0-
for-4, Roger Maris 0-for-1. Steve Bilko pinch hit in the ninth and struck
out.

Memories of that evening triggered memories from games I saw at Wrigley Field when the minor-league Angels played there.

My father didn't drink or smoke. When a cup of beer was being passed down our aisle from the vendor to a thirsty fan, Dad always leaned back in his seat as far as he could to avoid contact with the sinful suds. He tolerated second-hand smoke from cigarettes but cigars were cause for immediate action. He used our scorecard to clear the air.

Dad always wore a suit to games. He didn't say much except to comment on a good play or a bad call by an umpire.

We had our favorite players.

Gene Baker, a silky smooth shortstop, was one of them. Baker played three years for the Angels before he and Ernie Banks became the Chicago Cubs' first black players in September 1953. Baker switched to second base while teaching the younger Banks the art of playing shortstop.

Max West, a power-hitting outfielder, played seven years in the majors with the Boston Braves and Pittsburgh Pirates before moving into Wrigley in 1951, smashing thirty-five home runs each of his first two seasons and eighty-seven overall. "I liked the sound when you hit the ball," Max said of hitting at Wrigley. "The sound of the ball hitting the bat reverberated."

Bill "Poison" Moisan was a pitcher who won thirty-seven games for the Angels over four years, including ten in 1953. His pitching wasn't why he was nicknamed "Poison." It was Moisan's hitting. He was often used as a pinch-hitter in 1953 as he hit for a .284 average with four home runs and twenty-three RBIs. "One of my biggest thrills was a pinch-hit, walk-off home run against the Hollywood Stars at Wrigley," Moisan said.

We had a favorite fan, an elderly black woman called Angel Annie. She also was known as the "voice of Wrigley Field." For thirty-five years, Angel Annie attended nearly every game at the ballpark, entertaining fans and players alike with her yelps and hollers, once described as "a shouting voice somewhere between a police siren and a dynamite explosion."[2]

Near the end of the 1954 season, Angel Annie told a reporter, "I've been hollerin' since I was born and I won't quit till I die."[3]

Angel Annie, also known as Roberta King, died exactly four months after the news story and two months before Bilko and Buzz Clarkson arrived in L.A. She was eighty-seven.

The biggest Angels fan just missed seeing the two mightiest of all Angels' players.

My third and last visit to where Wrigley Field used to be was in 2008 on my way to the Pacific Coast League Historical Society's L.A. reunion held every May.

The gatherings remind Jerry Mezerow, an Angel fan and movie buff, of the movie *Dead Poets Society*. "It's an era gone by. But for a few hours, we're back in time—in most cases, a much better time—when our dads took us to games."

The reunions get smaller every year.

"It's thinning out," said John Schulian, a former sports columnist and an unapologetic sentimentalist when it comes to the old PCL. "It's like going to see an old jazz musician."

A month before the 2008 reunion, Schulian wrote in the *Los Angeles Times* about the last year of the PCL in 1957 and the end of the rivalry between the Angels and Stars: "The Dodgers would bring the major leagues the next year, as if the magic in baseball couldn't come from anywhere else. But the big leagues seemed to matter most to grown-ups and politicians, two groups that should never be considered one in the same. To a kid listening to the Stars on the radio, baseball was fine just the way it was."[4]

I looked around at the way it is now. There's a senior citizen center in addition to the soccer fields, basketball courts and Wrigley Little League Field that make up the recreational area that "rise and breathe where the ivy on the ballpark fences once climbed and reached for the same sun."[5]

That's what *L.A. Times* columnist John Hall envisioned in 1969 when the one-time "Pearl of Avalon" came tumbling down.

Talking with dozens of old Coast League players and poring through hundreds of newspaper and magazine stories from the 1950s made me curious about a few things.

One of them was a two-story apartment house on Forty-first Place that was a frequent target of home run balls over Wrigley's left-field wall.

"It is the place where television cameras at Wrigley Field automatically draw into focus every time Stout Steve Bilko comes to bat," *Los Angeles Times* columnist Ned Cronin wrote at the close of the 1956 season.[6]

The home run that is forever etched in my mind, however, is one of Clarkson's Buzz-bombs that ripped through the door of an apartment in the building. I'm not sure if this is because I was at Wrigley to see the bombing or the copy of two newspaper photos I have in a scrapbook. "Whatta wallop," the caption read below a shot of Buzz swinging and another of an artist's arrow tracing the path of the ball from home plate to the hole in the door of the house being examined by kids.

I found the house. It is surrounded by a tall white wrought iron fence. More wrought iron protected the front doors of the four apartments. But the windows were unprotected.

"Good thing Buzz and Bilko are gone," I thought to myself.

As I walked around, comments from the player interviews flooded my mind. I recalled a telephone conversation with Buzz shortly before I interviewed Bilko in Nanticoke, Pennsylvania, in 1976.

"Oh, he was something else," Buzz said of Bilko. "I never could understand the way he hit that ball that he didn't have a better major-league career. Boy, he had power to burn."

Figure 18.1. **The clock tower was the last identifying mark when the wrecker's ball leveled once-plush Los Angeles' Wrigley Field in March 1969.** *UCLA Charles E. Young Research Library Department of Special Collections, Los Angeles Times Photographic Archives.*

"Why do *you* think he didn't do better?" I asked.

Buzz's answer applied to his own career as well: "Probably they didn't give him a legitimate chance. The way he hit that ball out in the Coast League? *My!*

I remembered my brother, Don, out scrambling kids for baseballs hit into the right-field bleachers during batting practice. He came up with so many balls we never had to buy them.

Don attended the 2001 Coast League reunion with me.

"Thanks for the memories," he told Max West.

"Thanks for remembering," replied Max before posing for a picture with us.

One of the highlights of 1956 was the tape-measure home run Bilko swatted but didn't hang around after the game for the measuring ceremony that determined the ball traveled 451 feet. Steve rushed home to babysit his three kids so Mrs. Bilko could have a night out.

Lost among all of the home runs hit at Little Wrigley was the speed and base running ability of Gale Wade who led the 1956 Angels in stolen bases with sixteen.

Gale taught Maury Wills the art of stealing bases when they were teammates at Spokane in 1958 and four years later with the Dodgers, Wills set a modern era record of 104 stolen bases in a single season.

"Gale was the only player I ever knew that kept a book on a pitcher's move to first base," said Russ Kemmerer, a pitcher for the San Francisco Seals. "Not only was he fast, he timed you and pretty much knew how far he could go. Later Joe Morgan and Maury Wills developed techniques for base running and stealing bases but Gale was the first."

There are no signs, plaques or any other reminders of a famous ballpark and World War I memorial tower.

There's a sign reading "no golfing" on a light post in the area where several park benches are located. I thought of Bilko being called Little Wrigley's "home pro" and Bob Coats telling me he was Gene Mauch's caddy.

"He used to argue," Coats said. "I mean, just get beside himself. And his stomach would be killing him. So I'd get him a 7-Up or something to calm his stomach."

When I interviewed Raymond "Moe" Bauer, he showed me a newspaper photo of him and Arnold Palmer when they were honored as the "most outstanding" athletes of 1949–1950 at Wake Forest. In the picture, Moe watches as Palmer demonstrates his golf grip on a knife.

"Did you ever play golf with Arnold?" I asked.

"I wasn't playing golf at the time," Moe said. "I ran the golf course to get into shape."

I flashed back to the *Home Run Derby* series filmed at Wrigley Field in 1959. Harmon Killebrew was one of the sluggers featured. The so-called "Killer" out-homered Mantle 9–8 in one show and Rocky Colavito 6–5 in another.

After the 1956 Angels said goodbye to his perfect 5–0 record, Hy Cohen pitched for Memphis in the Southern Association. Several times he faced Killebrew, who played for Chattanooga.

"You wouldn't believe it but I used to strike that guy out four times a game—well, you know, a couple of times a game," Cohen said. "He never touched me."

Cohen became amused at the different directions their baseball careers took. "He's in the Hall of Fame and I'm playing poker."

I continued down memory lane, recalling the numerous barnstorming teams that visited Little Wrigley. In 1947, Bob Feller, the great Indians pitcher, headed a team of major league all-stars that played against the legendary Satchel Paige and a team of Negro League stars, including Piper Davis. Feller's team won both games in L.A. as the versatile Piper played three different positions.

Jim Murray, a *Los Angeles Times* sports columnist, once wrote, "To me, a ballpark is like an old song. It's fun. But it's also sad. You remember the darndest things about ballparks. Some of them have nothing to do with baseball."[7]

My thoughts turned briefly to Rev. Martin Luther King Jr. and a speech he gave at Little Wrigley in 1963 before a crowd of 30,000—the largest civil rights rally ever in L.A. "Injustice anywhere is a threat to justice everywhere," Rev. King declared. "Birmingham or Los Angeles, the cry is always the same. We want to be free . . . now is the time to lift this nation from the quicksand of racial injustice."[8]

Piper Davis, the 1956 Angels only black player, was respected and admired by his teammates, but they knew little about him and virtually nothing about what he did away from the ballpark. "He would often have to stay in different housing," said Bob Anderson, one of the Angels' kid pitchers. "That was a sad scenario."

In 1957, Piper went to Fort Worth in the Texas League where he and Gene Fodge, another Angel pitcher, were again teammates.

Gene related a conversation they had in Forth Worth.

"I've got to be at the ballpark at four o'clock tomorrow," Piper told Gene.

"Hell, we don't play until seven."

Gene arrived at around five o'clock to find Piper lying in the outfield on his back with his arms spread out and the palms of his hands facing upward.

"What the hell you doing?" Gene asked.

"Well, you see this here," Piper said pointing to the palms of his hands. "It's still as white as yours. I'm trying to get it evened out with the other side."

Early in the 1956 season, Angels' president John Holland invited the Yankees to play the Angels in an exhibition game at Little Wrigley during a two-day break in New York's September schedule. The Yankees declined the offer, citing the cross-country travel that might hurt their chances to win another American League pennant.

I always wondered what would've happened if the Angels and Yankees had played that game. I've even dreamed about it. In my dream, Piper comes to bat as a pinch-hitter with the bases loaded and two outs in the bottom of the ninth. The Yankees are leading 9–6. The sellout crowd is on its feet as Piper swings and misses at two fastballs. Yankee catcher Yogi Berra figures another fastball will catch Piper off guard. The pitch is on its way to the plate. It's a fastball—exactly what Piper would've called if he was catching. Piper swings and POW!

He watches the ball sail over the left-field wall and crash into the apartment house on Forty-first Place. It's a walk-off grand slam. The Angels win, 10–9.

The Yankees were one of the teams that thought Piper was too old to play white folks' ball. Piper lingers at home plate long enough to tell a puzzled Yogi, "Element of surprise, my dear brother! Element of surprise."

NOTES

1. *Los Angeles Times*, July 13, 1968, B2.
2. *Long Beach Independent-Press-Telegram*, Southland Magazine, September 5, 1954, 16.
3. Ibid.
4. *Los Angeles Times*, April 11, 2008, D5.
5. *Los Angeles Times*, January 29, 1969, G3.
6. *Los Angeles Times*, September 15, 1956, A3.
7. *Los Angeles Times*, April 30, 1961, G1.
8. *Los Angeles Times*, May 27, 1963, 2.

Appendix A

1956 Los Angeles Angels Batting Averages

INDIVIDUAL BATTING (10 or more games). Asterisk denotes left-handed batter, pound symbol denotes switch hitter, bold denotes league leader. *Source: 1957 Los Angeles Angels Yearbook.*

Player	G	AB	R	H	TB	2B	3B	HR	SH	SF	SB	BB	HB	RBI	SO	BA
Bilko, Steve	162	597	**163**	**215**	**410**	18	6	**55**	0	6	4	**104**	2	**164**	105	**.360**
Mauch, Gene	146	566	123	197	292	29	3	20	8	1	2	70	5	84	43	.348
Fanning, Jim	12	27	4	9	13	1	0	1	0	1	0	1	0	5	5	.333
Bolger, Jim	165	592	88	193	322	37	4	28	1	10	3	48	5	147	42	.326
Coats, Bob*	103	237	45	75	82	7	0	0	5	1	3	24	0	29	16	.316
Davis, Piper	64	152	19	48	75	9	0	6	1	1	1	5	1	24	17	.316
Speake, Bob*	158	580	107	174	284	29	3	25	1	8	14	74	3	111	100	.300
Wade, Gale*	101	383	77	112	194	8	7	20	3	2	16	43	4	67	62	.292
Freese, George	137	474	87	138	243	31	4	22	4	7	5	53	8	113	49	.291
Wise, Casey#	168	**705**	122	202	267	36	4	7	9	4	7	50	0	60	51	.287
Haas, Eddie	41	149	34	41	60	5	1	4	1	3	1	32	1	19	23	.275
Thorpe, Bob	35	62	6	17	25	3	1	1	1	0	0	3	0	9	18	.274
Hannah, Joe	93	239	29	65	82	12	1	1	2	1	0	34	1	33	46	.272
Tappe, Elvin	100	303	30	81	106	14	1	3	6	4	0	46	4	36	40	.267
Lauters, Don	39	100	15	26	40	6	1	2	3	1	0	7	1	6	25	.260
Pieretti, Marino	38	45	5	11	14	3	0	0	3	0	0	1	0	0	2	.244
Perkowski, Harry*	24	34	5	7	14	1	0	2	1	0	0	1	0	2	12	.206
Goryl, Johnny	12	21	4	4	8	1	0	1	1	1	0	4	0	4	4	.190
Drott, Dick	35	75	6	14	22	2	0	2	3	2	0	0	1	9	17	.187
Fodge, Gene	47	65	9	11	12	1	0	0	3	0	0	3	0	7	20	.169
Briggs, Johnny	19	31	3	5	9	1	0	1	0	0	0	1	0	1	12	.161

Bauer, Moe	49	19	3	3	3	0	0	0	0	0	0	2	1	0	5	.158
Adams, Red	15	34	2	4	4	0	0	0	0	0	0	1	0	1	7	.118
Myers, Richie	15	36	5	4	5	1	0	0	2	0	0	7	0	1	0	.111
Anderson, Bob	71	20	1	1	4	0	0	1	0	0	0	0	0	2	12	.050
TEAM HITTING	**168**	**5656**	**1000**	**1678**	**2611**	**255**	**36**	**202**	**57**	**53**	**56**	**623**	**36**	**933**	**771**	**.297**

Appendix B

1956 Los Angeles Angels Pitching Statistics

Appendix B

PITCHING (15 or more innings). Asterisk denotes left-handed pitcher, bold denotes league leader. Source: *1957 Los Angeles Angels Yearbook*

Player	G	GS	CG	W-L	PCT	IP	R	H	ER	HR	BB	HB	SO	WP	BK	SHO	ERA
Anderson	**70**	0	0	12-4	.750	105	43	103	31	5	52	1	61	12	0	0	2.65
Swanson	7	1	0	2-0	1.000	19	7	11	6	3	6	0	13	1	1	0	2.79
Bauer*	49	0	0	6-1	.857	80	36	85	28	4	25	1	32	2	0	0	3.16
Hillman	33	29	15	21-7	**.750**	210	90	207	79	16	60	3	130	3	0	3	3.38
Adams	15	12	5	6-2	.750	86	48	102	39	14	20	1	27	0	0	0	4.07
Fodge	44	25	11	19-7	.731	192	100	204	92	13	82	5	122	1	1	2	4.31
Drott	35	30	11	13-10	.565	197	119	198	96	23	108	6	**184**	9	1	1	4.39
Perkowski*	22	12	2	4-6	.400	90	57	106	48	10	41	3	52	0	0	0	4.78
Thorpe	29	20	6	7-7	.500	156	95	183	84	24	60	4	77	3	0	1	4.86
Pieretti	38	17	2	7-9	.438	156	99	191	85	16	53	4	68	3	0	0	4.90
Briggs	18	13	4	5-5	.500	80	56	109	50	9	27	0	37	1	0	0	5.62
Cohen	5	5	1	5-0	1.000	30	21	40	19	5	15	0	16	1	0	0	5.70

Appendix C
Steve Bilko Career Batting Statistics

Leagues in which Steve Bilko played

American Association	AA
American League	AL
Carolina League	CAR
Eastern Shore League	ESL
International League	IL
Inter-State League	ISL
National League	NL
Pacific Coast League	PCL
Piedmont League	PIED

Steve Bilko Career Batting Statistics. Based on statistics compiled by the Society of American Baseball Research (SABR)

Year	CLUB	LGE	G	AB	R	H	2B	3B	HR	RBI	SB	BB	SO	BA
1945	Allentown	ISL	1	1	0	1	0	0	0	1	0	0	0	1.000
1946	Salisbury	ESL	122	441	73	121	28	4	12	90	6	72	86	.274
1946	Allentown	ISL	1	1	0	0	0	0	0	0	0	0	0	.000
1947	Winston-Salem	CAR	116	438	109	148	26	3	29	120	12	77	80	.338
1948	Lynchburg	PIED	128	463	89	154	34	6	20	92	3	58	56	.333
1948	Rochester	IL	12	41	5	6	1	0	0	3	0	8	11	.146
1949	Rochester	IL	139	503	101	156	32	5	34	125	1	84	74	.310
1949	St. Louis	NL	6	17	3	5	2	0	0	2	0	5	6	.310
1950	St. Louis	NL	10	33	1	6	1	0	0	2	0	4	10	.290
1950	Rochester	IL	109	334	71	97	18	6	15	58	1	9	10	.290
1951	St. Louis	NL	21	72	5	16	4	0	2	12	0	9	10	.282
1951	Rochester	IL	73	273	41	77	14	6	8	50	0	37	51	.282
1951	Columbus	AA	26	74	13	21	2	0	1	6	0	12	18	.284
1952	Rochester	IL	82	286	55	92	22	5	12	55	0	36	40	.322
1952	St. Louis	NL	20	72	7	19	6	1	1	6	0	4	15	.264
1953	St. Louis	NL	154	570	72	143	23	3	21	84	0	70	125	.251
1954	St. Louis	NL	8	14	1	2	0	0	0	1	0	3	1	.143
1954	Chicago	NL	47	92	11	22	8	1	4	12	0	11	24	.239
1955	Los Angeles	PCL	168	622	105	204	35	3	37	124	4	73	104	.328
1956	Los Angeles	PCL	162	597	163	215	18	6	55	164	4	104	105	.360
1957	Los Angeles	PCL	158	536	111	161	22	1	56	140	8	108	150	.300

Year	Team	League												
1959	Spokane	PCL	135	478	76	146	24	1	26	92	2	72	98	.305
1960	Detroit	AL	78	222	20	46	11	2	9	25	0	27	31	.207
1961	Los Angeles	AL	114	294	49	82	16	1	20	59	1	58	81	.279
1962	Los Angeles	AL	64	164	26	47	9	1	8	38	1	25	35	.287
1963	Rochester	IL	101	261	41	68	17	1	8	37	1	58	72	.261
Minors			**1533**	**5349**	**1053**	**1667**	**293**	**47**	**313**	**1157**	**42**	**808**	**955**	**.312**
Majors			**600**	**1738**	**220**	**432**	**85**	**13**	**76**	**276**	**2**	**234**	**395**	**.249**

Bibliography

Beverage, Richard. *The Los Angeles Angels of the Pacific Coast League*. Jefferson, NC: McFarland, 2011.

Dobbins, Dick. *The Grand Minor League: An Oral History of the Old Pacific Coast League*. Emeryville, CA: Woodford Press, 1999.

Fullerton, Christopher D. *Every Other Sunday*. Birmingham, AL: Boozer Press, 1999.

Golenbock. Peter, *Wrigleyville: A Magical History Tour of the Chicago Cubs*. New York, NY: St. Martin's Griffin, 1999.

John, Tommy with Valenti, Dan. *T. J. My 26 Years in Baseball*. New York, NY: Bantam Books, 1991.

Kelley, Brent. *Voices from the Negro Leagues*. Jefferson, NC: McFarland & Company, Inc., 1998.

Kinsella, W. P. *Shoeless Joe*. Jefferson, NC: Ballantine Books, 1982.

Klima, John. *Willie's Boys*. Hoboken, NJ: John Wiley & Sons, 2009.

Mays, Willie with Sahadi, Lou. *Say Hey*. New York City: Pocket Books, 1988.

Mickelson, Ed, *Out Of The Park: Memoir of a Minor League Baseball All-Star*. Jefferson, NC: McFarland, 2007.

Moffi, Larry and Kronstadt, Jonathan., *Crossing the Line: Black Major Leaguers, 1947–1959*. Jefferson, NC: McFarland, 1994.

Schulz, Charles M. *What Makes This Country So Great?* Hallmark Cards, 1972

Schulian, John. *Twilight of the Long-ball Gods*. Lincoln: University of Nebraska Press, 2005.

Skipper, John C. *Take Me Out to the Cubs Game: 35 Former Ballplayers Speak of Losing at Wrigley*. Jefferson, NC: McFarland, 2000

Smith, Red. *Red Smith on Baseball*. Chicago: Ivan R. Dee, 2000.

Sutter, L. M. *Ball, Bat and Bitumen*. Jefferson, NC: McFarland, 2009

Tygiel, Jules. *Baseball's Great Experiment: Jackie Robinson and His Legacy*. New York City: Vintage Books, 1984.

Index

About the Author

Gaylon H. White went from sportswriting to speechwriting to scriptwriting before writing *The Bilko Athletic Club*.

The Los Angeles–born White started his career as a sportswriter for the *Denver Post, Arizona Republic*, and *Oklahoma Journal*. He became a speechwriter for top corporate executives and, then, a writer and producer of videos on design and innovation. White has authored nearly 100 articles for U.S. and international publications, many on baseball. He and his wife, Mary, live in Cartersville, Georgia.

For more photos and stories on Steve Bilko and the 1956 Los Angeles Angels, go to The Bilko Athletic Club website:

www.BilkoAthleticClub.com